Racial Formation

in the

United States

Racial Formation

in the

United States

From the 1960s to the 1990s

SECOND EDITION

Michael Omi & Howard Winant

ROUTLEDGE • **New York** • **London**

Published in 1994 by

Routledge
29 West 35 Street
New York, NY 10001

Published in Great Britain by

Routledge
11 New Fetter Lane
London EC4P 4EE

Library of Congress Cataloging-in-Publication Data

Omi, Michael
    Racial formation in the United States : from the 1960s to the 1990s / by Michael Omi and Howard Winant.
        p.   cm.
    Includes bibliographical references and index.
    ISBN 0-415-90904-X (cloth). — ISBN 0-415-90864-7 (paper)
    1. United States—Race relations.   2. United States—Social conditions—1960–1980.   3. United States—Social conditions—1980–
I. Winant, Howard.
    #184.A1047   1994
    305.8'00973—dc20   93-336254
                                                                    CIP

British Library cataloging in publication data also available

Table of Contents

Preface to the 1994 Edition

In this book we explore how concepts of race are created and changed, how they become the focus of political conflict, and how they have come to permeate U.S. society. Based on our account of the construction and transformation of racial meanings, we argue that today, as in the past, concepts of race structure both state and civil society. Race continues to shape both identities and institutions in significant ways.

Until we understand the concept of race, it is impossible effectively to analyze the familiar issues which involve race. It is hard to grasp the way racial identity is assigned and assumed, or to perceive the tacit racial dimensions of everyday experience, for example, without a clear sense of the socially constructed meaning of race. Similarly, without an awareness that the concept of race is subject to permanent political contestation, it is difficult to recognize the enduring role race plays in the social structure—in organizing social inequalities of various sorts, in shaping the very geography of American life, in framing political initiatives and state action. Nor is it possible to acknowledge or oppose *racism* without comprehending the sociohistorical context in which concepts of race are invoked.

We began working together on the project that would become *Racial Formation in the United States* in the late 1970s, and published the first edition in the mid-1980s. We initially conceived our task as a straightforward critique of the main social science literatures on race in the U.S. The inadequacies of these currents, both mainstream and radical, had become quite apparent in the 1970s. Mainstream approaches to racial theory and racial politics had become an embarrassment. Beginning in the 1970s, and with greater intensity in the 1980s, neoconservative racial doctrine, with its combination of theoretical endorsement and practical abandonment of racial equality, was used to cover the state's retreat from racial justice concerns. At the same time, the new right made a politics of subtextual race-baiting the centerpiece of a series of successful Republican campaigns not only for high office, but also to institutionalize ever more regressive social policies in the U.S.

While the right and center had retreated from democratic and egalitarian ideals with respect to race, the left had succumbed to a series of romantic illusions. Because the radical paradigms of race adopted by movement groups and progressive intellectuals had proved utopian, there was little analytical effort or theoretical ammunition available to counter the assaults of the right. By the early 1980s the various nationalisms which had emerged from the movement's black power phase had largely abandoned the quest for serious political alternatives. The limits of anticolonial ideologies imported from various third world conflicts had also become apparent. Similarly, Marxist approaches to race, unable to develop any class-based strategy for combating racial injustice and inequality, massively failed the test of political realism.

As we examined these currents—right, left, and center—we were struck by their reductionism. They shared a common tendency (perhaps the only thing they shared) to diminish the significance of race, to treat it as a mere manifestation of some other, supposedly more important, social relationship. Starting from a resistance to this reductionism, from an insistence that race be understood as a fundamental dimension of social organization and cultural meaning in the U.S., we developed our critique of the established views, both mainstream and radical. We also suggested the beginnings of an alternative approach, which we called *racial formation theory*, based on the idea that concepts of race were always politically contested. We identified the state as the preeminent—though by no means the only—site of racial contestation. Finally, we applied our racial formation approach to postwar U.S. racial politics from the 1960s to the 1980s. The "straightforward" critique of the social science literature on race had developed into something quite a bit bigger.

This new edition of *Racial Formation in the United States* appears a decade after we first presented this analysis of contemporary U.S. racial dynamics. There have been many developments since then, not only in U.S. racial politics, but also in racial theory. Drawing on a wide variety of approaches, from studies of social movements to studies in Gramsci, from critical theory to postcolonial theory, from cultural studies to feminist studies, a global network of scholars and activists has interrogated and debated the concept we designate as "race." We offer a second edition of *Racial Formation* in the hope of contributing to the burgeoning interest in racial issues.

In general we believe that the book's original formulations have stood up well. Thus we have not altered our critique of the main paradigms of race (Chapters 1–3). We think it remains sound and applicable to much of the literature even today. Since we have no wish to write and rewrite extended reviews of the vast literature on race, we would rather invite the reader to employ our categories and concepts to critique those works which interest her. Furthermore, a good deal of newer work has come out since the first edition of *Racial Formation* appeared in 1986, work which, we believe, avoids reductionist pitfalls and approximates our own position—notwithstanding particular differences and disagreements.[1]

Beyond some small updates, we have not changed the chapter on "The Racial State" (Chapter 5), whose model of an unstable equilibrium of racial conflict and contestation we continue to find useful. Nor have we greatly altered the two historical chapters which ended the first edition. The first of these (Chapter 6) covered the rise of the movement for racial justice and "The Great Transformation" it launched in U.S. politics. The second historical chapter (Chapter 7) analyzed the containment and ultimate destruction of the movement initiative in a "Racial Reaction" which began around 1970.

When we wrote and published the first edition, Ronald Reagan was President. Thus both Chapter 7 and the conclusion reflect on the mid-1980s racial situation from within, so to speak. Our analysis of that moment, we feel, has been borne out by many studies produced later. For example Thomas and Mary Edsall's *Chain Reaction*[2] underscored the points we were making about the centrality of race to the Republican ascendancy, and William Julius Wilson's *The Truly Disadvantaged*[3] analyzed in detail the debilitating effects on African Americans of the U.S.'s fall from economic preeminence. Thus we consider these chapters to retain their usefulness.

We have, however, made some major modifications in other sections of the book. We have completely reworked the theoretical chapter entitled "Racial Formation" (Chapter 4), to provide a more detailed account of racial formation processes. In this chapter we include new material on the historical development of race, on the question of racism, on race-class-gender interrelationships, on everyday life, and on hegemony. And we have written an epilogue, "Closing Pandora's Box: Race and the 'New Democrats,'" which extends our account of postwar racial politics up to the early 1990s.

In our 1986 "Acknowledgments" we noted that, in the U.S., work on matters of race must be carried out in a particularly conflictual atmosphere. The bitterness, pain, paranoia, and aggressiveness so often displayed in this field undoubtedly reflect the highly charged nature of this subject matter in U.S. society. Such difficulties quite effectively illustrate that there is no "ivory tower" for those in the universities who wish to understand the problems of the age, and more important, who hope to change the circumstances that produce them. It remains as true in 1994 as it was in 1986 that our collaboration contrasts as sharply as possible with both the miseries of the alienated academic life, and with the increasingly ravaged and competitive social landscape of U.S. society. We continue to enjoy the rare privilege of working together, of questioning each other and ourselves as deeply as we know how to do in the process of arduous intellectual labor, and of learning ever more to respect, trust, and love one another. Our deepest thanks go, then, awkwardly and in a deliberately public fashion, to each other.

Of course, in any intellectual—and emotional, and political—effort of this kind, one incurs enormous debts. We owe a tremendous vote of thanks to our friends and critics. Since the 1986 publication of the first edition of *Racial Formation in the United States,* we have been inundated with critical responses to our work, many favorable, some hostile. We have benefited greatly from these reactions. We would like to acknowledge some of the folks—friends and colleagues—whose continuing inspiration, support, and sometimes merciless commentaries have helped us produce this work: Tomás Almaguer, Margaret Anderson, Raphael Allen, Kimberly Benston, Bob Blauner, Sucheng Chan, Joe Feagin, Charles (Chip) Gallagher, Eddie Glaude, Evelyn Nakano Glenn, Michael Hanchard, Paul Jefferson, Lisa Lowe, Wahneema Lubiano, Lou Outlaw, Silvia Pedraza, Debbie Rogow, Stephen Small, Dana Y. Takagi, Fasaha M. Traylor, L. Ling-chi Wang, David Wellman, and Dianne Yamashiro-Omi.

Last but certainly not least, we would like to dedicate this edition to our children, Evan Minoru Omi, Johanna Celia Winant, Carmen Margaret Winant, and Gabriel Emmet Winant. May they live with dignity, respect, and justice in the society of the future.

Preface to the 1986 Edition

To study race in the United States is to enter a world of paradox, irony, and danger. In this world, arbitrarily chosen human attributes shape politics and policy, love and hate, life and death. All the powers of the intellect—artistic, religious, scientific, political—are pressed into service to explain racial distinctions, and to suggest how they may be maintained, changed, or abolished. The intellectual climate is anything but benign where racial studies are concerned. The ordinary competitiveness and isolation of academic work only adds to the peril.

In such an atmosphere, we have enjoyed a rare privilege: the opportunity to share a prolonged and difficult labor. For the past seven years, we have collaborated in the research and writing which have led to this book. The project has been a most demanding one. It has forced us to re-examine our beliefs, our politics, our lives. It has given us new respect, not only for the scholars whose work inspired us, but also for those with whom we most disagreed. Above all, it has taught us to love and trust each other.

We have drawn on the knowledge and skill of many friends and colleagues. Thanks to the following people for their tireless support, helpful comments, and merciless criticisms: Robert Allen, Carol Baker, Harold Baron, Mario Barrera, Gary Delgado, Doug Dowd, Jeff Escoffier, William Friedland, Hardy Frye, Frances Goldin, Amber Hollibaugh, Jim Jacobs, Andrés Jimenez, Michael Kazin, Robert Meeropol, James O'Connor, David Plotke, Juan Carlos Portantiero, Michael Rosenthal, Pamela Rosenthal, Alex Saragoza, Paul Scheifer, Gay Seidman, Nancy Shaw, Larry Shinagawa,

Preface to the 1986 Edition

Jim Shoch, Jere Takahashi, Ron Takaki, Dianne Yamashiro-Omi, and the West Coast editorial collective of *Socialist Review*.

The faculties and staffs of the Center for Latin American Studies and the Asian American Studies Program at the University of California, Berkeley, though aware that completion of this manuscript diverted the authors' attention from other duties, provided both tangible and emotional support for the project.

Finally, we would like to thank loved ones who made our work possible in more ways than we could ever express. We dedicate this book to Debbie Rogow and to Ben and Mabel Omi.

Michael Omi,
University of California, Berkeley

Howard Winant,
Temple University

Introduction

In January 1985, the chair of the U.S. Commission on Civil Rights, Clarence Pendleton, Jr., told President Reagan that members of the then recently reconstituted Commission were "working on a color blind society that has opportunities for all and guarantees success for none."[1] Pendleton's remarks echoed the President's own sentiments, which in turn have resonated with broad sectors of U.S. populace. The notion of a color-blind society where no special significance, rights, or privileges attach to one's "race" makes for appealing ideology. Taken at face value, the concept reaffirms values of "fair play" and "equal opportunity"—ideals, some would argue, which constitute the very essence of our democratic way of life.

Yet even a cursory glance at American history reveals that far from being color-blind, the United States has been an extremely "color-conscious" society. From the very inception of the Republic to the present moment, race has been a profound determinant of one's political rights, one's location in the labor market, and indeed one's sense of "identity." The hallmark of this history has been *racism*,[2] not the abstract ethos of equality, and while racial minority groups have been treated differently, all can bear witness to the tragic consequences of racial oppression. The U.S. has confronted each racially defined minority with a unique form of despotism and degradation. The examples are familiar: Native Americans faced genocide, blacks were subjected to racial slavery, Mexicans were invaded and colonized, and Asians faced exclusion.[3]

Optimistic observers of this history often acknowledge past atrocities, but offer a vision of the contemporary U.S. as an egalitarian society, one which

1

is trying to live up to its original principles by slowly extending and applying them to the gnawing issue of race. In such a vision recent history is seen as a period of enlightened progress—an unfolding drama of the social, political, and economic incorporation of minorities which will not be thwarted or reversed. The "color-blind" society, it is argued, will be the end result of this process.

Yet viewed more deeply, recent history—particularly the period from the 1960s to the 1980s—reveals a more complex and contradictory trajectory in which the pattern of race relations seems far less certain, and much less tranquil.

In the 1960s, race occupied the center stage of American politics in a manner unprecedented since the Civil War era a century earlier. Civil rights struggles and ghetto revolts, as well as controversies over state policies of reform and repression, highlighted a period of intense conflict in which the very *meaning* of race was politically contested. The 1970s, by contrast, were years of racial quiescence when the racial minority movements of the previous period seemed to wane. Racial oppression had hardly vanished, but conflicts over race receded as past reforms were institutionalized.

Issues of race have once again been dramatically revived in the 1980s, this time in the form of a "backlash" to the political gains of racial minority movements of the past. Conservative popular movements, academics, and the Reagan administration have joined hands to attack the legacy and logic of earlier movement achievements. They have done this, moreover, in a way which escapes obvious charges of "racism."

Such an intense ebb and flow in the politics of race truly begs for interpretation. This book developed from our desire to comprehend the recent tumultuous decades and to assess their meaning for a broader understanding of race in the U.S. We address three broad topics. First, we consider and critique recent theories of race in the U.S. Second, we advance an alternative conception, based in the concept of *racial formation*. Finally, we apply our racial formation approach to postwar U.S. racial history and politics.

Most racial theory fails to capture the centrality of race in American politics and American life. In general, theoretical work on race has not successfully grasped the shifting nature of racial dynamics in the postwar U.S., a failure which sparked important challenges as postwar racial events appeared to conflict with the predictions of theory. Most theories are marked by a tendency to *reduce* race to a mere manifestation of other supposedly more fundamental social and political relationships such as ethnicity or class. Our doubts about this literature derived from this reductionism— an inability to grasp the uniqueness of race, its historical flexibility and immediacy in everyday experience and social conflict.

Instead of exploring how groups become racially identified, how racial identities and meanings changed over time, or how racial conflicts shape the American polity and society, "mainstream" approaches consider race as a problem of policy, of social engineering, of state management. In the largest number of works, incorporation and assimilation of differences (or the problems involved in achieving this) is the principle governing not only social policy, but theory construction and analysis. "Radical" theories embrace class or nationalist perspectives which, while critical of the existing racial order, are often no more appreciative of the uniqueness and irreducibility of their subject than were the "established" analyses. Thus radicals too often submerge race in other social relations—most frequently class- or nation-based conflicts—thought to operate as the "motor force of history." Often influenced by movements and traditions whose reference points were located outside the U.S., many radical perspectives simply fail to address specific U.S. conditions.[4]

Part of the confusion resides in the fact that race in the U.S. is concurrently an obvious and complex phenomenon. Everyone "knows" what race is, though everyone has a different opinion as to how many racial groups there are, what they are called, and who belongs in what specific racial categories.

For example, consider the U.S. census. The racial categories used in census enumeration have varied widely from decade to decade. Groups such as Japanese Americans have moved from categories such as "non-white," "Oriental," or simply "Other" to recent inclusion as a specific "ethnic" group under the broader category of "Asian and Pacific Islanders." The variation both reflects and in turn shapes racial understanding and dynamics. It establishes often contradictory parameters of racial identity into which both individuals and groups must fit.[5]

How one is categorized is far from a merely academic or even personal matter. Such matters as access to employment, housing, or other publically or privately valued goods; social program design and the disbursement of local, state, and federal funds; or the organization of elections (among many other issues) are directly affected by racial classification and the recognition of "legitimate" groups. The determination of racial categories is thus an intensely political process.[6] Viewed as a whole, the census's racial classification reflects prevailing conceptions of race, establishes boundaries by which one's racial "identity" can be understood, determines the allocation of resources, and frames diverse political issues and conflicts.

Such an example underscores the fact that race and racial logic are ubiquitous. Yet existing racial theory, both mainstream and radical, has not grasped this reality. Consequently it minimizes the importance of race

3

in recent American political history. Our work is an effort to overcome these limitations.

We sought an approach that would remedy the defects of existing theory. Three crucial, and related, concerns shaped our theoretical orientation. The first was to assess the significance of the emergence of *new social movements* in the 1960s, heralded by the black movement. By challenging existing patterns of race relations, the black movement created new political subjects, expanded the terrain of political struggle beyond "normal" politics, and inspired and galvanized a range of "new social movements"[7] —student, antiwar, feminist, gay, environmental, etc. The black movement's ability to *rearticulate*[8] traditional political and cultural themes and in so doing mobilize a mass base of adherents is, we believe, a striking feature of racial politics in the postwar period.

The second concern was to locate race at the center of American political history, not in order to displace other important social relationships such as class and sex/gender, but to serve as a corrective to the reductionism characteristic of racial theory. Our theory of *racial formation* emphasizes the social nature of race, the absence of any essential racial characteristics, the historical flexibility of racial meanings and categories, the conflictual character of race at both the "micro-" and "macro-social" levels, and the irreducible political aspect of racial dynamics.

Our third concern was to suggest a new "expanded" model of the state and state activity, which would place socially based movements, rather than traditionally defined, economically based interest groups, at the center of contemporary political processes. In order to do this, we examined the *trajectory* of racial politics in the U.S.—the processes by which the state shapes and is shaped in turn by the racial contours of society and the political demands emanating from them.

While not possessing the ability to resolve all the problems inherent in the field of racial theory, our effort does provide an analytic framework with which to view the racial politics of the past three decades. Our argument is advanced in three parts.

Part One is an analytic assessment of contemporary racial theory. In each epoch of U.S. history, a certain school of racial theory has been dominant, serving as the racial "common sense" of its age. For much of our country's history, explicitly racist theories have played this role. During the postwar period, however, for the first sustained period in U.S. history, the dominant racial theory has upheld a notion of racial equality, albeit in various versions. In Chapter 1 we explore the particular approach to race— *ethnicity theory*—which since the early 1940s has been the main (though by no means the only) source of American racial concepts and values. Guided by ethnicity theory, Americans have come to view race as a variety of ethnicity, and to apply to racially defined groups certain standards and values whose pioneers and exemplars were European immigrants.

During its long reign, ethnicity theory has frequently been modified as its proponents attempted to account for new empirical phenomena or to address competing theoretical approaches. In the early postwar period, the ethnicity model encountered its main opponents in conservative quarters. Explicitly racial (and racist) perspectives on race, rooted in the formerly dominant paradigm of the prewar era, lived on in the South (and to some extent the Southwest). The early civil rights movement in the South, and the mobilization of Mexican Americans in the Southwest, destroyed these vestiges by the mid-1960s. Subsequently, the most severe challenge to ethnicity theory's dominance came from radical viewpoints, particularly *class*- and *nation*-based theories of race. These challenging approaches are the subjects of Chapters 2 and 3, respectively.[9]

Based on our criticism of existing racial theory (and also drawing upon it for the many partial insights it provides), Part Two advances an alternative theory of race and the racial state in the U.S. context. This approach is based on our conception of *racial formation*, which we present in Chapter 4, and on the socially based *trajectory* of racial politics, which we discuss in Chapter 5.

With these theoretical premises in place, we proceed in Part Three to analyze recent racial history, focusing on the expansion of politics to the terrain of social life, political competition among paradigms of race, postwar transformations of the racial state, and the nature of racial movements, both "radical democratic" and "reactionary."

The period from the 1960s to the 1980s represented anything but a slow, steady evolution to a "color-blind" society. It was a period of racial upsurge, failed consolidation, and reaction which, we believe, demonstrated the centrality of race in shaping American politics and culture. Today, faced with the antics of a Clarence Pendleton or the outlandish claims of Ronald Reagan that racial equality has been achieved, it is all too easy to regard race as an issue of the past. It is all too easy, even for those opposed to the right's racial policies, to suggest that today the crucial confrontation over America's future is taking place on some other ground. This book's conclusions, for the 1980s as much as for the 1960s, suggest the opposite. Race will *always* be at the center of the American experience.

PART ONE

Paradigms of Race
Ethnicity, Class, and Nation

Introduction

Theories of race—of its meaning, its transformations, the significance of racial events—have never been a top priority in social science. The great social theorists of the 19th century, towering figures such as Ferdinand Toennies, Auguste Comte, Karl Marx and Frederick Engels, Emile Durkheim, and Max Weber, were all consumed with analyzing the transition from feudalism to capitalism and interpreting the dynamic forces shaping the emergent capitalist order. Although they shared this central intellectual concern, these men could not agree on which structural relationships were the most important factors in explaining the new bourgeois industrial society.[1] What they could agree upon, though, was the belief that racial and ethnic social bonds, divisions, and conflicts were remnants of a preindustrial order which would decline in significance in the modern period. Marx and Engels, for example, predicted that as society split up into two great, antagonistic classes, social distinctions such as race and ethnicity would decrease in importance.

In the U.S., although the "founding fathers" of American sociology (men such as Lester Ward, William Graham Sumner, and Edward A. Ross) were explicitly concerned with the state of domestic race relations, racial theory remained one of the least developed fields of sociological inquiry. The pioneers were greatly influenced, not only by the Europeans, but also by the

Social Darwinist currents of the period. Their work contributed, some-times inadvertently but often by intention, to the racist hysteria of the late 19th and early 20th centuries. The epoch of the emergence of modern social science in the U.S. coincided with a sustained period of racial reaction, marked by the institutionalization of Jim Crow in the South and the suc-cess of the movement for Asian exclusion. Especially in this atmosphere, adherence to biologistic perspectives on race severely limited innovation and social scientific interest in this field.[2]

Starting in the 1920s, the Chicago school of sociology began to rework social scientific approaches to race. The Chicago sociologists, led by Robert E. Park, were the first *modern* analysts of the subject, and their thinking shaped the dominant theoretical and methodological assumptions about race relations for the greater part of this century. Park's *race-relations cycle*, with its four stages of contact, conflict, accommodation, and assim-ilation, is widely regarded as one of the most important contributions to the field. Park postulated the cycle as a law of historical development, a way of analyzing group relations and assessing a "minority" group's progress along a fixed continuum.[3]

Beginning with Park's concepts, a set of assumptions have gradually come to characterize the field and serve as guides for social scientists inves-tigating the nature of race in the United States. Blauner discusses these assumptions as follows:

> First, the view that racial and ethnic groups are neither central nor persistent elements of modern societies. Second, the idea that racism and racial oppression are not independent dynamic forces but are ultimately reducible to other causal determinants, usually economic or psychological. Third, the position that the most important aspects of racism are the attitudes and prejudices of Americans. And, finally, the so-called *immigrant analogy*, the assumption, critical in contemporary thought, that there are no essential long-term differences—in relation to the larger society—between the *third world* or racial minorities and the European ethnic groups.[4]

These assumptions are as much political and ideological as they are the-oretical. They neglect both the institutional and ideological nature of race in America, and the systemic presence of racial dynamics in such social spheres as education, art, social policy, law, religion, and science. Instead they focus attention on racial dynamics as the irrational products of indi-vidual pathologies.[5] Such assumptions make it impossible to grasp the specificity of racism and racial conflict in the U.S. They lead the analyst toward evolutionary models which optimistically predict the gradual absorption of distinct groups into the mainstream of American political, economic, and cultural life.[6] Theories based on these assumptions, therefore, reveal as much about the prevailing state of racial politics and racial ideology as they do about the nature of race relations.

Three Approaches to Race

Racial theory is shaped by actually existing race relations in any given historical period. Within any given historical period, a particular racial theory is dominant—despite often high levels of contestation. The dominant racial theory provides society with "common sense" about race, and with categories for the identification of individuals and groups in racial terms. Challenges to the dominant racial theory emerge when it fails adequately to explain the changing nature of race relations, or when the racial policies it prescribes are challenged by political movements seeking a different arrangement.

In Part One of this work, we examine recent racial theory in the U.S. We argue that this theory is encompassed by three paradigmatic approaches to race and race relations—approaches based on the categories of ethnicity, class, and nation. These approaches are *paradigms*[7] which have particular core assumptions and which highlight particular key variables. Racial paradigms serve as guides for research and have implicit and explicit policy and political action orientations.

There are, of course, limitations to this approach. We do not suggest that these three paradigms encompass all the racial theories generated during the period under consideration, but we do think that they embrace the vast bulk of them and demarcate the major lines of debate. Specific theories, and the paradigms themselves, are treated as *ideal types*: that is, the paradigms represent distillations for the purpose of analysis of complex and variegated theoretical arguments. A qualification to our approach, therefore, is the recognition that often a specific study cannot be neatly classified in one or the other paradigm. In many cases a particular work which we locate in one paradigm contains arguments which resemble those suggested by another paradigm. Any sophisticated theory, moreover, tries to take account of competing approaches by responding to particular elements—criticizing some, and integrating and synthesizing others.

Having made these qualifications, we suggest that in the contemporary period, race and racial dynamics in the U.S. have been theoretically understood by relying on one of three central categories: *ethnicity, class,* or

11

nation. The dominant paradigm of race for the last half-century has been that of *ethnicity.* Ethnicity theory emerged in the 1920s as a challenge to then predominant biologistic and Social Darwinist conceptions of race. Securing predominance by World War II, it shaped academic thinking about race, guided public policy issues, and influenced popular "racial ideology" well into the mid-1960s.

At that point ethnicity theory was challenged by *class-* and *nation*-based paradigms of race. These theoretical challenges originated with the black and other racial minority movements which rejected two central aspects of the ethnicity approach: the European immigrant analogy which suggested that racial minorities could be incorporated into American life in the same way that white ethnic groups had been, and the assumption of a fundamental, underlying American commitment to equality and social justice for racial minorities.

The appearance in the late 1970s and 1980s of a white "backlash" signalled the decline of these challenges and marked the resurgence of ethnicity theory. Although it has sustained major attacks and required reformulation in certain respects, the dominant paradigm of ethnicity has not been supplanted. Today ethnicity theory once again reigns supreme in the somewhat altered guise of *neoconservatism.*

In the following three chapters, we discuss the three paradigms of race as part of a broader understanding of the evolution of racial theory, ideology, and politics from the 1960s to the 1980s. Our concern here is not to elaborate our own approach to racial theory. That theoretical viewpoint, advanced in the concept of *racial formation,* is presented in Chapter 4. Nor will we dwell on the political dynamics of race during the period in question. That subject is considered theoretically in Chapter 5, and historically in Chapters 6 and 7. Rather, our immediate purpose is to elaborate and evaluate the existing range of racial theory. By locating established approaches to race in the three paradigms and discussing the development of the dominant approach and its challengers, we shall set the stage for the introduction of our own perspective in the next section of the book.

We argue that, in the absence of a clear conception of race itself, studies of race developed during the postwar period had perforce to rely on one of the three central categories of ethnicity, class, or nation in their interpretations of racial dynamics in the U.S. Race has not been afforded explicit theoretical primacy since the demise of the biologistic approaches of the previous eras. Thinking about race since that time has subordinated it to a supposedly "broader" category or conception. Thus the existing racial theories—both dominant and challenging—have all missed the manner in which race has been a *fundamental* axis of social organization in the U.S. It is for this reason that, in the following chapters and in this book as a whole, we attempt to develop an alternative conception which does not treat race epiphenomenally or subsume it within a supposedly more fundamental category.

1

Ethnicity

The definition of the terms "ethnic group" and "ethnicity" is muddy. "The connotation of an ethnic 'group,'" William Peterson writes in the *Harvard Encyclopedia of American Ethnic Groups*,

> . . . [I]s that its members are at least latently aware of common interests. Despite the difficulty of determining at what point people become a group, that is, the point at which coherence becomes established, it is important to retain the fundamental distinction between a group and a category. . . .[1]

Theoretically, the ethnicity paradigm represents the mainstream of the modern sociology of race. The paradigm has passed through three major stages: a pre-1930s stage in which the ethnic group view was an insurgent approach, challenging the biologistic (and at least implicitly racist) view of race which was dominant at that time; a 1930s to 1965 stage during which the paradigm operated as the progressive/liberal "common sense" approach to race, and during which two recurrent themes—assimilationism and cultural pluralism—were defined; and a post-1965 phase, in which the paradigm has taken on the defense of conservative (or "neoconservative") egalitarianism against what is perceived as the radical assault of "group rights."

The ethnicity-based paradigm arose in the 1920s and 1930s as an explicit challenge to the prevailing racial views of the period. The pre-existing biologistic paradigm had evolved since the downfall of racial slavery to explain racial inferiority as part of a natural order of humankind. Whites were considered the superior race; white skin was the norm while other skin colors were exotic mutations which had to be explained.[2] Race was equated with distinct hereditary characteristics. Differences in intelligence, temperament, and sexuality (among other traits) were deemed to be racial in character. Racial intermixture was seen as a sin against nature which would lead to the creation of "biological throwbacks." These were some of the assumptions in social Darwinist, Spencerist, and eugenicist thinking about race and race relations.[3]

But by the early decades of the 20th century biologism was losing coherence. It had come under attack by adherents of Progressivism, and had also been called into question by the work of the "Chicago school" of sociology. The Progressive attack was led by Horace Kallen, who also introduced the concept of *cultural pluralism*, which was to become a key current of ethnicity theory. The Chicago sociologists were led by Robert E. Park, who had been secretary to Booker T. Washington, and whose approach embodied the other major current of the ethnicity paradigm, *assimilationism*.[4]

In contrast to biologically oriented approaches, the ethnicity-based paradigm was an insurgent theory which suggested that race was a *social* category. Race was but one of a number of determinants of ethnic group identity or ethnicity. Ethnicity itself was understood as the result of a group formation process based on culture and descent.[5] "Culture" in this formulation included such diverse factors as religion, language, "customs," nationality, and political identification.[6] "Descent" involved heredity and a sense of group origins, thus suggesting that ethnicity was socially "primordial," if not biologically given, in character. While earlier theorists did indeed assume this,[7] later ethnicity theory came to question the validity of any primordial sense of identity or attachment, arguing instead that these concepts too were socially constructed.[8]

Early ethnicity-based theory, considered in the U.S. context, concentrated on problems of migration and "culture contact" (to use Park's phrase). The problems and foci generated by this approach have continued to preoccupy the school: incorporation and separation of "ethnic minorities," the nature of ethnic identity, and the impact of ethnicity on politics.[9]

With the advent of the vaguely egalitarian (racially speaking) vision of the New Deal[10] and of the antifascism of World War II (a war which was antiracist on the Atlantic front but decidedly racist on the Pacific front), the ethnic paradigm definitively dislodged the biologistic view in what appeared to be a triumph of liberalism. There remained, to be sure, many survivals from the old theoretical system (Jim Crow retained its grip on the South, for example, which would prove crucial for racial events in the 1950s and 1960s), but in the main, cultural and intellectual acceptance of the inevitability and even desirability of integration was achieved. Politically, the 1948 confrontation between integrationists and segregationists within the Democratic Party—a battle won decisively if not absolutely by the integrationists—symbolized the consensual shift.

Yet this victory was a hollow one where racial minorities were concerned, for the new paradigm was solidly based in the framework of European (white) ethnicity, and could not appreciate the extent to which racial inequality differed from ethnic inequality. Were the historical experiences which racial minority groups encountered similar to those of white Europeans? Were the trajectories for their perceived eventual incorporation and assimilation the same? To these questions ethnicity theorists generally answered yes. Many minority activists and movement groups, though, disagreed.

Theoretical Dominance

The chief debate between assimilationists and cultural pluralists *within* the ethnic group paradigm has been about the possibility of maintaining ethnic group identities over time, and consequently the viability of ethnicity in a society characterized by what one writer has labelled "Anglo-conformity,"[11] that is, the presence of a supposedly unitary majority culture. However, both currents agree on the existence of that culture, and both treat race as a component of ethnicity.

Insurgent ethnicity theory's main empirical reference point had been the study of immigration and the social patterns resulting from it. Park and his student Louis Wirth saw the development of ethnic enclaves and what Park called a "mosaic of segregated peoples" as stages in a cycle leading to assimilation.[12] Kallen's perspective, by contrast, had focused on the acceptance of different immigrant-based cultures. But both assimilationism and cultural pluralism had largely emphasized European, white immigrants, what Kallen called "the Atlantic migration." The origins of the concepts of "ethnicity" and "ethnic group" in the U.S., then, lay outside the experience of those identified (not only today, but already in Park's and Kallen's time), as *racial* minorities: Afro-Americans, Latin Americans, Native Americans, and Asian Americans (blacks, browns, reds, and yellows). The continuity of experience embodied in the application of the terms of ethnicity theory to both groups—to European immigrants and racial minorities—was not established; indeed it tended to rest on what we have labelled (following Blauner) the *immigrant analogy*.

The appearance of Gunnar Myrdal's *An American Dilemma* in 1944 marked the ascent of the ethnicity paradigm to a position of theoretical dominance.[13] This monumental study, funded by the Carnegie Commission, was the product of the labors not only of its director and principal author, but also of an unequalled array of talented students of racial issues in the U.S.[14] Myrdal both challenged biologistic theories of racism and asserted the desirability of assimilation for blacks.[15] He argued that the "American Creed" of democracy, equality, and justice had entered into conflict with black inequality, segregation, and racial prejudice in general. In order to resolve this conflict, America would be called upon, sooner or later, to extend its "creed" to include blacks. Myrdal's assessment was optimistic about the ultimate resolution of this battle—the contradictions would give way to racial equality and the eventual integration of blacks into the mainstream of American life.

The positions of many of his American advisors (particularly Park's students such as E. Franklin Frazier and "enlightened" liberals such as Arnold Rose), and Myrdal's own views as well, were predicated on the European immigrant model of assimilation. The U.S. had absorbed the immigrants, had eventually granted them their rights, and had seen them take their places as "Americans" despite the existence of considerable nativist hostility and prejudice against them. Was this not the essence of the "creed"? True, blacks presented this model with a stern challenge. Yet Myrdal and his associates firmly believed that black assimilation was an ineluctable imperative which presented the nation with a clear choice:

> If America in actual practice could show the world a progressive trend by which the Negro finally became integrated into modern democracy, all mankind would be given faith again—it would have reason to believe that peace, progress, and order are feasible. . . . *America is free to choose whether the Negro shall remain her liability or become her opportunity.*[16]

Assimilation was viewed as the most logical, and "natural," response to the dilemma imposed by racism. Indeed, Myrdal, drawing on the work of E. Franklin Frazier (as Daniel Patrick Moynihan was to do twenty years later) suggested that there was a "pathological" aspect to black culture which only full assimilation could cure.[17]

In its elevation to theoretical dominance with the Myrdal study, ethnicity theory derived its agenda from the political imperatives of the period: to condemn in the liberal terms of the war years the phenomenon of racial inequality, which smacked of the kinds of despotism the U.S. was fighting; to modernize and mobilize American society in preparation for its postwar role of world leadership; and to distribute the seemingly limitless resources deriving from U.S. hegemony—resources which were not only economic,

17

but also political and cultural—to all at home, even as they were to be offered to the vanquished as well as American allies abroad. The ethnicity-based theoretical tradition, derived from the experiences of European immigrants, was extended in the conclusions of *An American Dilemma* so that it might apply as well to nonwhites, especially blacks.

In the 1960s Nathan Glazer and Daniel Patrick Moynihan attempted a further innovation in ethnicity theory, stimulated by the burgeoning civil rights movement. Glazer and Moynihan wished both to validate the assimilationist bent of previous ethnic group-based theory, and to reintroduce the theme of "ongoing ethnicity" or cultural pluralism. In *Beyond The Melting Pot* (1963) they sought to link *cultural* pluralism with *political* pluralism, the dominant construct in American political science, and thus seemingly to reconcile the paradigm's problem of ethnic group identity—assimilation vs. cultural pluralism, incorporation vs. preservation—at a stroke.[18] Glazer and Moynihan argued that immigrating groups were transformed, if hardly "melted," by their experiences in New York, emerging as communities distinct not only from each other and their pre-existing sociocultural milieux, but also from their communities of origin.

> Ethnic groups, then, even after distinctive language, customs, and culture are lost . . . are continually recreated by new experiences in America. The mere existence of a name itself is perhaps sufficient to form group character in new situations, for the name associates an individual, who actually can be anything, with a certain past, country, or race.[19]

Assimilation, they argued, does take place as individuals acculturate and groups enter the political arena. Yet out of this very process a separate identity emerges, which must sustain itself culturally and deliver tangible political gains (as well as—ultimately—economic gains, e.g., "upward mobility") to the group. It was thus fundamental political interests, rather than factors such as primordial ties, cultural differences, or majoritarian resistance to incorporation which were ultimately decisive in the maintenance of ethnic identities. Continuing with the same passage:

> But as a matter of fact, someone who is Irish or Jewish or Italian generally has other traits than the mere existence of the name that associates him (sic) with other people attached to the group. A man is connected to his group by ties of family and friendship. But he is also connected by ties of *interest*. The ethnic groups in New York are also *interest groups*.[20]

18

This political focus initially seemed quite compatible with the racial conflicts of the 1950s and early 1960s. At that time ethnicity theory was grappling with black attempts to achieve equality through the civil rights movement. As seen through the lens of ethnicity, the civil rights movement was a drive for black integration and for the removal of any remaining forms of institutional/legal discrimination. From the perspective of writers such as Glazer and Moynihan or Milton Gordon, civil rights demands were intelligible and comprehensible within the ethnicity framework, and deserved the dominant paradigm's support. The civil rights movement was trying to create for blacks the same conditions that white ethnics had found: "opportunity" and relative equality (i.e., the absence of formal discriminatory barriers, however much attitudinal prejudice may have existed).[21] While debates about specific "affirmative" measures such as busing existed,[22] the ethnicity school supported such "negative" measures as the outlawing of discrimination to create and maintain conditions of equality.[23]

Although virulent forms of racism persisted in the South, the remedies for segregation were clear. The North, though, presented a different set of problems for the ethnicity theorists. At first glance, it was assumed that black equality had already been achieved there:

> One looked at the demands of the civil rights movement in 1963—
> equality in the vote, equality in the courts, equality in representation
> in public life, equality in accommodations—saw that they existed
> more or less in New York City, and concluded that the political
> course of the Northern Negro would be quite different from that of
> the Southern Negro. He (sic) would become part of the game of
> accommodation politics—he already was—in which posts and bene-
> fits were distributed to groups on the basis of struggle, of course,
> but also on the basis of votes, money, and political talent, and one
> concluded that in this game Negroes would not do so badly.[24]

In other words, blacks already had equal opportunity in the North; what more could they demand? Once equal opportunity legislation along with its judicial and administrative enforcement were accomplished facts, it fell to blacks to follow in their "predecessors'" footsteps. Through hard work, patience, delayed gratification, etc., blacks could carve out their own rightful place in American society. In the North, where blacks were still recent "immigrants" (from the South), this would involve some degree of assimilation.[25] It would involve the development of a new postimmigration cultural identity, and it would require engagement in mainstream pluralist politics. Race relations would thus continue in what Nathan Glazer was later to call the "American ethnic pattern."

Ethnicity

So, ethnicity theory assigned to blacks and other racial minority groups the roles which earlier generations of European immigrants had played in the great waves of the "Atlantic migration" of the 19th and early 20th centuries. But racial minorities refused to play their assigned roles. Structural barriers continued to render the immigrant analogy inappropriate and the trajectory of incorporation did not develop as the ethnicity paradigm had envisioned. Many blacks (and later, many Latinos, Indians, and Asian Americans as well) rejected *ethnic* identity in favor of a more radical *racial* identity which demanded group rights and recognition. Given these developments, ethnicity theory found itself increasingly in opposition to the demands of minority movements.[26] The ethnicity paradigm had to be reworked once again. The result was the phenomenon of *neoconservatism*.[27]

Therefore, beginning around 1970, ethnicity theorists developed a conservative egalitarian perspective which emphasized the dangerous radicalism and (in their view) antidemocratic character of "positive" or "affirmative" antidiscrimination policies. State activities should be restricted, they argued, to guarantees of equality for individuals.

This position was not new. As we have noted, Gordon had argued something similar as early as 1964. But the *doyens* of the ethnicity school, Glazer and Moynihan, were ambivalent about the group rights question in the 1960s. Indeed, Moynihan had *endorsed* positive antidiscrimination measures ("equality of result") in his famous "Report,"[28] though Glazer had warned about the principle's dangers early on.[29]

Some Critical Remarks on the Ethnicity Paradigm

Substantial criticism has been directed at the ethnicity school for its treatment of racially defined minorities as ethnically defined minorities, and for its consequent neglect of race *per se*. These arguments point to the limits of the immigrant analogy in addressing what was in many cases a qualitatively different historical experience—one which included slavery, colonization, racially based exclusion, and in the case of Native Americans, virtual extirpation. In addition, it has been argued, the paradigm tends to "blame the victims" for their plight and thus to deflect attention away from the ubiquity of racial meanings and dynamics. We share much of this critique, and will not recapitulate it here.[30] Instead we shall explore two less frequently noticed problems of the ethnicity approach to race: the social scientific, indeed methodological, limitations encountered by the ethnicity paradigm in its attempt to reduce race to an element of ethnicity, and the paradigm's consequent inability to deal with the particular characteristics of racial minority groups as a direct consequence of this reduction-ism. The first of these we call the "bootstraps model"; the second we refer to as "they all look alike."

The "Bootstraps Model". As we have noted, substantial reworking of the ethnicity paradigm took place in the later 1960s and early 1970s. By 1975 Glazer and Moynihan felt themselves able to offer a general hypothesis on the dynamics of group incorporation: "Ethnic groups bring different norms to bear on common circumstances with consequent different levels of success—hence *group* differences in status."[31]

The "group norms/common circumstances" correlation raises enormous problems, which can in turn be traced back to the immigrant analogy. The key factor in explaining the success that an ethnic group will have in becoming incorporated into majority society (a goal whose desirability is unquestioned) is the values or "norms" which the group brings to bear on the general social circumstances it faces just as all other minorities have done. Since the independent variable is the "norms," the idea that "differences in status" could be affected by factors outside or even unrelated to the group is ruled out at the level of assumptions. Everything is mediated through "norms" internal to the group. If Chicanos don't do well in school, this can-not, even hypothetically, be due to low-quality education; it has instead to do with Chicano values. After all, Jews and Japanese Americans did well in inferior schools, so why can't other groups? Ongoing processes of discrimination, shifts in the prevailing economic climate, the development of a sophisticated racial ideology of "conservative egalitarianism" (or should we say "benign neglect"?)—in other words, all the concrete sociopolitical dynamics within which racial phenomena operate in the U.S.—are ignored in this approach. It is the European immigrant analogy applied to all with-out reservation.[32]

"Common circumstances," by contrast, are relegated to the dependent variable. They are the universal conditions to which each ethnic group must accommodate. The assumption is made that each minority faces the majority society alone. Successful achievement of mobility—the achievement of high group status—reflects group willingness and ability to accept the norms and values of the majority. The "difference" that characterizes a minority group, once incorporated, will be outweighed by the "common-ality" it shares with the majority.

In other words, something akin to Milton Gordon's notion of "structural assimilation"[33] is assumed to take place as immigrant groups pass beyond their "fresh off the boat" status and gain the acceptance of the majority. Yet this assumption is quite unwarranted with respect to racial minori-ties, whose distinctiveness from the white majority is often not apprecia-bly altered by adoption of the norms and values of the white majority. It would in fact be just as plausible to assume the opposite: that in the case of racial minorities "common circumstances" consist in relatively permanent racial difference and non-incorporation.

The entire model for comparing and evaluating the success of ethnic groups in achieving higher status or in being incorporated into the majority society is limited by an unwillingness to consider whether there might be any special circumstances which racially defined minorities encounter in the U.S., circumstances which definitively distinguish their experiences from those of earlier European immigrants, and make the injunction to "pull yourselves up by your own bootstraps" impossible to fulfill.

"They All Look Alike". In what sense can racial minority groups be considered in ethnic group terms? In what sense is the category "black," for example, equivalent to the categories "Irish" or "Jewish" ?

The ethnicity paradigm does acknowledge black "uniqueness" because of the particular historical experience of institutionalized discrimination rooted in slavery. Yet there is something awkward, something one-dimensional, about ethnicity theory's version of black exceptionalism. *"Blacks" in ethnic terms are as diverse as "whites."* They resist comparison to the Jews and Irish, and even to Mexican Americans or Japanese Americans. The notion of "uniqueness" doesn't go far enough because it is still posed within the ethnic group framework, while "black," like "white," is a palpably racial category.

In fact, with rare exceptions, ethnicity theory isn't very interested in ethnicity *among* blacks. The ethnicity approach views blacks as one ethnic group among others. It does not consider national origin, religion, language, or cultural differences among blacks, as it does among whites, as sources of ethnicity. It would be quite interesting to see how ethnicity theory might address the range of subgroupings represented in the U.S. black community. What distinctions might it employ? Haitians? Jamaicans? Francophones? Georgians? Northern/Southern? The black community has been intensively studied from an ethnographic standpoint, so there is no lack of materials for analysis.[34] But ethnicity theory has not delved to any significant extent into the meaning of these "ethnic" distinctions.

There is, in fact, a subtly racist element in this substitution—in which whites are seen as variegated in terms of group identities, but blacks "all look alike." In our view, this is nothing intentional, but simply the effect of the application of a paradigm based in white ethnic history to a racially defined group. Blacks are thus aggregated—and treated as the great exception—because they are so clearly racially identified in the U.S.

But this issue cannot be confined to blacks. Similar problems can be discerned in ethnicity-based treatments of other racially based categories: Native Americans, Latin Americans, and Asian Americans. The aggregation of Americans of Filipino, Japanese, Korean, Chinese, and now Vietnamese, Laotian, Thai and Cambodian descent into the category "Asian American," for example, is clearly a racially based process. Ethnicity theorists might object that this is an improper exercise of "race-thinking," that there should be no recognition by the state of such a category, that these various groups should be able to maintain their ethnic identities and thus avoid "racialization,"[35] But the majority of Americans cannot tell the difference between members of these various groups. They are racially identified—their identities are racially constructed—by processes far more profound than mere state policy formation.

2

Class

The class paradigm of race includes those approaches which, in Stuart Hall's characterization, argue that "social divisions which assume a distinctively racial or ethnic character can be attributed or explained principally by reference to economic structures and processes."[1]

To equate Hall's "economic structures and processes" with *class*, whether understood in the Marxian sense of relationship to the means of production, or in the Weberian sense of relationship to the mode of distribution (giving rise to particular "life chances")[2], is to make a certain analytic leap. Indeed there is a significant economic literature on race, exemplified by the "neoclassical" approach of Gary Becker, which does not recognize the existence of classes at all, but confines itself narrowly to market relationships.

How, then, do we define the class paradigm of race, and how can the variety of approaches which emphasize "economic structures and processes" in their analyses of racial phenomena be categorized, linked, and compared? Without entering into the theoretical complexities involved in specifying the nature of "the economic,"[3] it is possible to proceed simply by recognizing that class theories principally explain race by reference to economic processes, understood in the standard sense of the creation and use of material resources. Thus the inclusion of "neoclassical" approaches in the class paradigm does not create insurmountable problems, precisely because such treatments seek to establish the roots *in exchange relationships* of racial inequality. Once we are dealing with any sort of unequal exchange we have a "class" system, although particular analysts might prefer not to use this designation.[4]

Given this qualification of the class paradigm, we suggest that there are three general approaches contained within it. We designate these as the market, stratification, and class-conflict approaches.[5] The three approaches look to different economic spheres—to market relations (exchange), systems of stratification (distribution), and processes of class conflict (production)—to provide their respective frameworks of analysis.

The Market Relations Approach

In the 1950s and 1960s, debates around the nature of racial inequality in the U.S. revealed some glaring problems in neoclassical economic thought. Market-based economic models appeared to lack the capacity to explain racial discrimination. Race appears as an anomaly in an equilibrium-oriented theoretical system—an obstacle to market processes. Neoclassical theory suggested that the market itself, unhampered by an interventionist state, would eliminate racial discrimination. Writers such as Milton Friedman argued that this was in fact taking place.[6]

Three sources of disruption of market equilibrium, potentially capable of generating racial inequality, were recognized: an irrational prejudice or "taste for discrimination"; monopolistic practices, which grant "privileges" or "special benefits" to strategically placed groups, and hence create various interests and incentives for maintaining (or transforming) racial inequality; and disruptive state practices which interfere with the supposed equilibrating tendencies of the market.[7] Focus on each of these three destabilizing forces generated a particular account of the social dynamics of race.

The irrational prejudice or "taste for discrimination" model suggests that a society segregated into black and white[8] sectors, linked as "trading partners" but separated by white "distaste" for physical proximity to blacks, will indeed be gradually integrated by market pressures. In a model such as Becker's, however, this will take place only if countervailing irrationalities can be tamed by limited and judicious state interventionism.[9]

The monopolistic practices model suggests a society structured in the interests of all whites, who gain thereby through a systematic transfer of resources from non-whites in a wide variety of fields. Whites, for example, can receive wages above the marginal utility rate for their labor and benefit from discriminatory pricing practices. Here too market forces are understood to be egalitarian, but the monopoly "cartel" which includes all whites is seen to impose inequalities in labor, capital, and consumption goods markets in order to maximize white gain. The political and cultural dynamics of race are merely the expressions of these fundamental relationships, and various conflicts which are not immediately given in market-based terms (e.g., busing), can be explained by reference to imputed market-based interests.

The disruptive state interventionism model suggests a society in which inequality is in the interests of some, but not all whites. State policies such as minimum wage laws, labor law, licensing procedures in labor-intensive trades (barbering, taxi-driving, trucking, etc.), are undertaken in response to the demands of white workers (or, often, white-dominated trade unions) anxious to protect their jobs from open competition on the part of non-whites. Thus the opportunities which white workers' immigrant parents and grandparents seized to lift themselves out of poverty and to create viable ethnic community institutions (particularly small businesses and trades) are denied to minorities today. In this view, minorities and capital share an interest in free market economics, which the state and white workers act to obstruct. This perspective argues that racial politics and ideologies of equality often mask the fact that concrete economic avenues for advancement are blocked.[10]

Market exchange theories of race necessarily try to reconcile racial inequality with the equilibrium assumptions of their model. Accounting for racial phenomena in terms of market relations is an onerous task, one which lends itself to a certain whimsicality in the formulation of hypotheses about why disequilibrating racially based interests arise. Market theories employ by far the purest form of economic determinism to be found in racial theory. These approaches conceive of racial phenomena rather monolithically in terms of (in)equality and discrimination in exchange. Racial interests are either cast in these terms or assumed to be irrational.

Certain elements of the market-based approach overlap with views deriving from other paradigms. For example, the disruptive state interventionism model of Sowell and Williams agrees with neoconservative ethnicity theories of race that racial policies should be guided by principles of individualism, and opposes demands for "equality of result." In similar fashion, the monopolistic practices model shares certain elements with nation-based analyses of race, especially those which stress the operation of "white skin privilege"[11] or of a "colonial labor principle" which allocates rights and resources differentially to groups on the basis of race. There are innumerable theoretical coincidences, along with patterns of agreement and influence, in the vast literature on race. These resemblances, however, should not be mistaken for theoretical accord. Market-based theories (which are class-oriented, economic theories) are based on quite different perceptions of what race *means* than are ethnicity- or nation-based approaches.

Stratification Theory

Stratification approaches deal with the social distribution of resources—chiefly, though not exclusively, economic ones. Individuals receiving roughly equal incomes, or partaking of equal quantities of wealth, are deemed to have similar "life chances" and assigned to groups in a "status order" or ranked hierarchy of "classes." Various degrees of "mobility" are postulated among the ranks of the hierarchy and numerous non-economic factors are analyzed as playing important roles in the stratification system's maintenance and modification over time.

Politics are also a crucial factor. In stratification theory the relationships of elites and masses, the dynamics of authority systems and forms of domination, and the overall shape of sociopolitical conflict are central preoccupations. In most respects these extra-economic factors reinforce the distribution dynamic. Patterns of elite rule, for example, are frequently "traced back" to the distribution of economic resources.

William J. Wilson's *The Declining Significance of Race* (1978) represents a sophisticated application of stratification theory to racial issues—in this case, to the interpretation of emerging class cleavages within the black community. While Wilson accepts an economically determined stratification theory for previous epochs of U.S. history (an "economic system," he suggests, shaped the "polity" and thereby structured and enforced "racial norms"), he argues that the contemporary period is one in which the state has developed "autonomy" in handling racial problems.[12] This does not negate the existence of an economically determined status order. Rather, it detaches "class" (i.e., status) categories from racial ones. According to Wilson, although black "life-chances" were formerly determined by racial stratification, since 1965 they have been shaped directly by "class" stratification. After state-enforced racial inequality was eliminated by civil rights legislation, blacks were admitted to the society-wide system of stratification, rather than being confined to a specific location by segregation. The results are a black community which is stratified into a small privileged "class" whose opportunities are equivalent to those of whites with similar high levels of training and skills, and a massive black "underclass" which is relegated to permanent marginality.

Wilson's book has been received by critics in a highly partisan fashion. Many radical writers have castigated the work, although some have found in it the justification for orthodoxy.[13] Conservative writers have appropriated Wilson's notion of a shift from racially based to class-based sources of black poverty to argue against egalitarian state interventionism itself. This is far from Wilson's own position. He appeals for state policies which will ameliorate the catastrophic impact of increased class cleavages in the black community, calling, for instance, for expansion of day-care services available to low-income single mothers.[14]

Despite the many merits of Wilson's analysis, certain serious flaws remain. He appears to believe that since the mid-1960s a genuinely egalitarian racial state has existed in the U.S., and further, that support for its policies is now a permanent feature of U.S. politics. Yet one has only to consider electoral dynamics, or recent shifts in civil rights policy which legitimate a notion of "reverse discrimination" (that is, the supposedly invidious effects on *whites* of affirmative action and similar policies), to recognize that the ongoing (post-1965) racial contestation for and within the state is far from over.

Wilson's argument that the contemporary black community is stratified into a relatively small privileged "class" and a large black "underclass" suggests that race is no longer a salient linkage between those who have "made it" and their less fortunate "underclass" brethren. We consider, on the contrary, that the fate of the black middle class remains tied to the lower class precisely through racial dynamics which are structured into the U.S. economy, culture, and politics. First of all, personal, familial, and community ties continue to interconnect the two strata despite attempts on the part of a few black intellectuals and some in the privileged strata to create a distinct "black bourgeois" community and culture.[15] Secondly, the very existence of educational and job opportunities of which middle class blacks took advantage depended, and continues to depend, on the political action of the black majority.[16] Futhermore, many "privileged" blacks work in industries and economic sectors whose economic and political *raison d'être* is linked to the black "masses." Government workers, educators, and other tertiary sector workers, for example, may have achieved middle-class status and incomes, but their employment relates directly to the management, marketing, and servicing of the black community as a whole.[17] An extended period of reaction which included significant curtailment of the welfare state, underfunding of public education, restriction of health and social security benefits, etc., would prove massively detrimental, not only to the black "underclass," but to "middle-class" blacks as well.

As in the case of market-based theories, stratification theories overlap with viewpoints originating in other paradigms. Where they emphasize "caste," that is, the closing-off of "mobility" in a status order with racial characteristics, they resemble certain nation-based views which deny the potential for integration across racial (or colonizer/colonized) lines.[18] Where they focus on those characteristics of the system which facilitate "mobility," such as the avenues available to various minority groups for economic advancement, they resemble ethnicity-based views. Within the class paradigm, there is also considerable variation among stratification analyses. For example, they may tend toward market-based approaches, if decisionistic models of trade and association are judged to generate status disparities relatively automatically;[19] or they may tend towards class-conflict perspectives, if segmentations or splits in the labor market are thought to play a major role in assigning particular locations in the status order to different racial groups.

Class Conflict Theory

"Classical" Marxism never explicitly addressed issues of race and racial conflict, but it did consider the problem of divisions within the working class and the nature of "national oppression." As such, the Marxian legacy has had a profound impact on both class-based and nation-based paradigms of race.

Class conflict theories of race in the 1960s, rooted in an idea central to Marxist analysis—the concept of exploitation—posed a fundamental challenge to ethnicity theory. Exponents of the class conflict paradigm recognize the existence of racial oppression, but regard class divisions as the fundamental source of exploitation in society. Class conflict theory asserts the centrality of the "social relations of production" in structuring classes and class relationships.[20] This view then proceeds to situate racial conflict within the class dynamics of society as a whole. There are many ways of doing this, including crudely economic determinist as well as highly mediated "neo-Marxist" conceptions of the class-race relationship.

Effects of class conflict upon race relations are noted at all "levels" of society, but as in the market-based and stratification variants, class conflict theory infers racially oriented political interests from economic ones. An interest in shaping labor or immigration policy, for example, may be attributed to capitalists who seek higher profits and more effective controls over the labor process through strategies of "divide and rule"[21] or to white labor's efforts to limit competition from lower-paid minority workers.[22] Ideologies of racial inferiority are explained in a similar manner, as "grounded" in racially defined economic interests.

It is not coincidental that class conflict approaches strongly resemble market-based perspectives since both rely on conceptions of the *labor market* to situate their views of the race-class relationship. This emphasis on the labor market derives from the tendency, explicit in all "classical-" and much "neo-" Marxism, to understand class as a production relation. Within

this framework it is quite difficult to specify *anything* about actual production relationships that is specifically racial.[23]

If we rule out mechanistic and dogmatic class conflict theories, the field
can be understood as ranging from attempts, such as those of Cox and
Reich, to establish a capitalist class interest in racial inequality,[24] to efforts,
such as that of Bonacich and Prager, to demonstrate a working-class interest therein.[25]

Class conflict theories of race may be divided into two opposing tendencies, each focused on the labor market. These two viewpoints are, first,
a "divide and rule" conception which rests on the notion of labor market
segmentation as the key determinant of racially based inequalities in production relations; and second, an "exclusionism" perspective which suggests
that a *split* labor market is the central source of these inequalities. Despite
the diametric opposition of the two positions, there is agreement between
them on the primacy of class conflict over racial conflict. But it must be
stressed that in both of these approaches, racially differentiated relationships to the means of production are the result, not of production relationships themselves, but of market or exchange relationships.

Segmentation theory has been developed in the Marxian tradition most
centrally by Michael Reich (in collaboration with David M. Gordon and
Richard Edwards), and in the institutionalist or stratification tradition by
Michael Piore and Peter Doeringer.[26]

Reich, Gordon, and Edwards have developed the segmentation perspective in two basic ways: first, Reich has explored the microeconomics
of racial inequality in a rigorous critique of the neoclassical or market-
based approach.[27] Second, Gordon, Edwards, and Reich have chronicled
the historical evolution of labor control and labor market processes in the
U.S., linking these to long-run trends or "swings" in the capitalist accumulation process. This evolution, they argue, has culminated in a segmented labor system in the contemporary period.[28]

In his microeconomic analysis, Reich develops evidence for the "divide
and rule" hypothesis by measuring the effects of racial (in)equality on wage
levels and on the distribution of social spending in such areas as education
and welfare. He effectively demonstrates the limits of the market-based
approach by introducing class variables (measurements of class cohesion
and class segmentation across racial lines) which account far better for
empirically observed inequalities than do pure market-based variables.
Finally, he attempts to synthesize the class conflict and neoclassical modes
of analysis. Concerned to emphasize the structural aspects of discrimination, Reich employs a "bargaining power theory." Because a working class
which lacks unity will exercise less leverage over employers, Reich argues,

"Capitalists benefit from racial divisions whether or not they have individually or collectively practiced racial discrimination."[29]

The problem with this is that it relegates subjectivity to the sidelines of the model. Class organization—across racial lines—is seen as the objective and primary necessity which all workers face. Racially based organization and identification is implicitly a form of "false consciousness." This may work fine in the abstract, but concretely it would require the suppression of racially defined experience in order to operate. Historically speaking, the call for class unity across racial lines has amounted in practice to an argument that non-whites give up their racially based demands in favor of "class" unity on white terms. This will not be achieved by appeals to "class unity" or by reliance on "bargaining power theory," which merely offer an abstraction to minorities confronted by racial inequities in the workplace.

In Reich's study, then, economic interests come strongly to the fore, and political/ideological factors appear as mere manifestations of underlying economic relationships. But in practice economic interests are defined politically and ideologically. The identities which social actors take on are defined ideologically; they are the essence of ideology. Am I a worker first or a Chicano first? By placing so much emphasis on the structural nature of racial inequality (which he does to combat conspiratorial and cartelization theories of discrimination), Reich upholds a rather strong economic determinism of his own. This problem is not limited to his treatment, of course, but is endemic to the class paradigm in general.

In *Segmented Work, Divided Workers*, Gordon, Edwards, and Reich attempt a synthesis of a different sort: here accumulation processes and the dynamics of capitalist labor control are seen to be woven together. Two themes drawn from this ambitious work and essential to the segmentation framework are particularly relevant to the present study: the argument that labor market segmentation "played a major role in channeling the effects of past and present race and sex discrimination,"[30] and the contention that the segmentation system began to "decay" in the early 1970s. Because the authors focus their account on labor relations, processes, and structures of control, it is quite understandable that they should seek to locate "black" labor within the segmentation model they defined earlier[31] (and refine substantially in this work). There should be no illusions, however, that this focus addresses the basic dynamics of race. Indeed when the authors assert that "black protest" in the 1960s placed strains on the segmentation system, this political intervention by blacks appears as entirely exogenous to their model. They note that "blacks became increasingly intolerant of low-wage labor and lack of opportunities for advancement,"[32] but *why* this should have occurred is not explained.

Class

Although Gordon, Reich, and Edwards place great emphasis on the role played by labor market segmentation in structuring the post–World War II accumulation process, they make no special effort to explore the racial dimensions of this segmentation. Race (along with sex) merely furnishes one of the major axes upon which the working class is assumed to be divided.

This line of argument carries less weight today than it might have in the past. In the contemporary U.S., as an analysis like Wilson's shows, race cuts *across* class lines as well as dividing classes internally. It is thus extremely important to understand the different axes along which "workers" (or if you prefer, "social actors") are organized, linked in the system of social reproduction, and "constructed" as ideological subjects. Only on the basis of such an analysis is it possible to understand how political opposition takes shape, how, for example, black struggles for integration of public facilities in the South during the 1950s could have expanded into the confrontation with the overall capitalist accumulation process which Gordon, Reich, and Edwards themselves note.

Today it is more difficult than ever to understand race in terms of an economically determined formula of class belonging (for example, that class is determined by relationship to the means of production). It would be more accurate to say that race and class are competing modalities by which social actors may be organized.

Problems of this sort have led Gordon, Edwards, and Reich to conclude that the segmentation system has begun a phase of "decay." "Decay," in their theory, is the breakdown phase into which each epochal arrangement of the capitalist accumulation/labor control system enters as internal conflicts and external pressures challenge its organizational and reproductive capacity. In the 1960s and early 1970s, Gordon, Edwards, and Reich assert, the signs of decay were becoming apparent in the system of labor market segmentation. Although they previously informed us that "black protest" strained the system, the major reasons cited for the onset of decay are located at the point of production: productivity slowdowns, increased rank and file militance, etc.[33] The fact that the authors make no effort to interpret these phenomena in terms of the racial conflicts and protests which characterized this period, and which they recognize as a key source of political opposition at this time, testifies to the limited explanatory capacity of the segmentation model in accounting for racial dynamics.

The *split labor market* approach has been most effectively advanced by Edna Bonacich.[34] Her conception stresses the existence of a group of "dominant workers" which is threatened by the competition of "cheap labor." *Class* conflict takes place between capital and the "dominant" group, which seeks to maintain its wage levels, defend whatever control it may have of production processes, etc. *Racial/ethnic* conflict takes place between "dominant" and "subordinate" workers as the former seek to prevent the latter from bidding down the price of their labor.

The exclusionist movements that arise as a result are not racially motivated or "nationalist" *per se*, but "the product of historical accident which produced a correlation between ethnicity and the price of labor."[35] They are the result of pre-existing differences between the costs of racially (and ethnically) defined labor, differences which in turn stem from the existence of a worldwide division of labor, migration patterns, unequal exchange and uneven development processes, etc.[36]

Far from enhancing capitalist control over labor, as the segmented labor market is said by its theorists to do, the split labor market is seen as problematic for capital. Bonacich argues that while the existence of a cheap labor pool creates an obvious incentive for lowering wage costs and thus boosting profits, the resistance of dominant labor to these tactics forces capitalists into accommodations they would otherwise not choose to make:

> Capital turns toward the cheap labor pool as a more desirable
> work force, a choice consistent with the simple pursuit of higher
> profits. Higher priced labor resists being displaced, and the racist
> structures they erect to protect themselves are anatagonistic to the
> interests of capital.[37]

Bonacich confronts the "divide and rule" approach of the segmentation theorists with the following counterarguments: 1. Labor is already differentiated in price before employers can engage it; 2. Offering a positive incentive to dominant workers would be inconsistent with the pronounced capitalist preference for tactics of virulent struggle; 3. Indeed, cheap labor would be (and historically has been) a better target than "dominant" labor for "bribes" and similar tactics.[38]

The split labor market approach fares no better than the segmentation argument in accounting for the complexities of U.S. race relations. While it recognizes that in practice class modalities of organization are often less salient than racial ones, the "exclusionism" perspective is as absolute as the "divide and rule" view in imputing political interests and ideological meanings to the various economically defined class and racial actors it depicts. This eliminates the possibility that "class unity" might prevail at one moment or on one terrain, while racial conflict might rule the day on another. The "split" labor market approach, as much as the "segmentation" one, refuses to engage concrete politics and ideologies of race, insisting instead on imposing a highly schematic and economically determined model of the race/class relationship.

Class

Whether understood as "dual," "segmented," or "split," the labor market exhibits a great variety of forms and axes of differentiation: "internal labor markets,"[39] "monopoly, competitive, and state" sectors,[40] gender-based categories, undocumented workers' jobs, "upper primary" and "subordinate primary" categories, etc.[41] These overlap and cut across racial lines of division. It thus becomes problematic to assert for example that "dominant" (or "primary sector") labor is white, unionized, or even (given recent debates on the question) more "skilled." Segmented or split labor markets organized along racial lines cannot be demonstrated to exist in the U.S. today with the same degree of definition they might have possessed in the past. As Lever-Tracy observes with respect to immigrant labor,

> To explain the finer contours of segmentation, the concentration of immigrant workers in some productive jobs or their exclusion from others, the formation or the avoidance of ethnic work groups, and so on, requires knowledge of the various strategies pursued by employers and by workers (both native and immigrant) in their conflicts with each other.[42]

In short, segmentations and splits must be understood politically and ideologically, rather than as "objective" systems of division within the labor market, and beyond this, within the working class as a whole.

If "strategies" (or more broadly, political and ideological factors) are recognized to be central to these conflicts, it is clear that any correspondence between racially defined groupings and sectors of the labor market—"dominant-subordinate," "core-peripheral," "primary-secondary," or "monopoly-competitive-state"—is at best highly inaccurate, and at worst quite spurious. Indeed it is rather obvious that racial categories cut across class lines and will not serve adequately to classify social actors even in terms of class membership, not to mention among classes.[43] Nor is the concept of "labor market" equivalent to that of "working class."

The "class conflict" perspective on race is thus no more workable than the market- or stratification-based approaches; it does, however, bring to the fore the necessity of understanding classes as the "effects of struggles."

Racial dynamics must be understood as determinants of class relationships and indeed class identities, not as mere consequences of these relationships. Recent analyses of class-formation processes have suggested as much.[44] Once it is recognized that classes too are not objectively given entities, but formed and transformed over time, it becomes possible to view sectoral organization in production much more flexibly. We can then investigate how, at any historical point, sectoral lines of demarcation, both within and among classes, are themselves the objects of political struggle, how they are secured by "coercion" against challenge, and made flexible and adaptable by "consent."[45] Such an approach could explore the meaning of class for racial minorities in terms which avoid mere assimilation of racial categories into class ones.[46]

As the segmentation theorists have recognized, capitalist interests in profit-maximization and (very importantly) in control of production processes have at times been furthered by "balkanization" of the labor force, at other times by its homogenization. Yet there is little in either the segmentation or the split labor market analyses which comprehends class formation in broad enough terms to suggest a theory of racial dynamics. Race remains an exogenous element to both conceptions. Both adopt a "zero-sum" approach in which either capitalists or white workers "gain" what minority workers "lose." On this economic "base," which has much more in common with market-based theory than with a class formation perspective, an epiphenomenal racial "superstructure" is quite easily erected, in which political interests and racial as well as subjective identities are assigned to the various actors (themselves defined in simplistic terms) in the more "fundamental" drama of class conflict. In our view, as will be seen, such an approach hardly begins to inquire into the sources and contours of racial dynamics.

3

Nation

The emergence of black nationalism in the mid-1960s ruptured the tenuous unity of liberal and radical factions within the civil rights movement and signalled a growing disillusionment with the moderate political agenda of nonviolence and integration. The rise and popularity of black nationalism initiated an intense theoretical and strategic debate about the nature of racism and the future of black politics in the U.S.

The nation-based analysis of black oppression and resistance had, of course, its historical antecedents. The refusal of integrationist solutions could be traced back at least to the repatriation movements of the mid-19th century, led by men such as Martin Delany and Paul Cuffe.[1] The Pan-Africanist and Marxist-Leninist traditions had also elaborated nationalist analyses, and a substantial current of cultural nationalism existed whose components could be discerned in Du Bois's *The Souls of Black Folk*,[2] in the Harlem Renaissance of the 1920s, and in the influential writings of Harold Cruse during the 1950s and 1960s.[3] Strong nationalist traditions could also be found in other minority communities, notably among Puerto Ricans, Mexican Americans, and Native Americans.

The nation-based paradigm, to a far greater extent than the ethnicity- or class-based approaches, is a theoretical convergence, a resultant of disparate currents. Nationalist currents have always existed in the U.S.—in the form of minority-based political movements—responding to perceived failures of racial accommodation and integration. Nation-based approaches to race also have a long theoretical tradition, which analyzes in diverse ways the realities of racial separation and white supremacy. In the postwar period, nation-based approaches have taken on an additional theoretical dimension: the critical rejection of ethnicity-based racial theory.

Despite the wide range of specific approaches, nation-based theory is fundamentally rooted in the dynamics of *colonialism*. Colonialism in the age of capitalism differed from previous imperial systems in that it came to encompass the entire world. Launched from Europe in the 15th century, it reached its zenith in the 19th century, by which time all nations and territories had been assigned a place in "the modern world system."[4] Although in a state of disarray and breakdown today, the legacy of the colonial order remains in a variety of forms, extending from the position of international frontiers drawn in much of the colonized world by the ruling powers, to the existence of spheres of influence descended from systems of colonial rule,[5] and indeed to the very contours of the international division of labor, based on unequal exchange and the domination of the "periphery" by the "core." In the nation-based paradigm, racial dynamics are understood as products of colonialism and, therefore, as outcomes of relationships which are global and epochal in character.

Framing the paradigm in this way has several advantages. First, it emphasizes the relationships among the different elements of racial oppression—inequality, political disenfranchisement, territorial and institutional segregation, cultural domination—in contrast to the ethnicity or class paradigms which focus on a few aspects (or even one "fundamental" aspect) of the social order in an attempt to explain racial dynamics. Recognition of the centrality of the colonial heritage also provides an alternative to other, more taxonomic approaches to nation-based theories of race. Many writers have delineated, for example, "varieties of black nationalism": bourgeois, proletarian, reformist, revolutionary, cultural, religious, economic, educational, etc.[6] While efforts to catalog the range of nationalist positions within specific minority group traditions, and to trace debates within these traditions, obviously have merit,[7] they often reveal a notable lack of specificity about the *meaning* of nation-based categories in such approaches. Nationalism is easily reduced to minority militance or separatism, for example, if no effort is made to specify its historical and theoretical origins in particular minority experiences of colonialism.

While not comparable in many respects, we include Pan-Africanism, cultural nationalism, Marxist debates on "The National Question," and perspectives focusing on internal colonialism as specific analyses of race and racism which take shape within the nation-based paradigm. What these approaches share is their reliance on elements derived from the dynamics of colonialism to demonstrate the continuity of *racial* oppression from its origins in the *national* oppression prevailing in colonialism's heyday. Chief among these is the use of racial categories to distinguish members of the oppressor and oppressed "nations"—the colonizers and the colonized. Several consequences of these arguments may be specified: the explicit demand for organizations and movements uniformly composed of the "colonized" (i.e., the victims of racial oppression), the need for "cultural autonomy" to permit the development of those unique characteristics which the colonized group has developed or preserved through the ordeal of subjugation, or the necessity of "national liberation" to uproot the colonial heritage and restructure society on a non-racial basis.

Pan-Africanism

The roots of Pan-Africanism can be traced back to the black repatriation movements of Martin Delany, Paul Cuffe, and others in the mid-19th century. In the 20th century, Pan-Africanism took shape on two fronts: the first was a series of international conferences held in Europe and the U.S. from 1900 to 1945, most of them organized by W. E. B. Du Bois.[8] These conferences were oriented primarily toward decolonization of Africa and had relatively little U.S. domestic impact.

The second front of Pan-Africanist activity was the formation, largely in the U.S., of the Universal Negro Improvement Association, led by Marcus Garvey.[9] The UNIA had unprecedented success in mobilizing blacks, numbering millions of adherents at its height in the 1920s. Garvey sought to unite blacks throughout the world in a movement for the "redemption" of Africa, which he envisioned as a "racial empire." For him and his followers, Africa existed not only on the continent, but in the diaspora which slavery had visited on its inhabitants and their descendants. Thus the fates of blacks throughout the world were linked. The liberation and reconstruction of the African homeland would allow blacks finally to overcome the racial oppression which had sustained colonialism.

Garvey was greatly influenced by the doctrines of Booker T. Washington, specifically those promoting separate economic development. Garvey's economic argument, however, went beyond Washington's in two respects: first, he denounced the exploitation of Africa and African labor throughout the world.[10] Second, he saw the black population of the U.S. not only in the "self-help" terms of Washington, but as

> . . . a vanguard for Africa's redemption. . . . He believed that if the Negroes were economically strong in the United States, they would be able to redeem Africa and establish a worldwide confraternity of black people.[11]

For all its excesses and errors, the most notorious being its *rapproche-ment* with the Ku Klux Klan,[12] the Garvey movement represents one of the founding pillars of modern Pan-Africanism,[13] and stands as a crucial source for much other black nationalism as well.[14] Indeed it still represents the highwater mark of mass black political mobilization, rivalled only by the movements of the 1960s. In this respect it is entirely appropriate to treat Garveyism as the archetype of the Pan-Africanist tradition in the U.S.[15]

Pan-Africanism maintained a limited foothold in the U.S. through the contributions of Du Bois, George Padmore, and C. L. R. James. When Malcolm X broke with the Nation of Islam in 1964 to form the Organization of Afro-American Unity, making a series of well-publicized trips to Africa and attempting to enlist the support of African governments in denouncing U.S. racism at the United Nations, he dramatically stimulated black interest in African issues. With the advent of "black power," the contributions of Malcolm, Nkrumah, Frantz Fanon, and later, Amilcar Cabral and Walter Rodney received new attention in the U.S., and contributed to the Pan-African canon. Stokely Carmichael in particular moved to embrace Pan-Africanism after 1967.[16]

Pan-Africanism enjoyed a further resurgence in the early 1970s. By this time, however, the fractured movement was only clinging to providing what in retrospect can only be seen as illusions of unity among black nationalists: the reference point of Africa had become symbolic. The precise character of the illusion was that U.S. political reference points could be subordinated to African ones. In 1975 even this fell apart in debates over the Angolan revolution. "Left" Pan-Africanists supported the MPLA, thereby accepting (often dogmatically) some version of Marxism and rejecting the racial determinism of "right" Pan-Africanists, who sided with UNITA.[17]

The power of the Pan-Africanist perspective remains its ability to link the specific forms of oppression which blacks face in various societies with the colonialist exploitation and underdevelopment of Africa. The impact this theoretical current had in the U.S. stemmed from its argument that black identity conferred membership in a single worldwide black "nation"—the African diaspora itself.

Cultural Nationalism

Cultural nationalism has had a particularly strong hold in the black community, where its roots can be traced back at least to the Harlem Renaissance of the 1920s.[18] As a broader phenomenon, however, cultural nationalist perspectives have been enunciated and practiced in nearly all racially defined communities.[19] Cultural nationalism has focused less on the political and economic elements of the nation-based approach than it has on *cultural* elements which give rise to collective identity, community, and a sense of "peoplehood."

Probably the most devoted and incisive cultural nationalist theorist has been Harold Cruse. In two early and highly original essays entitled "Rebellion or Revolution?" and in his massive and controversial *The Crisis of the Negro Intellectual*,[20] Cruse argued that "The only observable way in which the Negro rebellion can become revolutionary in terms of American conditions is for the Negro movement to project the concept of Cultural Revolution."[21]

Cruse stressed the unique conditions facing American blacks, conditions which, while related to those encountered by other victims of colonialism, were unlike those of the African continent, the West Indies, or elsewhere. Cruse also accepted certain "domestic colonialism" concepts; indeed, he gave voice to them as early as 1962.[22] Anticipating the "black power" view, he criticized the civil rights movement in the early 1960s for being dominated by liberal ideas and demands:

> This Negro rebellion, mistakenly called by some the Negro revolution, is not revolutionary because it projects no new ideas beyond what have already been ratified in the democratic philosophy of the American Constitution.[23]

He proposed that the movement "incorporate . . . a cultural program along with its economic, social, and political programs."[24] A "cultural program," in Cruse's view, would recognize both the unique characteristics of black cultural traditions, and the essential part that these cultural elements—for example in music, art, or language—played in the cultural life of the U.S. Cruse suggested that the black movement focus its demands on "the creation and distribution of cultural production in America."[25] The ultimate aim of this challenge, Cruse argued, was "the revolutionizing . . . of the entire apparatus of cultural communication and placing it under public ownership."[26]

This approach, needless to say, raised as many questions as it answered. How the cultural apparatus could be so transformed, how blacks could affect cultural production under the proposed new "revolutionary" conditions, and what would be the ultimate social and political impact of such a change, were only a few of the issues Cruse did not address. What was significant about his work, however, was not its immediate practical application. Rather, his accomplishment lay in the development of a culturally based radical perspective. His positions anticipated debates between integrationists and nationalists in the later 1960s and 1970s. He thus re-opened questions that had lain dormant for nearly half a century.[27] In many ways Cruse explored the terrain upon which later, lesser figures of this current, such as Ron Karenga, Imamu Amiri Baraka, and Haki Mad-hubuti would stand.[28]

Many black nationalists embraced African values, traditions, culture, and language through Pan-Africanism, while others became adherents of groups such as Karenga's U.S. organization or Baraka's Spirit House in Newark, without becoming Pan-Africanists politically. Cultural national-ism had many indirect effects on black "lifestyle": clothes, hair, language, and art reflected the perspective's upsurge. African heritage was often invoked to support domestic ideological and political aims.[29]

Cultural nationalism was by no means limited to the black movement. In the Chicano movement, for example, it arose in the early 1970s, basing itself in the concept of *Aztlán*, particularly as developed in quasi-mythical form by Rodolfo "Corky" Gonzales. The appeal of *Aztlán*, the lost Mex-ico of the North, evoked traditional Mexican cultural values untainted by Anglo domination. This symbolism was then applied to present-day real-ities of Chicano life.[30] Such reference systems represented less any real pos-sibility of forging a separate Afro-American or Chicano "nation" within the territorial boundaries of the U.S. (despite occasional illusions to the con-trary), than efforts to unify previously fragmented minority groups by forg-ing collective cultural identities.

Black cultural nationalism degenerated in the late 1960s and early 1970s as its discourse and symbolism was increasingly coopted and commodified. There was, it turned out, nothing particularly radical about afros, dashikis, or the concept of "soul." As Adolph L. Reed, Jr. noted:

> [T]he intellectual climate which came to pervade the movement was best summarized in the nationalists' exhortation to "think black" .... Truth became a feature of the speaker's "blackness," i.e., valid-ity claims were to be resolved not through discourse but by the claimant's manipulation of certain banal symbols of legitimacy.[31]

Demographic, economic, and political fissures within the black com-munity—whose "unity" and "peoplehood" had been central features of cultural nationalist theory—increasingly became too obvious to ignore. In the face of these changes, leading adherents moved on to new political horizons. Some, notably Baraka, made spectacular and belated conversions to Marxism-Leninism and Maoism, subsuming their original "racial" proj-ects under broader "class" ones.

Interestingly, cultural nationalists have always manifested a certain disdain for political activity, especially normal politics, whether reform-oriented or radical. Their preference has been for building "countercultural" institutions, and, where necessary, for elite-led negotiations with the white power structure. A willful neglect of key political determinants of race—the racial state, class conflict, the politics of alliance and coalitions—ultimately doomed many cultural nationalist projects to irrelevance as U.S. racial formation processes overtook their models. Cultural nationalist projects which sought to create minority "nations" founded on common cultural reference points were never politically viable. The real accomplishment of cultural nationalist currents was in the nature of "consciousness-raising." They underscored the centrality of cultural domination in the logic of racial oppression, and stressed the importance of "cultures of resistance" in unifying and promoting collective identity among the oppressed.

The "National Question" and Marxist Debates

Classical Marxism viewed nations and national boundaries as increasingly meaningless as world capitalism inexorably penetrated every corner of the planet. Marx and Engels stated this perspective clearly in *The Communist Manifesto* and viewed it as a "progressive" feature of the unfolding capitalist order:

> National differences and antagonisms between peoples are daily
> more and more vanishing, owing to the development of the bour-
> geoisie, to freedom of commerce, to the world market, to unifor-
> mity in the mode of production and in the conditions of life
> corresponding thereto.[32]

It is far from clear that this view was their final word on the subject, for the idea of the abolition of national boundaries and antagonisms is contradicted by other writings of Marx during the same period.[33] When Marx begins to write on the national question (with specific reference to Ireland), he argues that the bourgeoisie not only maintains but *heightens* national antagonisms. National hostilities are engendered by 1. the struggle to control world markets, which creates conflicts among capitalist powers; 2. the exploitation of colonies, which creates antagonism between "oppressed" and "oppressor" nations; and 3. the use of nationalism as an ideological tool to detract proletarian attention from class antagonisms.

This contradictory stance towards the persistence or demise of nations is further complicated by an implicit "stage" theory of development which views colonial penetration and plunder as "progressive" events in so far as they rupture traditional social relations and supplant them with capitalist ones.

The dilemma of what posture Marxists should take towards forms of oppression which were not obviously class-based was not resolved by Marx and Engels and formed the basis for significant debates on the "national question" during the Second International. The polemical exchange between Lenin and Luxemburg on the national question revolves around the "right of nations to self-determination." Lenin argued that all nations should be free from national oppression and enjoy the right to determine their own destiny.[34] Luxemburg was critical of this "right to self-determination," which led in her view to a certain pandering to the aspirations of the national bourgeoisies of the "oppressed" countries. Both Lenin and Luxemburg attempted to steer a course between positions which asserted an unqualified right to national/cultural autonomy and a position which completely denied the legitimacy of nationalist aspirations.[35]

The legacy of these debates on the national question was subsequently invoked to analyze the situation of blacks in the U.S. Prior to 1928, the Communist Party of the United States attributed no special role or status to blacks (or other "national minorities") within the general class struggle. Comintern discussions between 1928–30, however, resulted in the thesis that blacks in the southern region known as the Black Belt (named for the soil) constituted a nation and were therefore entitled to "self-determination"—including the right of political secession. Blacks in the North were considered an oppressed "national minority" whose salvation was to be sought in solidarity with white workers in the struggle for socialism.

The criteria for this thesis were drawn from a pamphlet by Joseph Stalin, who in 1908 had proposed four defining characteristics of a nation: "A nation is a historically constituted, stable community of people, formed on the basis of a common language, territory, economic life, and psychological make-up manifested in a common culture."[36] The "Black Nation Thesis" was meant to resolve contradictions within the party due to racism and to compete for black support with Garveyism and other supposedly "bourgeois" separatist trends.

The Communist Party adhered only fitfully to this increasingly marginal analysis. Between 1936 and the early 1950s, the right to self-determination was subordinated to the New Deal and the war against fascism. Between 1955–59, the party moved to discard the Thesis entirely, recognizing that black migration from the South had eroded its political viability. After dying this slow death, the Thesis was exhumed by various Marxist-Leninist groups in the 1970s.[37]

There is no consensus about the application, or indeed the meaning, of the Black Nation Thesis on the Marxist-Leninist left. Thus, debates both recapitulate discussions in the Second (and Third) Internationals, and overlap with ongoing academic debate. There has been discussion on: 1. the application of Stalin's criteria (Do blacks constitute a nation?); 2. the material basis of racism (Is racism merely a capitalist tool to divide the working class? Are blacks "superexploited"?); 3. the nature of nationalism (Is nationalism reactionary or revolutionary in character and in what instances?); 4. the right of self-determination (Does this include separatism?).

Lacking an orthodox Marxist theory of racism, and unable to examine U.S. society without a comforting pillow of citations from the "classics," Marxist-Leninist groups have performed some strenuous theoretical contortions in their efforts to apply the literature on the "national question" to racial dynamics in the U.S. In these approaches national categories are frequently substituted for racial ones. This done, the corresponding political rights (e.g., self-determination for "legitimate" nations) can be asserted. The result has been confusion and endless debate over the appropriate criteria for "nationhood."[38] For Marxist-Leninists, nation-based approaches became little more than a convenient way to deal with the messy and untheorized problem of race and racism.[39]

Internal Colonialism

The internal colonialism perspective has been applied to national movements in many countries, among them France,[40] Peru,[41] South Africa,[42] and Great Britain.[43] In the U.S. the concept achieved great currency in the late 1960s and early 1970s (although earlier formulations, such as that of Cruse, can be found), when various writers employed it to account for the upsurge in racial minority militance. Radical nationalist movements (re)surfaced in black, Chicano, Native American, Puerto Rican, and Asian American communities at this time; these groups generally rejected reform-oriented politics, preferring to link their struggles with those of such national liberation movements as the Vietnamese, Algerian, or Chinese revolutions.

Internal colonialism approaches attempted the synthesis of different aspects of racial oppression: economic, political, and cultural, through the invocation of a colonial model. In most cases they appealed as well to nationalist forms of mobilization against this generalized system of oppression. Among the elements of internal colonialism which analysts identified were:

1. A colonial *geography* emphasizing the territoriality or spatial arrangement of population groups along racial lines;
2. A dynamic of *cultural domination and resistance,* in which racial categories are utilized to distinguish between antagonistic colonizing and colonized groups, and conversely, to emphasize the essential cultural unity and autonomy of each;
3. A system of *superexploitation,* understood as a process by which extra-economic coercion is applied to the racially identified colonized group, with the aim of increasing the economic resources appropriated by the colonizers;
4. Institutionalization of *externally based control,* such that the racially identified colonized group is organized in essential political and administrative aspects by the colonizers or their agents.

In some cases militant groups themselves adopted analyses of their conditions and demands based on internal colonialism arguments; in others, scholarly treatments brought these perspectives to bear. Notable studies were devoted to the black[44] and Chicano[45] communities.

Robert Blauner's *Racial Oppression in America* is probably the most familiar general discussion of race in the U.S. written from an internal colonialism perspective, and the one most tailored to U.S. conditions.[46] Blauner has two central preoccupations: the first is to provide theoretical arguments with which to counter the dominant ethnicity paradigm of race in the U.S. As we have seen, that approach sought to incorporate racial categories within ethnic ones, and thus to locate racial minorities in an analytical framework defined by the dynamics of assimilation and cultural pluralism. It generalized from European immigrant experiences in the U.S. to formulate racial theory in ethnic terms. A critical dialogue with Nathan Glazer, the chief spokesperson for the ethnicity paradigm, punctuates several chapters of Blauner's book.[47]

The second overriding commitment in Blauner's work is a commitment to the radical nationalist politics of the 1960s, which Blauner admirably recognizes to have shaped his analysis in counterpoint with the sociological literature he seeks to criticize.[48] He explicitly seeks to provide radical nationalist practice with the theory that it lacks. In adopting the movements of his times, however, Blauner is also forced to transfer their weaknesses from the realm of practice to that of theory.

Blauner effectively employs the distinction between "colonized and immigrant minorities" to criticize the ethnic group paradigm. "Colonized" minorities are those whose presence in the U.S. was the result of "forced entry," a criterion that serves well in general (though not absolutely) to distinguish between those whose entry was the direct result of processes of colonialism and those (Europeans) who "became ethnic groups and minorities within the United States by the essentially voluntary movements of individuals and families."[49]

In respect to Blauner's second point of emphasis, derived chiefly from the militant black politics of the late 1960s (his "basic thesis that the most important expressions of protest in the black community reflect the colonized status of Afro-America"),[50] the internal colonialism approach fares poorly. None of the protest phenomena Blauner cites (ghetto riots, cultural nationalism, ghetto-based "community control" movements) necessitates the internal colonialism perspective as a framework of explanation. Rioting has been explained as an extension of "normal" politics when institutionalized channels of political expression are blocked.[51] What is "nationalist" about cultural movements among the oppressed is a matter of considerable ambiguity and debate. Ghetto community control demands have proved subject to quite moderate (or "reformist") interpretation, besides proving to be at best "too little, too late" as key decisions about the cities' fate are made elsewhere.[52] At worst such demands provide grounds for rearticulation in new right or neoconservative analyses and programs, for example to provide codewords for opposition to busing or welfare rights.[53]

Blauner's approach also neglects class cleavages within minority communities, inter-minority group rivalries, and the extensive interpenetration in the U.S. of minority and majority societies, which, though hardly as complete as an ethnicity theorist like Glazer might wish to argue, casts into doubt the internal colonialism analogy in respect to territoriality, at the very least.[54] This interpenetration, in our view, also suggests limits to other elements of the nation-based paradigm in the U.S. context. Cultural domination/cultural autonomy, for example, appears to be but one element of a broader cultural dynamic that includes both the distinctiveness and the interaction of majority- and minority-based cultural elements. Superexploitation does not encompass contemporary economic developments which include marginalization and permanent dependency for many on the one hand, and significant "upward mobility" for some on the other.

In many respects, then, the patent limitations of the analogy to Vietnam or Algeria, an analogy which was politically and not analytically grounded, doomed the internal colonialist version of nation-based racial theory.

Some Critical Remarks on the Nation-Based Paradigm

How effectively does the nation-based paradigm account for racial dynamics? In fact, the connection is tenuous. The analogy between U.S.

conditions and colonial systems of discrimination composed of colonizers and colonized—systems which made use of racial distinctions—does not automatically carry over into postcolonial society. Even the specifically national aspects of the internal colonialism perspective (geography, culture, extra-economic coercion, and external political rule), are rather easily dispensed with, as Burawoy shows in his critique of Blauner.[55] As applied to the contemporary U.S. (with significant exceptions such as Native American conditions or the case of Puerto Rico), the appeal of nationalism, in political practice or in theory, appears to be limited. Unlike many of the old colonial nations, and possibly because it was created out of a colony, the U.S. political scene allows radical nationalism little space.[56] Even black nationalism, the most vibrant and multifaceted minority movement of this kind, has been mainly a refuge for activists and intellectuals disaffected by the intransigence of the racial order and disillusioned by moderate programs for change.

What is important in the nation-based account is the paradigm's retention of an explanatory framework *based* on race (even if race is seen through the distorted "national" lens). Nation-based theories of race, while not free of epiphenomenalism, contrast sharply with both the ethnicity and class approaches in this respect. Perhaps it is the very inability of the nation-based account to specify precisely what exactly is "national" about racial oppression in the U.S. which leads it to lend a certain "primacy" and integrity to racial phenomena. The ethnicity and class paradigms, working from more secure assumptions about the "primacy" of their paradigmatic categories, tend to dissolve the unity of racially constituted groups.

While the nation-based account fails to demonstrate the existence of racial minority or colonized "nations" internal to the U.S. and structurally separated from the majority society, some applications of this paradigm do facilitate comprehensiveness in the study of racial dynamics. Nation-based approaches may unite the micro- and macro-levels of racially shaped experience, for example, or permit comparisons among different groups. Thus the nation-based approach serves in some ways as an inadequate but partial prototype for the approach we present in the following chapter in respect to "racial formation."

Toward a Racial Formation Perspective

The ethnic group-, class-, and nation-based perspectives all neglect the specificity of race as an autonomous field of social conflict, political organization, and cultural/ideological meaning. Authors working within each paradigm locate the fundamental elements of race, not surprisingly, on their own home ground.

For ethnicity theory, this terrain is that of the *dynamics of incorporation* of minority groups into the dominant society. Ethnicity theory is therefore primarily concerned with questions of group identity; with the resolution of tensions between the twin pressures of assimilation (dissolution of group identity) and cultural pluralism (preservation of group identity); and with the prospects for political integration via normal political channels. The terrain of ethnicity was first explored in U.S. history by immigrating Europeans, and later mapped by intellectuals whose visceral loyalties and social scientific guideposts were framed in terms of the histories of these immigrant groups. For these writers there exists an intense will to pound the square peg of race into the round hole of ethnicity.

For practitioners of class theory, the terrain upon which race may best be encountered is that of *inequality*: racial dynamics are understood primarily in terms of the social allocation of advantage and disadvantage, winners and losers, and the origins and structure of discrimination. Racial inequality is an outcome, not a cause; its roots lie elsewhere: in market imperfections, political power structures, or the search for secure means of labor control. From the perspective of the class paradigm, racial dynamics manifest these more fundamental processes; only secondarily may they take on "a life of their own," or a "relative autonomy."

For nation-based writers, the terrain upon which race may best be analyzed is territorial, geographical, in a particularly epochal sense. The European powers divided up the world in the heyday of colonialism, assigning power and privilege to the planet's North, and misery and exploitation to its South. With the rule of Europeans and their descendants over the "natives" of the rest of the globe and their descendants went a highly flexible and adaptive, but nevertheless inexorable "color code," a system of racial distinctions that was (usually) effective in reinforcing colonial domination. The "real" issues, though, weren't racial, but *national* oppression and liberation, or (at a minimum) cultural autonomy and the right to self-determination. Thus race was assigned epiphenomenal status once again, this time as a manifestation of deeper "national" conflicts.

None of these paradigms can stand alone. There is necessarily overlap among them. Certain class approaches, as we have noted, reinforce the ethnicity school's conservative individualist model of equality. Certain nation-based analyses adopt a version of Marxism. Each paradigm has perforce to cope with the great historical and sociological weight of the others' central foci: ethnicity theory and class theory must address the issue of colonialism, for example. In our ideal-typical approach, we have necessarily given greater weight to the uniqueness of each paradigm than to continuity among the paradigms. Each does stand on its own particular ground, each does adopt a specific frame of reference which distinguishes it from the others, but each paradigm must also address a unitary social and historical problematic—that of race in the U.S. Hence the phenomenon of partial encounters and partial "misses" among the competing paradigms.

Though none of the three paradigms can grasp the nettle of race, each is able to develop certain fascinating insights into racial phenomena. The ethnicity school can document in rich detail the contingency and adaptability of racial identities (considered of course in ethnic group terms), basing its work on the transformations which European immigrants underwent. Thus certain apparent anomalies—the "success," for example, of Japanese Americans—can to some extent be addressed within the ethnicity framework. Ethnicity theory, especially in its post-1965 incarnation, comes closest to our concept of "racial formation," though of course this term does not appear in the ethnicity framework. Writers working within this paradigm note the frequent shifts of ethnic identity and the political significance of its contingency, but still fail to recognize at all adequately, either historically or in the present, the qualitative differences between white and non-white groups' encounters with U.S. society. Or to put it another way, they fail to grasp the extent to which U.S. society is racially structured from top to bottom.

In similar fashion, various class theories of race have been able to explain shifts in patterns of exploitation, mobility, and social control with great insight.[1] Yet these same approaches generally fail to notice the political and cultural dimensions of these shifts—often their most salient features. Thus William Julius Wilson, probably the most incisive class theorist of race, accepts the existence of an egalitarian racial state after 1965, and Harold Baron links his conception of a new racial order to advanced capitalist reproduction imperatives in functionalist fashion.

The great insight of nation-based approaches has always been their ability to connect U.S. conditions with global patterns based in the legacy of colonialism. Yet this link has often proved tenuous. A sort of "exceptionalism" turns out to be necessary if one is to address racial dynamics in the U.S. (and probably in respect to any particular nation's racial dynamics); this is what we seek to provide with our "racial formation" perspective.

No new theory can be proposed simply to dispense with these paradigms; there is too much of value within them. Nor is this our aim in suggesting a perspective based on the concept of racial formation in order to understand U.S. racial dynamics, especially in recent decades. Rather we wish to detach racial theory from epiphenomenalism, from entanglements which in our view are superfluous and stifling, in order to grasp the complexities of racial identity, politics, and social structure in the U.S. We believe that much new insight is to be gained in that process, to which, in Part Two, we now turn.

PART TWO

4

Racial Formation

In 1982–83, Susie Guillory Phipps unsuccessfully sued the Louisiana Bureau of Vital Records to change her racial classification from black to white. The descendant of an 18th-century white planter and a black slave, Phipps was designated "black" in her birth certificate in accordance with a 1970 state law which declared anyone with at least 1/32nd "Negro blood" to be black.

The Phipps case raised intriguing questions about the concept of race, its meaning in contemporary society, and its use (and abuse) in public policy. Assistant Attorney General Ron Davis defended the law by pointing out that some type of racial classification was necessary to comply with federal record-keeping requirements and to facilitate programs for the prevention of genetic diseases. Phipps's attorney, Brian Begue, argued that the assignment of racial categories on birth certificates was unconstitutional and that the 1/32nd designation was inaccurate. He called on a retired Tulane University professor who cited research indicating that most Louisiana whites have at least 1/20th "Negro" ancestry.

In the end, Phipps lost. The court upheld the state's right to classify and quantify racial identity.[1]

Phipps's problematic racial identity, and her effort to resolve it through state action, is in many ways a parable of America's unsolved racial dilemma. It illustrates the difficulties of defining race and assigning individuals or groups to racial categories. It shows how the racial legacies of the past—slavery and bigotry—continue to shape the present. It reveals both the deep involvement of the state in the organization and interpretation of race, and the inadequacy of state institutions to carry out these functions. It demonstrates how deeply Americans both as individuals and as a civilization are shaped, and indeed haunted, by race.

Having lived her whole life thinking that she was white, Phipps suddenly discovers that by legal definition she is not. In U.S. society, such an event is indeed catastrophic.[2] But if she is not white, of what race is she? The *state* claims that she is black, based on its rules of classification,[3] and another state agency, the court, upholds this judgment. But despite these classificatory standards which have imposed an either-or logic on racial identity, Phipps will not in fact "change color." Unlike what would have happened during slavery times if one's claim to whiteness was successfully challenged, we can assume that despite the outcome of her legal challenge, Phipps will remain in most of the social relationships she had occupied before the trial. Her socialization, her familial and friendship networks, her cultural orientation, will not change. She will simply have to wrestle with her newly acquired "hybridized" condition. She will have to confront the "Other" within.

The designation of racial categories and the determination of racial identity is no simple task. For centuries, this question has precipitated intense debates and conflicts, particularly in the U.S.—disputes over natural and legal rights, over the distribution of resources, and indeed, over who shall live and who shall die.

A crucial dimension of the Phipps case is that it illustrates the inadequacy of claims that race is a mere matter of variations in human physiognomy, that it is simply a matter of skin color. But if race cannot be understood in this manner, how *can* it be understood? We cannot fully hope to address this topic—no less than the meaning of race, its role in society, and the forces which shape it—in one chapter, nor indeed in one book. Our goal in this chapter, however, is far from modest: we wish to offer at least the outlines of a theory of race and racism.

What Is Race?

There is a continuous temptation to think of race as an *essence*, as something fixed, concrete, and objective. And there is also an opposite temptation: to imagine race as a mere *illusion,* a purely ideological construct which some ideal non-racist social order would eliminate. It is necessary to challenge both these positions, to disrupt and reframe the rigid and bipolar manner in which they are posed and debated, and to transcend the presumably irreconcilable relationship between them.

The effort must be made to understand race as an unstable and "decentered" complex of social meanings constantly being transformed by political struggle. With this in mind, let us propose a definition: *race is a concept which signifies and symbolizes social conflicts and interests by referring to different types of human bodies*. Although the concept of race invokes biologically based human characteristics (so-called "phenotypes"), selection of these particular human features for purposes of racial signification is always and necessarily a social and historical process. In contrast to the other major distinction of this type, that of gender, there is no biological basis for distinguishing among human groups along the lines of race.[4] Indeed, the categories employed to differentiate among human groups along racial lines reveal themselves, upon serious examination, to be at best imprecise, and at worst completely arbitrary.

If the concept of race is so nebulous, can we not dispense with it? Can we not "do without" race, at least in the "enlightened" present? This question has been posed often, and with greater frequency in recent years.[5] An affirmative answer would of course present obvious practical difficulties: it is rather difficult to jettison widely held beliefs, beliefs which moreover are central to everyone's identity and understanding of the social world. So the attempt to banish the concept as an archaism is at best counterintuitive. But a deeper difficulty, we believe, is inherent in the very formulation of this schema, in its way of posing race as a *problem*, a misconception left over from the past, and suitable now only for the dustbin of history.

A more effective starting point is the recognition that despite its uncertainties and contradictions, the concept of race continues to play a fundamental role in structuring and representing the social world. The task for theory is to explain this situation. It is to avoid both the utopian framework which sees race as an illusion we can somehow "get beyond," and also the essentialist formulation which sees race as something objective and fixed, a biological datum.[6] Thus we should think of race as an element of social structure rather than as an irregularity within it; we should see race as a dimension of human representation rather than an illusion. These perspectives inform the theoretical approach we call racial formation.

Racial Formation

We define *racial formation* as the sociohistorical process by which racial categories are created, inhabited, transformed, and destroyed. Our attempt to elaborate a theory of racial formation will proceed in two steps. First, we argue that racial formation is a process of historically situated *projects* in which human bodies and social structures are represented and orga-nized. Next we link racial formation to the evolution of hegemony, the way in which society is organized and ruled. Such an approach, we believe, can facilitate understanding of a whole range of contemporary controver-sies and dilemmas involving race, including the nature of racism, the rela-tionship of race to other forms of differences, inequalities, and oppression such as sexism and nationalism, and the dilemmas of racial identity today.

From a racial formation perspective, race is a matter of both social struc-ture and cultural representation. Too often, the attempt is made to under-stand race simply or primarily in terms of only one of these two analytical dimensions.[7] For example, efforts to explain racial inequality as a purely social structural phenomenon are unable to account for the origins, pat-terning, and transformation of racial difference.

Conversely, many examinations of racial difference—understood as a matter of cultural attributes *à la* ethnicity theory, or as a society-wide signification system, *à la* some poststructuralist accounts—cannot com-prehend such structural phenomena as racial stratification in the labor market or patterns of residential segregation.

An alternative approach is to think of racial formation processes as occurring through a linkage between structure and representation. Racial *projects* do the ideological "work" of making these links. *A racial project is simultaneously an interpretation, representation, or explanation of racial dynamics, and an effort to reorganize and redistribute resources along par-ticular racial lines.* Racial projects connect what race *means* in a particu-lar discursive practice and the ways in which both social structures and everyday experiences are racially *organized,* based upon that meaning. Let us consider this proposition, first in terms of large-scale or macro-level social processes, and then in terms of other dimensions of the racial for-mation process.

Racial Formation as a Macro-Level Social Process

To *interpret the meaning of race is to frame it social structurally.* Con-sider for example, this statement by Charles Murray on welfare reform:

> My proposal for dealing with the racial issue in social welfare is to repeal every bit of legislation and reverse every court decision that in any way requires, recommends, or awards differential treatment according to race, and thereby put us back onto the track that we left in 1965. We may argue about the appropriate limits of govern-ment intervention in trying to enforce the ideal, but at least it

should be possible to identify the ideal: Race is not a morally admissible reason for treating one person differently from another. Period.[8]

Here there is a partial but significant analysis of the meaning of race: it is not a morally valid basis upon which to treat people "differently from one another." We may notice someone's race, but we cannot act upon that awareness. We must act in a "color-blind" fashion. This analysis of the meaning of race is immediately linked to a specific conception of the role of race in the social structure: it can play no part in government action, save in "the enforcement of the ideal." No state policy can legitimately require, recommend, or award different status according to race. This example can be classified as a particular type of racial project in the present-day U.S.—a "neoconservative" one.

Conversely, *to recognize the racial dimension in social structure is to interpret the meaning of race.* Consider the following statement by the late Supreme Court Justice Thurgood Marshall on minority "set-aside" programs:

> A profound difference separates governmental actions that them-
> selves are racist, and governmental actions that seek to remedy the
> effects of prior racism or to prevent neutral government activity
> from perpetuating the effects of such racism.[9]

Here the focus is on the racial dimensions of *social structure*—in this case of state activity and policy. The argument is that state actions in the past and present have treated people in very different ways according to their race, and thus the government cannot retreat from its policy responsibilities in this area. It cannot suddenly declare itself "color-blind" without in fact perpetuating the same type of differential, racist treatment.[10] Thus, race continues to signify difference and structure inequality. Here, racialized social structure is immediately linked to an interpretation of the meaning of race. This example too can be classified as a particular type of racial project in the present-day U.S.—a "liberal" one.

To be sure, such political labels as "neoconservative" or "liberal" cannot fully capture the complexity of racial projects, for these are always multiply determined, politically contested, and deeply shaped by their historical context. Thus, encapsulated within the neoconservative example cited here are certain egalitarian commitments which derive from a previous historical context in which they played a very different role, and which are rearticulated in neoconservative racial discourse precisely to oppose a more open-ended, more capacious conception of the meaning of equality. Similarly, in the liberal example, Justice Marshall recognizes that the contemporary state, which was formerly the architect of segregation and the chief enforcer of racial difference, has a tendency to reproduce those patterns of inequality in a new guise. Thus he admonishes it (in dissent, significantly) to fulfill its responsibilities to uphold a robust conception of equality. These particular instances, then, demonstrate how racial projects are always concretely framed, and thus are always contested and unstable. The social structures they uphold or attack, and the representations of race they articulate, are never invented out of the air, but exist in a definite historical context, having descended from previous conflicts. This contestation appears to be permanent in respect to race.

These two examples of contemporary racial projects are drawn from mainstream political debate; they may be characterized as center-right and center-left expressions of contemporary racial politics.[11] We can, however, expand the discussion of racial formation processes far beyond these familiar examples. In fact, we can identify racial projects in at least three other analytical dimensions: first, the political spectrum can be broadened to include radical projects, on both the left and right, as well as along other political axes. Second, analysis of racial projects can take place not only at the macro-level of racial policy-making, state activity, and collective action, but also at the micro-level of everyday experience. Third, the concept of racial projects can be applied across historical time, to identify racial formation dynamics in the past. We shall now offer examples of each of these types of racial projects.

The Political Spectrum of Racial Formation

We have encountered examples of a neoconservative racial project, in which the significance of race is denied, leading to a "color-blind" racial politics and "hands off" policy orientation; and of a "liberal" racial project, in which the significance of race is affirmed, leading to an egalitarian and "activist" state policy. But these by no means exhaust the political possibilities. Other racial projects can be readily identified on the contemporary U.S. scene. For example, "far right" projects, which uphold biologistic and racist views of difference, explicitly argue for white supremacist policies. "New right" projects overtly claim to hold "color-blind" views, but covertly manipulate racial fears in order to achieve political gains.[12] On the left, "radical democratic" projects invoke notions of racial "difference" in combination with egalitarian politics and policy.

Further variations can also be noted. For example, "nationalist" projects, both conservative and radical, stress the incompatibility of racially defined group identity with the legacy of white supremacy, and therefore advocate a social structural solution of separation, either complete or partial.[13] As we saw in Chapter 3, nationalist currents represent a profound legacy of the centuries of racial absolutism that initially defined the meaning of race in the U.S. Nationalist concerns continue to influence racial debate in the form of Afrocentrism and other expressions of identity politics.

Taking the range of politically organized racial projects as a whole, we can "map" the current pattern of racial formation at the level of the public sphere, the "macro-level" in which public debate and mobilization takes place.[14] But important as this is, the terrain on which racial formation occurs is broader yet.

Racial Formation as Everyday Experience

At the micro-social level, racial projects also link signification and structure, not so much as efforts to shape policy or define large-scale meaning, but as the applications of "common sense." To see racial projects operating at the level of everyday life, we have only to examine the many ways in which, often unconsciously, we "notice" race.

One of the first things we notice about people when we meet them (along with their sex) is their race. We utilize race to provide clues about *who* a person is. This fact is made painfully obvious when we encounter someone whom we cannot conveniently racially categorize—someone who is, for example, racially "mixed" or of an ethnic/racial group we are not familiar with. Such an encounter becomes a source of discomfort and momentarily a crisis of racial meaning.

Our ability to interpret racial meanings depends on preconceived notions of a racialized social structure. Comments such as, "Funny, you don't look black," betray an underlying image of what black should be. We expect people to act out their apparent racial identities; indeed we become disoriented when they do not. The black banker harassed by police while walking in casual clothes through his own well-off neighborhood, the Latino or white kid rapping in perfect Afro patois, the unending *faux pas* committed by whites who assume that the non-whites they encounter are servants or tradespeople, the belief that non-white colleagues are less qualified persons hired to fulfill affirmative action guidelines, indeed the whole gamut of racial stereotypes—that "white men can't jump," that Asians can't dance, etc., etc.—all testify to the way a racialized social structure shapes racial experience and conditions meaning. Analysis of such stereotypes reveals the always present, already active link between our view of the social structure—its demography, its laws, its customs, its threats—and our conception of what race means.

Conversely, our ongoing interpretation of our experience in racial terms shapes our relations to the institutions and organizations through which we are imbedded in social structure. Thus we expect differences in skin color, or other racially coded characteristics, to explain social differences. Temperament, sexuality, intelligence, athletic ability, aesthetic preferences, and so on are presumed to be fixed and discernible from the palpable mark of race. Such diverse questions as our confidence and trust in others (for example, clerks or salespeople, media figures, neighbors), our sexual preferences and romantic images, our tastes in music, films, dance, or sports, and our very ways of talking, walking, eating, and dreaming become racially coded simply because we live in a society where racial awareness is so pervasive. Thus in ways too comprehensive even to monitor consciously, and despite periodic calls—neoconservative and otherwise—for us to ignore race and adopt "color-blind" racial attitudes, skin color "differences" continue to rationalize distinct treatment of racially identified individuals and groups.

To summarize the argument so far: the theory of racial formation suggests that society is suffused with racial projects, large and small, to which all are subjected. This racial "subjection" is quintessentially ideological. Everybody learns some combination, some version, of the rules of racial classification, and of her own racial identity, often without obvious teaching or conscious inculcation. Thus are we inserted in a comprehensively racialized social structure. Race becomes "common sense"—a way of comprehending, explaining, and acting in the world. A vast web of racial projects mediates between the discursive or representational means in which race is identified and signified on the one hand, and the institutional and organizational forms in which it is routinized and standardized on the other. These projects are the heart of the racial formation process.

Under such circumstances, it is not possible to represent race discursively without simultaneously locating it, explicitly or implicitly, in a social structural (and historical) context. Nor is it possible to organize, maintain, or transform social structures without simultaneously engaging, once more either explicitly or implicitly, in racial signification. Racial formation, therefore, is a kind of synthesis, an outcome, of the interaction of racial projects on a society-wide level. These projects are, of course, vastly different in scope and effect. They include large-scale public action, state activities, and interpretations of racial conditions in artistic, journalistic, or academic fora,[15] as well as the seemingly infinite number of racial judgments and practices we carry out at the level of individual experience.

Since racial formation is always historically situated, our understanding of the significance of race, and of the way race structures society, has changed enormously over time. The processes of racial formation we encounter today, the racial projects large and small which structure U.S. society in so many ways, are merely the present-day outcomes of a complex historical evolution. The contemporary racial order remains transient. By knowing something of how it evolved, we can perhaps better discern where it is heading. We therefore turn next to a historical survey of the racial formation process, and the conflicts and debates it has engendered.

The Evolution of Modern Racial Awareness

The identification of distinctive human groups, and their association with differences in physical appearance, goes back to prehistory, and can be found in the earliest documents—in the Bible, for example, or in Herodotus. But the emergence of a modern conception of race does not occur until the rise of Europe and the arrival of Europeans in the Americas. Even the hostility and suspicion with which Christian Europe viewed its two significant non-Christian "Others"—the Muslims and the Jews— cannot be viewed as more than a rehearsal for racial formation, since these antagonisms, for all their bloodletting and chauvinism, were always and everywhere religiously interpreted.[16]

It was only when European explorers reached the Western Hemisphere, when the oceanic seal separating the "old" and the "new" worlds was breached, that the distinctions and categorizations fundamental to a racialized social structure, and to a discourse of race, began to appear. The European explorers were the advance guard of merchant capitalism, which sought new openings for trade. What they found exceeded their wildest dreams, for never before and never again in human history has an opportunity for the appropriation of wealth remotely approached that presented by the "discovery."[17]

But the Europeans also "discovered" people, people who looked and acted differently. These "natives" challenged their "discoverers'" pre-existing conceptions of the origins and possibilities of the human species.[18] The representation and interpretation of the meaning of the indigenous peoples' existence became a crucial matter, one which would affect the outcome of the enterprise of conquest. For the "discovery" raised disturbing questions as to whether *all* could be considered part of the same "family of man," and more practically, the extent to which native peoples could be exploited and enslaved. Thus religious debates flared over the attempt to reconcile the various Christian metaphysics with the existence of peoples who were more "different" than any whom Europe had previously known.[19]

In practice, of course, the seizure of territories and goods, the introduction of slavery through the *encomienda* and other forms of coerced native labor, and then through the organization of the African slave trade— not to mention the practice of outright extermination—all presupposed a worldview which distinguished Europeans, as children of God, full-fledged human beings, etc., from "Others." Given the dimensions and the ineluctability of the European onslaught, given the conquerors' determination to appropriate both labor and goods, and given the presence of an axiomatic and unquestioned Christianity among them, the ferocious division of society into Europeans and "Others" soon coalesced. This was true despite the famous 16th-century theological and philosophical debates about the identity of indigenous peoples.[20]

Indeed debates about the nature of the "Others" reached their practical limits with a certain dispatch. Plainly they would never touch the essential: nothing, after all, would induce the Europeans to pack up and go home. We cannot examine here the early controversies over the status of American souls. We simply wish to emphasize that the "discovery" signalled a break from the previous proto-racial awareness by which Europe contemplated its "Others" in a relatively disorganized fashion. In other words, the "conquest of America" was not simply an epochal historical event—however unparalleled in its importance. It was also the advent of a consolidated social structure of exploitation, appropriation, domination. Its representation, first in religious terms, but soon enough in scientific and political ones, initiated modern racial awareness.

The conquest, therefore, was the first—and given the dramatic nature of the case, perhaps the greatest—racial formation project. Its significance was by no means limited to the Western Hemisphere, for it began the work of constituting Europe as the metropole, the center, of a group of empires which could take, as Marx would later write, "the globe for a theater."[21] It represented this new imperial structure as a struggle between civilization and barbarism, and implicated in this representation all the great European philosophies, literary traditions, and social theories of the modern age.[22] In short, just as the noise of the "big bang" still resonates through the universe, so the overdetermined construction of world "civilization" as a product of the rise of Europe and the subjugation of the rest of us, still defines the race concept.

From Religion to Science

After the initial depredations of conquest, religious justifications for racial difference gradually gave way to scientific ones. By the time of the Enlightenment, a general awareness of race was pervasive, and most of the great philosophers of Europe, such as Hegel, Kant, Hume, and Locke, had issued virulently racist opinions.

The problem posed by race during the late 18th century was markedly different than it had been in the age of "discovery," expropriation, and slaughter. The social structures in which race operated were no longer primarily those of military conquest and plunder, nor of the establishment of thin beachheads of colonization on the edge of what had once seemed a limitless wilderness. Now the issues were much more complicated: nation-building, establishment of national economies in the world trading system, resistance to the arbitrary authority of monarchs, and the assertion of the "natural rights" of "man," including the right of revolution.[23] In such a situation, racially organized exploitation, in the form of slavery, the expansion of colonies, and the continuing expulsion of native peoples, was both necessary and newly difficult to justify.

The invocation of scientific criteria to demonstrate the "natural" basis of racial hierarchy was both a logical consequence of the rise of this form of knowledge, and an attempt to provide a more subtle and nuanced account of human complexity in the new, "enlightened" age. Spurred on by the classificatory scheme of living organisms devised by Linnaeus in *Systema Naturae* (1735), many scholars in the 18th and 19th centuries dedicated themselves to the identification and ranking of variations in humankind. Race was conceived as a *biological* concept, a matter of species. Voltaire wrote that "the negro race is a species of men (sic) as different from ours ... as the breed of spaniels is from that of greyhounds," and in a formulation echoing down from his century to our own, declared that

> If their understanding is not of a different nature from ours ... ,
> it is at least greatly inferior. They are not capable of any great
> application or association of ideas, and seem formed neither for the
> advantages nor the abuses of philosophy.[24]

Jefferson, the preeminent exponent of the Enlightenment doctrine of "the rights of man" on North American shores, echoed these sentiments:

> In general their existence appears to participate more of sensation
> than reflection. ... [I]n memory they are equal to whites, in reason
> much inferior ... [and] in imagination they are dull, tasteless, and

anomalous. . . . I advance it therefore . . . that the blacks, whether originally a different race, or made distinct by time and circumstances, are inferior to the whites. . . . Will not a lover of natural history, then, one who views the gradations in all the animals with the eye of philosophy, excuse an effort to keep those in the department of Man (sic) as distinct as nature has formed them?[25]

Such claims of species distinctiveness among humans justified the inequitable allocation of political and social rights, while still upholding the doctrine of "the rights of man." The quest to obtain a precise scientific definition of race sustained debates which continue to rage today. Yet despite efforts ranging from Dr. Samuel Morton's studies of cranial capacity[26] to contemporary attempts to base racial classification on shared gene pools,[27] the concept of race has defied biological definition.

In the 19th century, Count Joseph Arthur de Gobineau drew upon the most respected scientific studies of his day to compose his four-volume *Essay on the Inequality of Races* (1853–1855).[28] He not only greatly influenced the racial thinking of the period, but his themes would be echoed in the racist ideologies of the next one hundred years: beliefs that superior races produced superior cultures and that racial intermixtures resulted in the degradation of the superior racial stock. These ideas found expression, for instance, in the eugenics movement launched by Darwin's cousin, Francis Galton, which had an immense impact on scientific and sociopolitical thought in Europe and the U.S.[29] In the wake of civil war and emancipation, and with immigration from southern and Eastern Europe as well as East Asia running high, the U.S. was particularly fertile ground for notions such as social darwinism and eugenics.

Attempts to discern the *scientific meaning* of race continue to the present day. For instance, an essay by Arthur Jensen which argued that hereditary factors shape intelligence not only revived the "nature or nurture" controversy, but also raised highly volatile questions about racial equality itself.[30] All such attempts seek to remove the concept of race from the historical context in which it arose and developed. They employ an *essentialist* approach which suggests instead that the truth of race is a matter of innate characteristics, of which skin color and other physical attributes provide only the most obvious, and in some respects most superficial, indicators.

From Science to Politics

It has taken scholars more than a century to reject biologistic notions of race in favor of an approach which regards race as a *social* concept. This trend has been slow and uneven, and even today remains somewhat embattled, but its overall direction seems clear. At the turn of the century Max Weber discounted biological explanations for racial conflict and instead highlighted the social and political factors which engendered such conflict.[31] W. E. B. Du Bois argued for a sociopolitical definition of race by identifying "the color line" as "the problem of the 20th century."[32] Pioneering cultural anthropologist Franz Boas rejected attempts to link racial identifications and cultural traits, labelling as pseudoscientific any assumption of a continuum of "higher" and "lower" cultural groups.[33] Other early exponents of social, as opposed to biological, views of race included Robert E. Park, founder of the "Chicago school" of sociology, and Alain Leroy Locke, philosopher and theorist of the Harlem Renaissance.[34]

Perhaps more important than these and subsequent intellectual efforts, however, were the political struggles of racially defined groups themselves. Waged all around the globe under a variety of banners such as anticolonialism and civil rights, these battles to challenge various structural and cultural racisms have been a major feature of 20th-century politics. The racial horrors of the 20th century—colonial slaughter and apartheid, the genocide of the holocaust, and the massive bloodlettings required to end these evils—have also indelibly marked the theme of race as a political issue *par excellence*.

As a result of prior efforts and struggles, we have now reached the point of fairly general agreement that race is not a biologically given but rather a socially constructed way of differentiating human beings. While a tremendous achievement, the transcendence of biologistic conceptions of race does not provide any reprieve from the dilemmas of racial injustice and conflict, nor from controversies over the significance of race in the present. Views of race as socially constructed simply recognize the fact that these conflicts and controversies are now more properly framed on the terrain of politics. By privileging politics in the analysis which follows we do not mean to suggest that race has been displaced as a concern of scientific inquiry, or that struggles over cultural representation are no longer important. We do argue, however, that race is now a preeminently political phenomenon. Such an assertion invites examination of the evolving role of racial politics in the U.S. This is the subject to which we now turn.

Dictatorship, Democracy, Hegemony

For most of its existence both as European colony and as an independent nation, the U.S. was a *racial dictatorship*. From 1607 to 1865—258 years—most non-whites were firmly eliminated from the sphere of politics.[35] After the Civil War there was the brief egalitarian experiment of Reconstruction which terminated ignominiously in 1877. In its wake followed almost a century of legally sanctioned segregation and denial of the vote, nearly absolute in the South and much of the Southwest, less effective in the North and far West, but formidable in any case.[36] These barriers fell only in the mid-1960s, a mere quarter-century ago. Nor did the successes of the black movement and its allies mean that all obstacles to their political participation had now been abolished. Patterns of racial inequality have proven, unfortunately, to be quite stubborn and persistent.

It is important, therefore, to recognize that in many respects, racial dictatorship is the norm against which all U.S. politics must be measured. The centuries of racial dictatorship have had three very large consequences: first, they defined "American" identity as white, as the negation of racialized "otherness"—at first largely African and indigenous, later Latin American and Asian as well.[37] This negation took shape in both law and custom, in public institutions and in forms of cultural representation. It became the archetype of hegemonic rule in the U.S. It was the successor to the conquest as the "master" racial project.

Second, racial dictatorship organized (albeit sometimes in an incoherent and contradictory fashion) the "color line" rendering it the fundamental division in U.S. society. The dictatorship elaborated, articulated, and drove racial divisions not only through institutions, but also through psyches, extending up to our own time the racial obsessions of the conquest and slavery periods.

Third, racial dictatorship consolidated the oppositional racial consciousness and organization originally framed by marronage[38] and slave revolts, by indigenous resistance, and by nationalisms of various sorts. Just as the conquest created the "native" where once there had been Pequot, Iroquois, or Tutelo, so too it created the "black" where once there had been Asante or Ovimbundu, Yoruba or Bakongo.

The transition from a racial dictatorship to a racial democracy has been a slow, painful, and contentious one; it remains far from complete. A recognition of the abiding presence of racial dictatorship, we contend, is crucial for the development of a theory of racial formation in the U.S. It is also crucial to the task of relating racial formation to the broader context of political practice, organization, and change.

In this context, a key question arises: in what way is racial formation related to politics as a whole? How, for example, does race articulate with other axes of oppression and difference—most importantly class and gender—along which politics is organized today?

The answer, we believe, lies in the concept of *hegemony*. Antonio Gramsci —the Italian communist who placed this concept at the center of his life's work—understood it as the conditions necessary, in a given society, for the achievement and consolidation of rule. He argued that hegemony was always constituted by a combination of coercion and consent. Although rule can be obtained by force, it cannot be secured and maintained, especially in modern society, without the element of consent. Gramsci conceived of consent as far more than merely the legitimation of authority. In his view, consent extended to the incorporation by the ruling group of many of the key interests of subordinated groups, often to the explicit disadvantage of the rulers themselves.[39] Gramsci's treatment of hegemony went even farther: he argued that in order to consolidate their hegemony, ruling groups must elaborate and maintain a popular system of ideas and practices—through education, the media, religion, folk wisdom, etc.—which he called "common sense." It is through its production and its adherence to this "common sense," this ideology (in the broadest sense of the term), that a society gives its consent to the way in which it is ruled.[40]

These provocative concepts can be extended and applied to an understanding of racial rule. In the Americas, the conquest represented the violent introduction of a new form of rule whose relationship with those it subjugated was almost entirely coercive. In the U.S., the origins of racial division, and of racial signification and identity formation, lie in a system of rule which was extremely dictatorial. The mass murders and expulsions of indigenous people, and the enslavement of Africans, surely evoked and inspired little consent in their founding moments.

Over time, however, the balance of coercion and consent began to change. It is possible to locate the origins of hegemony right within the heart of racial dictatorship, for the effort to possess the oppressor's tools—religion and philosophy in this case—was crucial to emancipation (the effort to possess oneself). As Ralph Ellison reminds us, "The slaves often took the essence of the aristocratic ideal (as they took Christianity) with far more seriousness than their masters."[41] In their language, in their religion with its focus on the Exodus theme and on Jesus's tribulations, in their music with its figuring of suffering, resistance, perseverance, and transcendence, in their interrogation of a political philosophy which sought perpetually to rationalize their bondage in a supposedly "free" society, the slaves incorporated elements of racial rule into their thought and practice, turning them against their original bearers.

Racial rule can be understood as a slow and uneven historical process which has moved from dictatorship to democracy, from domination to hegemony. In this transition, hegemonic forms of racial rule—those based on consent—eventually came to supplant those based on coercion. Of course, before this assertion can be accepted, it must be qualified in important ways. By no means has the U.S. established racial democracy at the end of the century, and by no means is coercion a thing of the past. But the sheer complexity of the racial questions U.S. society confronts today, the welter of competing racial projects and contradictory racial experiences which Americans undergo, suggests that hegemony is a useful and appropriate term with which to characterize contemporary racial rule.

Our key theoretical notion of racial projects helps to extend and broaden the question of rule. Projects are the building blocks not just of racial formation, but of hegemony in general. Hegemony operates by simultaneously structuring and signifying. As in the case of racial opposition, gender- or class-based conflict today links structural inequity and injustice on the one hand, and identifies and represents its subjects on the other. The success of modern-day feminism, for example, has depended on its ability to reinterpret gender as a matter of both injustice and identity/difference.

Today, political opposition necessarily takes shape on the terrain of hegemony. Far from ruling principally through exclusion and coercion (though again, these are hardly absent) hegemony operates by including its subjects, incorporating its opposition. *Pace* both Marxists and liberals, there is no longer any universal or privileged region of political action or discourse.[42] Race, class, and gender all represent potential antagonisms whose significance is no longer given, if it ever was.

Thus race, class, and gender (as well as sexual orientation) constitute "regions" of hegemony, areas in which certain political projects can take shape. They share certain obvious attributes in that they are all "socially constructed," and they all consist of a field of projects whose common feature is their linkage of social structure and signification.

Going beyond this, it is crucial to emphasize that race, class, and gender, are not fixed and discrete categories, and that such "regions" are by no means autonomous. They overlap, intersect, and fuse with each other in countless ways. Such mutual determinations have been illustrated by Patricia Hill Collins's survey and theoretical synthesis of the themes and issues of black feminist thought.[43] They are also evident in Evelyn Nakano Glenn's work on the historical and contemporary racialization of domestic and service work.[44] In many respects, race is gendered and gender is racialized. In institutional and everyday life, any clear demarcation of specific forms of oppression and difference is constantly being disrupted.

There are no clear boundaries between these "regions" of hegemony, so political conflicts will often invoke some or all these themes simultaneously. Hegemony is tentative, incomplete, and "messy." For example, the 1991 Hill-Thomas hearings, with their intertwined themes of race and gender inequality, and their frequent genuflections before the altar of hard work and upward mobility, managed to synthesize various race, gender, and class projects in a particularly explosive combination.[45]

What distinguishes political opposition today—racial or otherwise—is its insistence on identifying itself and speaking for itself, its determined demand for the transformation of the social structure, its refusal of the "common sense" understandings which the hegemonic order imposes. Nowhere is this refusal of "common sense" more needed, or more imperilled, than in our understanding of racism.

What Is Racism?

Since the ambiguous triumph of the civil rights movement in the mid-1960s, clarity about what racism means has been eroding. The concept entered the lexicon of "common sense" only in the 1960s. Before that, although the term had surfaced occasionally,[46] the problem of racial injustice and inequality was generally understood in a more limited fashion, as a matter of prejudiced attitudes or bigotry on the one hand,[47] and discriminatory practices on the other.[48] Solutions, it was believed, would therefore involve the overcoming of such attitudes, the achievement of tolerance, the acceptance of "brotherhood," etc., and the passage of laws which prohibited discrimination with respect to access to public accommodations, jobs, education, etc. The early civil rights movement explicitly reflected such views. In its espousal of integration and its quest for a "beloved community" it sought to overcome racial prejudice. In its litigation activities and agitation for civil rights legislation it sought to challenge discriminatory practices.

The later 1960s, however, signalled a sharp break with this vision. The emergence of the slogan "black power" (and soon after, of "brown power," "red power," and "yellow power"), the wave of riots that swept the urban ghettos from 1964 to 1968, and the founding of radical movement organizations of nationalist and Marxist orientation, coincided with the recognition that racial inequality and injustice had much deeper roots. They were not simply the product of prejudice, nor was discrimination only a matter of intentionally informed action. Rather, prejudice was an almost unavoidable outcome of patterns of socialization which were "bred in the bone," affecting not only whites but even minorities themselves.[49] Discrimination, far from manifesting itself only (or even principally) through individual actions or conscious policies, was a structural feature of U.S. society, the product of centuries of systematic exclusion, exploitation, and disregard of racially defined minorities.[50] It was this combination of relationships—prejudice, discrimination, and institutional inequality—which defined the concept of racism at the end of the 1960s.

Such a synthesis was better able to confront the political realities of the period. Its emphasis on the structural dimensions of racism allowed it to address the intransigence which racial injustice and inequality continued to exhibit, even after discrimination had supposedly been outlawed[51] and bigoted expression stigmatized. But such an approach also had clear limitations. As Robert Miles has argued, it tended to "inflate" the concept of racism to a point at which it lost precision.[52] If the "institutional" component of racism were so pervasive and deeply rooted, it became difficult to see how the democratization of U.S. society could be achieved, and difficult to explain what progress had been made. The result was a levelling critique which denied any distinction between the Jim Crow era (or even the whole *longue durée* of racial dictatorship since the conquest) and the present. Similarly, if the prejudice component of racism were so deeply inbred, it became difficult to account for the evident hybridity and interpenetration that characterizes civil society in the U.S., as evidenced by the shaping of popular culture, language, and style, for example. The result of the "inflation" of the concept of racism was thus a deep pessimism about any efforts to overcome racial barriers, in the workplace, the community, or any other sphere of lived experience. An overly comprehensive view of racism, then, potentially served as a self-fulfilling prophecy.

Yet the alternative view—which surfaced with a vengeance in the 1970s—urging a return to the conception of racism held before the movement's "radical turn," was equally inadequate. This was the neoconservative perspective, which deliberately restricted its attention to injury done to the individual as opposed to the group, and to advocacy of a color-blind racial policy.[53] Such an approach reduced race to ethnicity,[54] and almost entirely neglected the continuing organization of social inequality and oppression along racial lines. Worse yet, it tended to rationalize racial injustice as a supposedly natural outcome of group attributes in competition.[55]

The distinct, and contested, meanings of racism which have been advanced over the past three decades have contributed to an overall crisis of meaning for the concept today. Today, the absence of a clear "common sense" understanding of what racism means has become a significant obstacle to efforts aimed at challenging it. Bob Blauner has noted that in classroom discussions of racism, white and non-white students tend to talk past one another. Whites tend to locate racism in color consciousness and find its absence color-blindness. In so doing, they see the affirmation of difference and racial identity among racially defined minority students as racist. Non-white students, by contrast, see racism as a system of power, and correspondingly argue that blacks, for example, cannot be racist because they lack power. Blauner concludes that there are two "languages" of race, one in which members of racial minorities, especially blacks, see the centrality of race in history and everyday experience, and another in which whites see race as "a peripheral, nonessential reality."[56]

Given this crisis of meaning, and in the absence of any "common sense" understanding, does the concept of racism retain any validity? If so, what view of racism should we adopt? Is a more coherent theoretical approach possible? We believe it is.

We employ racial formation theory to reformulate the concept of racism. Our approach recognizes that racism, like race, has changed over time. It is obvious that the attitudes, practices, and institutions of the epochs of slavery, say, or of Jim Crow, no longer exist today. Employing a similar logic, it is reasonable to question whether concepts of racism which developed in the early days of the post–civil rights era, when the limitations of both moderate reform and militant racial radicalism of various types had not yet been encountered, remain adequate to explain circumstances and conflicts a quarter-century later.

Racial formation theory allows us to differentiate between race and racism. The two concepts should not be used interchangeably. We have argued that race has no fixed meaning, but is constructed and transformed sociohistorically through competing political projects, through the necessary and ineluctable link between the structural and cultural dimensions of race in the U.S. This emphasis on projects allows us to refocus our understanding of racism as well, for racism can now be seen as characterizing some, but not all, racial projects.

A racial project can be defined as *racist* if and only if it *creates or reproduces structures of domination based on essentialist*[57] *categories of race.* Such a definition recognizes the importance of locating racism within a fluid and contested history of racially based social structures and discourses. Thus there can be no timeless and absolute standard for what constitutes racism, for social structures change and discourses are subject to rearticulation. Our definition therefore focuses instead on the "work" essentialism does for domination, and the "need" domination displays to essentialize the subordinated.

Further, it is important to distinguish racial awareness from racial essentialism. To attribute merits, allocate values or resources to, and/or represent individuals or groups on the basis of racial identity should not be considered racist in and of itself. Such projects may in fact be quite benign.

Consider the following examples: first, the statement, "Many Asian Americans are highly entrepreneurial"; second, the organization of an association of, say, black accountants.

The first racial project, in our view, signifies or represents a racial category ("Asian Americans") and locates that representation within the social structure of the contemporary U.S. (in regard to business, class issues, socialization, etc.). The second racial project is organizational or social structural, and therefore must engage in racial signification. Black accountants, the organizers might maintain, have certain common experiences, can offer each other certain support, etc. Neither of these racial projects is essentialist, and neither can fairly be labelled racist. Of course, racial representations may be biased or misinterpret their subjects, just as racially based organizational efforts may be unfair or unjustifiably exclusive. If such were the case, if for instance in our first example the statement in question were "Asian Americans are naturally entrepreneurial," this would by our criterion be racist. Similarly, if the effort to organize black accountants had as its rationale the raiding of clients from white accountants, it would by our criterion be racist as well.

Similarly, to allocate values or resources—let us say, academic scholarships—on the basis of racial categories is not racist. Scholarships are awarded on a preferential basis to Rotarians, children of insurance company employees, and residents of the Pittsburgh metropolitan area. Why then should they not also be offered, in particular cases, to Chicanos or Native Americans?

In order to identify a social project as racist, one must in our view demonstrate a link between essentialist representations of race and social structures of domination. Such a link might be revealed in efforts to protect dominant interests, framed in racial terms, from democratizing racial initiatives.[58] But it might also consist of efforts simply to reverse the roles of racially dominant and racially subordinate.[59] There is nothing inherently white about racism.[60]

Obviously a key problem with essentialism is its denial, or flattening, of differences within a particular racially defined group. Members of subordinate racial groups, when faced with racist practices such as exclusion or discrimination, are frequently forced to band together in order to defend their interests (if not, in some instances, their very lives). Such "strategic essentialism" should not, however, be simply equated with the essentialism practiced by dominant groups, nor should it prevent the interrogation of internal group differences.[61]

Without question, any abstract concept of racism is severely put to the test by the untidy world of reality. To illustrate our discussion, we analyze the following examples, chosen from current racial issues because of their complexity and the rancorous debates they have engendered:

• Is the allocation of employment opportunities through programs restricted to racially defined minorities, so-called "preferential treatment" or affirmative action policies, racist? Do such policies practice "racism in reverse"? We think not, with certain qualifications. Although such programs necessarily employ racial criteria in assessing eligibility, they do not generally essentialize race, because they seek to overcome specific socially and historically constructed inequalities.[62] Criteria of effectiveness and feasibility, therefore, must be considered in evaluating such programs. They must balance egalitarian and context-specific objectives, such as academic potential or job-related qualifications. It should be acknowledged that such programs often do have deleterious consequences for whites who are not personally the source of the discriminatory practices the programs seek to overcome. In this case, compensatory measures should be enacted to vitiate the charge of "reverse discrimination."[63]

- Is all racism the same, or is there a distinction between white and non-white versions of racism? We have little patience with the argument that racism is solely a white problem, or even a "white disease."[64] The idea that non-whites cannot act in a racist manner, since they do not possess "power," is another variant of this formulation.[65]

For many years now, racism has operated in a more complex fashion than this, sometimes taking such forms as self-hatred or self-aggrandizement at the expense of more vulnerable members of racially subordinate groups.[66] Whites can at times be the victims of racism— by other whites or non-whites—as is the case with anti-Jewish and anti-Arab prejudice. Furthermore, unless one is prepared to argue that there has been no transformation of the U.S. racial order over the years, and that racism consequently has remained unchanged—an essentialist position *par excellence*—it is difficult to contend that racially defined minorities have attained no power or influence, especially in recent years.

Having said this, we still do not consider that all racism is the same. This is because of the crucial importance we place in situating various "racisms" within the dominant hegemonic discourse about race. We have little doubt that the rantings of a Louis Farrakhan or Leonard Jeffries—to pick two currently demonized black ideologues—meet the criteria we have set out for judging a discourse to be racist. But if we compare Jeffries, for example, with a white racist such as Tom Metzger of the White Aryan Resistance, we find the latter's racial project to be far more menacing than the former's. Metzger's views are far more easily associated with an essentializing (and once very powerful) legacy: that of white supremacy and racial dictatorship in the U.S., and fascism in the world at large. Jeffries's project has far fewer examples with which to associate: no more than some ancient African empires and the (usually far less bigoted) radical phase of the black power movement.[67] Thus black supremacy may be an instance of racism, just as its advocacy may be offensive, but it can hardly constitute the threat that white supremacy has represented in the U.S., nor can it be so easily absorbed and rearticulated in the dominant hegemonic discourse on race as white supremacy can. All racisms, all racist political projects, are not the same.

- Is the redrawing—or gerrymandering—of adjacent electoral districts to incorporate large numbers of racially defined minority voters in one, and largely white voters in the other, racist? Do such policies amount to "segregation" of the electorate? Certainly this alternative is preferable to the pre–Voting Rights Act practice of simply denying racial minorities the franchise. But does it achieve the Act's purpose of fostering electoral equality across and within racial lines? In our view such practices, in which the post–1990 redistricting process engaged rather widely—are vulnerable to charges of essentialism. They often operate through "racial lumping," tend to freeze rather than overcome racial inequalities, and frequently subvert or defuse political processes through which racially defined groups could otherwise negotiate their differences and interests. They worsen rather than ameliorate the denial of effective representation to those whom they could not effectively redistrict—since no redrawing of electoral boundaries is perfect, those who get stuck on the "wrong side" of the line are particularly disempowered. Thus we think such policies merit the designation of "tokenism"—a relatively mild form of racism—which they have received.[68]

Parallel to the debates on the concept of race, recent academic and political controversies about the nature of racism have centered on whether it is primarily an ideological or structural phenomenon. Proponents of the former position argue that racism is first and foremost a matter of beliefs and attitudes, doctrines and discourse, which only then give rise to unequal and unjust practices and structures.[69] Advocates of the latter view see racism as primarily a matter of economic stratification, residential segregation, and other institutionalized forms of inequality which then give rise to ideologies of privilege.[70]

From the standpoint of racial formation, these debates are fundamentally misguided. They frame the problem of racism in a rigid "either-or" manner. We believe it is crucial to disrupt the fixity of these positions by simultaneously arguing that ideological beliefs have structural consequences, and that social structures give rise to beliefs. Racial ideology and social structure, therefore, mutually shape the nature of racism in a complex, dialectical, and overdetermined manner.

Even those racist projects which at first glance appear chiefly ideological turn out upon closer examination to have significant institutional and social structural dimensions. For example, what we have called "far right" projects appear at first glance to be centrally ideological. They are rooted in biologistic doctrine, after all. The same seems to hold for certain conservative black nationalist projects which have deep commitments to biologism.[71] But the unending stream of racist assaults initiated by the far right, the apparently increasing presence of skinheads in high schools, the proliferation of neo-Nazi computer bulletin boards, and the appearance of racist talk shows on cable access channels, all suggest that the organizational manifestations of the far right racial projects exist and will endure.[72] Perhaps less threatening but still quite worrisome is the diffusion of doctrines of black superiority through some (though by no means all) university-based African American Studies departments and student organizations, surely a serious institutional or structural development.

By contrast, even those racisms which at first glance appear to be chiefly structural upon closer examination reveal a deeply ideological component. For example, since the racial right abandoned its explicit advocacy of segregation, it has not seemed to uphold—in the main—an ideologically racist project, but more primarily a structurally racist one. Yet this very transformation required tremendous efforts of ideological production. It demanded the rearticulation of civil rights doctrines of equality in suitably conservative form, and indeed the defense of continuing large-scale racial inequality as an outcome preferable to (what its advocates have seen as) the threat to democracy that affirmative action, busing, and large-scale "race-specific" social spending would entail.[73] Even more tellingly, this project took shape through a deeply manipulative coding of subtextual appeals to white racism, notably in a series of political campaigns for high office which have occurred over recent decades. The retreat of social policy from any practical commitment to racial justice, and the relentless reproduction and divulgation of this theme at the level of everyday life—where whites are now "fed up" with all the "special treatment" received by non-whites, etc.—constitutes the hegemonic racial project at this time. It therefore exhibits an unabashed structural racism all the more brazen because on the ideological or signification level, it adheres to a principle of "treating everyone alike."

In summary, the racism of today is no longer a virtual monolith, as was the racism of yore. Today, racial hegemony is "messy." The complexity of the present situation is the product of a vast historical legacy of structural inequality and invidious racial representation, which has been confronted during the post–World War II period with an opposition more serious and effective than any it had faced before. As we will survey in the chapters to follow, the result is a deeply ambiguous and contradictory spectrum of racial projects, unremittingly conflictual racial politics, and confused and ambivalent racial identities of all sorts. We begin this discussion by addressing racial politics and the state.

5

The Racial State

Introduction: The Trajectory of Racial Politics

Two recent incidents reveal some of the ironies and incongruities of contemporary racial politics:

- In 1989, the Republican National Committee established a tax-exempt foundation called Fairness for the 90s. The group's mission was to provide money and technical assistance to black and Latino organizations seeking to create minority-dominated legislative and congressional districts. In anticipation of the legislative redistricting that would follow the 1990 census, the Republicans offered black and Latino leaders and organizers the prospect of creating "safe seats" for minority legislators. The Republicans went so far as to ally themselves with black and Latino plaintiffs in redistricting suits brought under the Voting Rights Act. What accounted for the strange bedfellows of redistricting politics? The answer was simple: Republicans sought to segregate racial minority voters into separate districts, to divide white from nonwhite Democrats, and so to increase their opportunities to win legislative seats in adjoining white districts.[1]

- In the late 1980s, Asian American academic leaders, civil rights organizations, and university students began to suspect that informal quotas for Asian American admissions had been put in place in the leading U.S. universities in violation of civil rights laws. As they mobilized to confront this situation and initiated negotiations with university administrators on various campuses, they suddenly received support from an unsolicited, and unexpected, quarter. In November, 1988, Ronald Reagan's neoconservative Deputy Attorney General for Civil Rights, William Bradford Reynolds, not only agreed that such quotas had been established, but blamed these restrictive practices on the existence of affirmative action admissions policies. "The phenomenon of a 'ceiling' on Asian American admissions is the inevitable result of the 'floor' that has been built for a variety of other favored racial groups," Reynolds said. Asian Americans were alarmed that the issue of "quotas" would be used as part of a broader attack on preferential policies for underrepresented minorities.[2]

As these examples illustrate, advocacy groups and movement organizations which seek to represent racially defined minority interests, mobilize minority group members politically, and articulate minority viewpoints, are frequently faced with bitterly ironic political choices. No sooner did egalitarian and antidiscrimination policies emerge from the political tempests of the 1960s than they began to "decay." From the early 1970s of Richard Nixon to the early 1990s of Bill Clinton, the state has sought to absorb, to marginalize, and to transform (or "rearticulate") the meaning of the reforms won in the earlier decade.

How have these transformations occurred? What are the dynamics of the relationships between the state and racial minorities? Why does a pattern of alternating activism and quiescence characterize both state racial activities and movement ebbs and flows? In this chapter we consider these questions in an effort to understand the *trajectory* which contemporary racial politics—and thus racial formation processes—follow in the contemporary U.S.

By "trajectory" we mean the pattern of conflict and accommodation which takes shape over time between racially based social movements and the policies and programs of the state. We consider the central elements of this trajectory to be the state and social movements, linked in a single historical framework of racial formation.

Social movements and the state are interrelated in a complex way. Racial movements arise, and race becomes a political issue, when state institutions are thought to structure and enforce a racially unjust social order.[3] State institutions acquire their racial orientations from the processes of conflict with and accommodation to racially based movements. Thus "reform," "reaction," "radical change," or "backlash"—indeed every transformation of the racial order—is constructed through a process of clash and compromise between racial movements and the state.

These are the dynamics of present-day racial politics in the U.S. Yet there is nothing permanent or sacred about this pattern. Indeed, the existence of political channels for the expression of racial conflict is a relatively recent phenomenon. The broad sweep of U.S. history is characterized not by racial democracy, but by racial despotism, not by trajectories of reform, but by implacable denial of political rights, dehumanization, extreme exploitation, and policies of minority extirpation. Democracy has never been in abundant supply where race is concerned. The very emergence of political channels through which reform can at times be achieved is an immense political victory for minorities, and for democracy itself.[4]

In order to understand the interaction of today's racial state and minority movements, we must examine the origins of racial politics in the U.S. In the next two sections of this chapter, we survey the historical context from which modern racial politics emerged, and the role of the state in the process of racial formation. We then proceed to a theoretical sketch of the contemporary political dynamics of race.

Historical Change in the U.S. Racial Order

Since the earliest days of colonialism in North America, an identifiable racial order has linked the system of political rule to the racial classification of individuals and groups. The major institutions and social relationships of U.S. society—law, political organization, economic relationships, religion, cultural life, residential patterns, etc.—have been structured from the beginning by the racial order.

Clearly the system of racial subjection has been more monolithic, more absolute, at some historical periods than others.[5] Where political opposition was banned or useless, as it was for slaves in the South and for Native Americans during much of the course of U.S. history, transformation of the racial order, or resistance to it, was perforce military (or perhaps took such economic forms as sabotage). An oppositional racial ideology requires some political space, a certain minimal conceptual flexibility about race, upon which to fasten in order to recast racial meanings and constitute alternative racial institutions. During much of U.S. history, this political and ideological space was extremely limited.

But even at its most oppressive, the racial order was unable to arrogate to itself the entire capacity for the production of racial meanings, of racial subjects. Racial minorities were always able to counterpose their own cultural traditions, their own forms of organization and identity, to the dehumanizing and enforced "invisibility" imposed by the majority society.

As the voluminous literature on black culture under slavery shows, black slaves developed cultures of resistance based on music, religion, African traditions, and family ties through which they sustained their own ideological project: the development of a "free" black identity and a collectivity dedicated to emancipation.[6] The examples of Geronimo, Sitting Bull, and other Native American leaders were passed down from generation to generation as examples of resistance, and the Ghost Dance and Native American Church were employed by particular generations of Indians to maintain a resistance culture.[7] Rodolfo Acuña has pointed out how the same "bandits" against whom Anglo vigilantes mounted expeditions after the Treaty of Guadalupe-Hidalgo—Tibúrcio Vasquez, Joaquín Murieta— became heroes in the Mexicano communities of the Southwest, remembered in folktales and celebrated in *corridos*.[8] We do not offer these examples to romanticize brutal repression or to give the air of revolutionary struggle to what were often grim defeats; we simply seek to affirm that even in the most uncontested periods of American racism, oppositional cultures were able, often at very great cost, to maintain themselves.

Without reviewing the vast history of racial conflict, it is still possible to make some general comments about the manner in which the racial order was historically consolidated. Gramsci's distinction between "war of maneuver" and "war of position" will prove useful here.

For much of American history, no political legitimacy was conceded to alternative or oppositional racial ideologies, to competing racially defined political projects. The absence of democratic rights, of property, of political and ideological terrain upon which to challenge the monolithic character of the racial order, forced racially defined opposition both *outward*, to the margins of society, and *inward*, to the relative safety of homogeneous minority communities.

Slaves who escaped, forming communities in woods and swamps; Indians who made war on the U.S. in defense of their peoples and lands; Chinese and Filipinos who drew together in Chinatowns and Manilatowns in order to gain some measure of collective control over their existence—these are some examples of the movement of racial opposition *outward*, away from political engagement with the hegemonic racial state.

These same slaves, Indians, and Asians, as well as many others, banned from the political system and relegated to what was supposed to be a permanently inferior sociocultural status, were forced *inward* upon themselves as individuals, families, and communities. Tremendous cultural resources were nurtured among such communities; enormous labors were required to survive and to develop elements of an autonomy and opposition under such conditions. These circumstances can best be understood as combining with the violent clashes and the necessity of resistance (to white-led race riots, military assaults, etc.) which characterized these periods, to constitute a racial *war of maneuver*.

However democratic the U.S. may have been in other respects (and it is clear that democracy has always been in relatively short supply), in its treatment of racial minorities it has been to varying degrees *despotic* for much of its history. "War of maneuver" describes a situation in which subordinate groups seek to preserve and extend a definite territory, to ward off violent assault, and to develop an internal society as an alternative to the repressive social system they confront.

More recent history suggests that war of maneuver is being replaced by *war of position* as racially defined minorities achieve political gains.[9] A strategy of *war of position* can only be predicated on political struggle— on the existence of diverse institutional and cultural terrains upon which oppositional political projects can be mounted, and upon which the racial state can be confronted. Prepared in large measure by the practices undertaken under conditions of war of maneuver, minorities were able to make sustained strategic incursions into the mainstream political process beginning with World War II. "Opening up" the state was a process of democratization which had effects both on state structures and on racial meanings. The postwar black movement, later joined by other racially based minority movements, sought to transform dominant racial ideology in the U.S., to locate its elements in a more egalitarian and democratic framework, and thereby to reconstruct the social meaning of race. The state was the logical target for this effort.

Historical Development of the Racial State

The state from its very inception has been concerned with the politics of race. For most of U.S. history, the state's main objective in its racial policy was repression and exclusion. Congress' first attempt to define American citizenship, the Naturalization Law of 1790, declared that only free "white" immigrants could qualify. The extension of eligibility to all racial groups has been slow indeed. Japanese, for example, could become naturalized citizens only after the passage of the McCarran-Walter Act of 1952.[10]

Historically, a variety of previously racially undefined groups have required categorization to situate them within the prevailing racial order.

The Racial State

Throughout the 19th century, many state and federal legal arrangements recognized only three racial categories: "white," "Negro," and "Indian." In California, the influx of Chinese and the debates surrounding the legal status of Mexicans provoked a brief juridical crisis of racial definition. California attempted to resolve this dilemma by assigning Mexicans and Chinese to categories within the already existing framework of "legally defined" racial groups. In the wake of the Treaty of Guadalupe Hidalgo (1848), Mexicans were defined as a "white" population and accorded the political-legal status of "free white persons." By contrast, the California Supreme Court ruled in *People v. Hall* (1854) that Chinese should be considered "Indian" [!] and denied the political rights accorded to whites.[11]

The state's shifting racial perspective is also revealed by the census. Latinos surfaced as an ethnic category, "Persons of Spanish Mother Tongue," in 1950 and 1960. In 1970 they appeared as "Persons of Both Spanish Surname and Spanish Mother Tongue," and in 1980 the "Hispanic" category was created.[12] Such changes suggest the state's inability to "racialize" a particular group—to institutionalize it in a politically organized racial system. They also reflect the struggles through which racial minorities press their demands for recognition and equality, and dramatize the state's uncertain efforts to manage and manipulate those demands.[13]

The state is the focus of collective demands both for egalitarian and democratic reforms and for the enforcement of existing privileges. The state "intervenes" in racial conflicts, but it does not do so in a coherent or unified manner. Distinct state institutions often act in a contradictory fashion.[14]

Does the state, however clumsily, actually capture, steer, or organize the realities of racial identity and racial conflict? There is some validity to the idea of a racially "interventionist" state. With this theoretical concept, it is possible to investigate certain racial dimensions of state policy. The 1960s civil rights reforms, for example, can be interpreted as federal intervention in the area of racial discrimination.

Yet this approach does not reveal how the state itself is racially structured; it depicts the state as intervening, but not *intervened*, structuring, but not *structured*. Such a state is not basically shaped by race since it intervenes in race relations from *outside* them. The treatment afforded to racial politics is thus confined to "normal" political arenas.

In contrast to this, we suggest that the state *is* inherently racial. Far from *intervening* in racial conflicts, the state is itself increasingly the preeminent site of racial conflict. In the following sections of this chapter, we examine this expanding involvement of the state in the racial formation process. We first present a model of the racial state, and then consider contemporary patterns of change in the racial order, focusing on the interaction between state and social movements.

A Model of the Racial State

The state is composed of *institutions*, the *policies* they carry out, the *conditions and rules* which support and justify them, and the *social relations* in which they are imbedded.[15]

Every state *institution* is a racial institution, but not every institution operates in the same way. In fact, the various state institutions do not serve one coordinated racial objective; they may work at cross-purposes.[16] Therefore, race must be understood as occupying varying degrees of centrality in different state institutions and at different historical moments.

To illustrate this point, let us contrast two agencies of the federal state, the Department of Housing and Urban Development (HUD) and the National Science Foundation (NSF). HUD must deal directly with questions of residential segregation, urban development pressures, housing subsidization programs, and the like; it is staffed by numerous minority-group members, and is subject to constant pressures from lobbies, community groups, and local and state governments (many of which address racial issues or are organized along racial lines). Thus it can be expected to be more racially oriented than the National Science Foundation, where staffing along professional/academic lines, a technical mandate, and a politically more limited range of constituents limit the racial agenda. Nevertheless, in certain areas (e.g., hiring policies, funding priorities, positions taken in respect to racially oriented scientific disputes—does Shockley get a grant?)[17] the NSF too is a racial institution.

Through *policies* which are explicitly or implictly racial, state institutions organize and enforce the racial politics of everyday life. For example, they enforce racial (non)discrimination policies, which they administer, arbitrate, and encode in law. They organize racial identities by means of education, family law, and the procedures for punishment, treatment, and surveillance of the criminal, deviant and ill.[18]

State institutions and their policies take shape under a series of *conditions and rules*. These "rules of the game" integrate the disparate racial policies of different state agencies, define the scope of state activity, establish "normal" procedures for influencing policy, and set the limits of political legitimacy in general. To speak, for example, of an agency's "mandate," of a policy's "constituency," or of an epochal political "project" (the "Keynesian welfare state," the "conservative opportunity society")[19] is to accept a set of political rules about who is a political actor, what is a political interest, and how the broad state/society relationship is to be organized.[20]

The specific *social relations* through which state activity is structured constitute the materiality of politics. Examples include the complex linkages of agencies and constituencies,[21] the dynamics of coalitions and gov-

ositional blocs, and the varieties of administrative control
ate agencies throughout civil society.[22] Racial politics are
in this respect. For example, civil rights organizations, lob-
groups, and "social programs" with significant constituency bases,
legal mandates, etc., may engage the state in the "normal" politics of interest-group liberalism,[23] adopt movement tactics of direct action and confrontation "from without," or—as is most likely—combine these tactics.

The state is also imbedded in another kind of social relations: the cultural and technical norms which characterize society overall. These affect
the organizational capacities of state agencies, their coordination, both
with "external" social actors and with each other, and the practices of
their own personnel.[24] In racial terms, these relationships are structured
by "difference" in certain ways: for example, minority officials may establish caucuses or maintain informal networks with which to combat the
isolation frequently encountered in bureaucratic settings.

Despite all the forces working at cross-purposes within the state—disparate demands of constituents, distinct agency mandates and preroga-
tives, unintended and cross-cutting consequences of policy, etc.—the state
still preserves an overall unity. This is maintained in two ways: first, strategic unity is sought at the apex of the apparatus by key policy makers, and
in legislative and judicial agencies by established decision rules.[25] Second,
unity is imposed on the state by its thorough interpenetration with society.
In advanced capitalist societies *hegemony* is secured by a complex system
of compromises, legitimating ideologies (e.g., "the rule of law"), by adherence to established political rules and bureaucratic regularities, etc.[26] Under
all but the most severe conditions (economic collapse, war), this severely
limits the range and legitimacy of both dominant and oppositional political initiatives, no matter how heavy the conflicts among contemporary
U.S. political institutions and their constituents may appear to be.[27]

The Trajectory of Racial Politics

It is useful to think of the U.S. racial order as an "unstable equilibrium."[28] The idea of politics as "the continuous process of formation and
superseding of unstable equilibria" has particular resonance, we think, in
describing the operation of the racial state.[29] The racial order is equilibrated by the state—encoded in law, organized through policy-making,
and enforced by a repressive apparatus. But the equilibrium thus achieved
is unstable, for the great variety of conflicting interests encapsulated in
racial meanings and identities can be no more than pacified—at best—by

the state. Racial conflict persists at every level of society, varying over time and in respect to different groups, but ubiquitous. Indeed, the state is itself penetrated and structured by the very interests whose conflicts it seeks to stabilize and control.[30]

This unstable equilibrium has at times in U.S. history gone undisturbed for decades and even centuries, but in our epoch its degree of "stability" has lessened. Under "normal" conditions, state institutions have effectively routinized the enforcement and organization of the prevailing racial order. Constituency relationships and established political organizations are at least implicitly and frequently explicitly racial.[31] Challenges to the racial order are limited to legal and political marginality. The system of racial meanings, of racial identities and ideology, seems "natural." Such conditions seemed generally to prevail from the end of Reconstruction to the end of World War I, for example.

Now let us imagine a situation in which this unstable equilibrium is disrupted. There can be many reasons for this, and the disruption may take many shapes, for example the emergence of a mass-based racial movement such as took place in the 1960s, or of a powerful counter-egalitarian thrust such as appeared in the 1870s (with the beginnings of Asian exclusion and Jim Crow), or in the 1980s (with the institutionalization of new right and neoconservative interpretations of race). We shall be concerned with movement phenomena presently. Here we are interested chiefly in the effects on the state of racial disequilibrium.

Under conditions of disrupted equilibrium, inter-institutional competition and conflict within the state is augmented, as some agencies move toward accommodation of challenging forces while others "dig in their heels." Re-composition of constituencies and political alliances takes place. Opposition groups may resort to "direct action," and explicitly seek to politicize racial identities further; challenge will also take the route of "normal politics" (legislation, legal action, electoral activity, etc.), assuming this possibility is open to racially identified minorities. Strategic unity will therefore become more necessary for the governing forces or bloc.

The establishment or restoration of conditions of unstable equilibrium— let us say by means of reform policies—suggests an opposite cyclical phase. Such a situation guarantees the relative unity of the racial state by reducing the stakes of intra-state, or inter-institutional, conflict. It poses formidable obstacles to the fomenting of oppositional political projects. It minimizes the government's need to strategize and promises the automatic reproduction of the prevailing order, obviously an optimum situation from the standpoint of the dominant racial groups.

Disruption and restoration of the racial order suggests the type of cyclical movement or pattern we designate by the term *trajectory*. Both racial movements and the racial state experience such transformations, passing through periods of rapid change and virtual stasis, through moments of massive mobilization and others of relative passivity. While the movement and state versions of the overall trajectory are independently observable, they could not exist independently of each other. Racially based political movements as we know them are inconceivable without the racial state, which provides a focus for political demands and structures the racial order. The racial state, in its turn, has been historically constructed by racial movements; it consists of agencies and programs which are the institutionalized responses to racial movements of the past.

The point at which we begin to examine the trajectory of racial politics, then, is arbitrary. Let us assume, therefore, a beginning point of *unstable equilibrium₁*. At this historical point, the racial order is (relatively) undisturbed by conflict and mobilization. The racial state is able to function (again, relatively) automatically in its organization and enforcement of the racial order. We first address the racial movement version of the trajectory, and then that of the racial state.

Racial movements come into being as the result of political projects, political interventions led by "intellectuals."[32] These projects seek to transform (or rearticulate) the dominant racial ideology. They thereby summarize and explain problems—economic inequality, absence of political rights, cultural repression, etc.—in racial terms. The result of this ideological challenge is a disparity, a conflict, between the pre-existing racial order, organized and enforced by the state, and an oppositional ideology whose subjects are the real and potential adherents of a racially defined movement. When this conflict reaches a certain level of intensity, a phase of *crisis* is initiated.

During a period of crisis, racial movements experiment with different strategies and tactics (electoral politics, "spontaneity," cultural revitalization efforts and alternative institution-building, lobbying, direct action, etc.). We assume that at least some of these are successful in mobilizing political pressure, either through "normal" political channels or through disruption of those channels.[33] Indeed the success of a racial movement probably depends on its ability to generate a wide and flexible variety of strategies, ideological themes, and political tactics, as both the minority movements of the 1960s and the new right/neoconservative movements of the present have demonstrated.

In response to political pressure, state institutions adopt policies of absorption and insulation.[34] *Absorption* reflects the realization that many demands are greater threats to the racial order before they are accepted than after they have been adopted in suitably moderate form. *Insulation* is a related process in which the state confines demands to terrains that are, if not entirely symbolic, at least not crucial to the operation of the racial order. These policies then become ideological elements which are employed both by movements and state institutions. State agencies might argue, for example, that they have already met reasonable movement demands, while movement groups might claim that reforms don't address the problem, don't go far enough, etc.

Once the general contours of state reformism are clear, movements undergo internal divisions. A certain segment of the movement is absorbed ("coopted," in 1960s parlance) along with its demands, into the state, and there constitutes the core staff and agenda of the new state programs or agencies with which reform policies are to be implemented. The remaining active segment of the movement is "radicalized," while its more passive membership drops away to take up the roles and practices defined by a rearticulated racial ideology in the newly restabilized racial order (*unstable equilibrium$_2$*).

Considering the trajectory of racial politics from the standpoint of the state, *unstable equilibrium$_1$* at first coexists with a series of effectively marginalized political projects located outside the "normal" terrain of state activity. In racial terms the state's trajectory of reform is initiated when movements challenge the pre-existent racial order. Crisis ensues when this opposition upsets the pre-existing *unstable equilibrium$_1$*. The terms of challenge can vary enormously, depending on the movement involved. Opposition can be democratic or authoritarian, primarily based in "normal" politics or in disruption; opposition can even reject explicit political definition, as in the case of cultural movements.

Crisis generates a series of conflicts within and among state agencies as particular demands are confronted and the terms of the state response (repression, concessions, symbolic responses, etc.) are debated. Agency and constituent groups, confronted by racial opposition, explore the range of potential accommodations, the possibilities for reconsolidating the racial order, and their possible roles in a racial ideology "rearticulated" in light of oppositional themes. "Hard-liners" and "moderates" appear, and compromises are sought both with the opposition and within the state itself.

Ultimately a series of reforms is enacted which partially meets oppositional demands. Reform policies are initiated and deemed potentially effective in establishing a new *unstable equilibrium$_2$*. These policies are then regularized in the form of agencies and programs whose constituency bases, like those of other state apparatuses, will consist of former adherents and sympathizers of the movement (as well as "free riders," of course). A new racial ideology is articulated, often employing themes initially framed by the oppositional movements.

The concept of the trajectory of racial politics links the two central actors in the drama of contemporary racial politics—the racial state and racially based social movements, and suggests a general pattern of inter-action between them. Change in the racial order, in the social meaning and political role played by race, is achieved only when the state has initiated reforms, when it has generated new programs and agencies in response to movement demands. Movements capable of achieving such reforms only arise when there is significant "decay" in the capacities of pre-existing state programs and institutions to organize and enforce racial ideology. Contemporary patterns of change in the racial order illustrate this point clearly.

Contemporary Change in the U.S. Racial Order

In the period with which we are concerned, the "rules of the game" by which racial politics are organized have become tremendously complex. In the pre–World War II period change in the racial order was epochal in scope, shaped by the conditions of "war of maneuver" in which minorities had very little access to the political system, and understood in a context of assumed racial inequalities (i.e., comprehensive and generally unexamined racism). Today all of this has been swept away.

In the present day, racial change is the product of the interaction of racially based social movements and the racial state. In the postwar period, minority movements, led by the black movement, radically challenged the dominant racial ideology. As a result of this challenge, the racial order anchored by the state was itself destabilized, and a comprehensive process of reform was initiated. Later still, the reformed racial state became the target for further challenge, this time from the right. Racial politics now take place under conditions of "war of position," in which minorities have achieved significant (though by no means equal) representation in the political system, and in an ideological climate in which the *meaning* of racial equality can be debated, but the desirability of some form of equality is assumed. The new "rules of the game" thus contain *both* the legacy of movement efforts to rearticulate the meaning of race and to mobilize minorities politically on the basis of the new racial ideologies thus achieved, *and* the heritage of deep-seated racism and inequality.

As we have argued, social movements create collective identity, collective subjectivity, by offering their adherents a different view of themselves and their world; different, that is, from the characteristic worldviews and self-concepts of the social order which the movements are challenging. Based upon that newly forged collective identity, they address the state politically, demanding change. This is particularly true of contemporary

racial movements. In fact these movements largely established the parameters within which popular and radical democratic movements (so-called
"new social movements") operate in the U.S.

Racial movement mobilization and "normal" politics (the state, electoral activity, constituency formation, administrative and judicial systems,
etc.) are now linked in a reciprocal process. Demands for state reform—
for the transformation of racial society as a whole—are the consequences
of transformations in collective identity, indeed in the meaning of race
itself, "translated" from the cultural/ideological terrain of everyday life
into the terms of political discourse. Such "translations" may come from
movements themselves, or they may originate in "normal" political processes
as electoral bases are sought, judicial decisions handed down, administrative procedures contested, etc. Our conception of the "trajectory" of racial
movements and state reform policies suggests that the transformation of the
racial order occurs by means of an alternately equilibrated and disrupted
relationship between the formation of racial ideology and the elaboration
of state policy.

Today racial movements not only pose new demands originating outside
state institutions, but may also frame their "common identity" in response
to state-based racial initiatives. The concept of "Asian American," for
example, arose as a political label in the 1960s. This reflected the similarity of treatment that various groups such as Chinese Americans, Japanese
Americans, Korean Americans, etc. (groups which had not previously considered themselves as having a common political agenda) received at the
hands of state institutions. The census, the legislatures, the courts, the educational system, the military, the welfare state apparatus—each in its own
way a racial institution—are all sources of such racial change.

At the same time racial movements (both radical and conservative) continue to present the state with political demands. We understand this
process as the *rearticulation* of racial ideology. Racially based movements
begin as political projects which both build upon and break away from
their cultural and political predecessors. Movement projects take shape in
the interaction of civil society and the racial state. Movements set out to
question the meaning of race and the nature of racial identity (e.g., "blackness," "Chicanismo," "minority" status; or for that matter, "majority" status, "whiteness"), while state initiatives seek to reinforce or transform the
"unstable equilibrium" of racial politics in response to movement demands.
Such "projects" challenge pre-existing racial ideology. They are efforts to
rearticulate the meaning of race, and responses to such efforts.

The rearticulation of pre-existing racial ideology is a dual process of
disorganization of the dominant ideology and of *construction* of an alternative, oppositional framework.

The dominant ideology can be disorganized in various ways. An insurgent movement may question whether the dominant racial ideology properly applies to the collective experience of its members. Examples of this interrogation of the pre-existing system of racial categories and beliefs may be found, not only in militant movement rhetoric,[35] but also in popular and intellectual discourse. During the 1960s, for instance, minority economists, political scientists, sociologists and psychologists rejected dominant social science perspectives on racial grounds:

> For years, traditional (white) social science research—especially on political life and organizations—told us how politically workable and healthy the society was, how all the groups in society were getting pretty much their fair share, or moving certainly in that direction. There was a social scientific myth of consensus and progress developed.[36]

Similarly, during the 1970s, conservative, whites-oriented racial movements, such as those of the "new right" or the "unmeltable" ethnics, developed counter-egalitarian challenges to the reforms which minority movements had achieved in the previous decade.[37] In this way the overarching racial ideology—in which racial minorities and the white majority alike recognize themselves—is called into question.

Insurgent racial movements also try to redefine the essential aspects of group identity. Demands for "self-determination" (which of course are linked to important democratic traditions in the U.S.) attain currency, while past organizational efforts are criticized. For example, militants of the 1960s attacked the political accommodations and compromises into which pre-existing community organizations and leaderships had entered. The NAACP and Urban League, the G.I. Forum and LULAC were criticized as "Uncle Toms" and "Tio Tacos" who had succumbed to "cooptation."[38] Militants also denounced various cultural practices in minority communities which were judged to reinforce submission and dependence. Malcolm X, for instance, excoriated the black practice of "conking" (i.e., straightening) the hair with lye.[39]

The construction of an oppositional movement employs a wide variety of ideological themes. Racially based movements have as their most fundamental task the creation of new identities, new racial meanings, and a new collective subjectivity. Not only does the articulation of a new racial ideology involve the recombination of pre-existent meanings and identities, but it also draws on quite heterodox and unexpected sources.[40]

The disorganization of the dominant racial ideology, the construction of a new set of racial meanings and identities, the transition from political project to oppositional movement, is a complex, uneven process, marked by considerable instability and tension. Change is being demanded, but any change in the system of racial meanings will affect all groups, all identities. Challenging the dominant racial ideology inherently involves not only reconceptualizing one's own racial identity, but a reformulation of the meaning of race in general. To challenge the position of blacks in society is to challenge the position of whites.[41]

Racial movements, built on the terrain of civil society, necessarily confront the state as they begin to upset the unstable equilibrium of the racial order. Once an oppositional racial ideology has been articulated, once the dominant racial ideology has been confronted, it becomes possible to demand reform of state racial policies and institutions. There has been a change in the "rules of the game." A new political terrain has been opened up.

By the same token, once such challenges have been posed and become part of the established political discourse, they in turn become subject to rearticulation. The state reforms won by minority movements in the 1960s, and the racial definitions and meanings embodied in these reforms, provided a formidable range of targets for "counter-reformers" in the 1970s and 1980s. "New right" and neoconservative currents, armed with the still-dominant social-scientific paradigm of ethnicity theory, were able to carry on their own political "project." They were able to rearticulate racial ideology and restructure racial politics once again.

In the next chapters, we consider in detail the process by which the particular trajectory of racial politics—which involved both democratizing and authoritarian movements, both state reform and state reaction—developed in the postwar U.S.

PART THREE

6

The Great Transformation

Introduction

The racial upsurges of the 1950s and 1960s were among the most tempestuous events in postwar American history. The struggles for voting rights, the sit-ins and boycotts to desegregate public facilities, the ghetto rebellions of the mid-1960s, and the political mobilizations of Latinos, Indians, and Asian Americans, dramatically transformed the political and cultural landscape of the U.S. The postwar period has indeed been a racial crucible. During these decades, new conceptions of racial identity and its meaning, new modes of political organization and confrontation, and new definitions of the state's role in promoting and achieving "equality" were explored, debated, and contested on the battlegrounds of politics.

The racial minority movements responsible for these developments achieved limited but very real reforms in their struggle for racial justice and equality. By the 1970s however, through repression, cooptation, and fragmentation, these movements experienced a sharp decline, losing their vitality and coherence. In the ensuing context of the economic, political, and cultural crises of the period, even the moderate gains they had achieved came under attack by an alliance of right-wing and conservative forces.

In this chapter, we examine the minority movement upsurge of the 1950s and 1960s. We do not seek to reprise the history of these decades, but to employ our theory of *racial formation* to interpret the events of the period. We suggest that two important changes characterize the racial politics of the 1950s and 1960s: the first of these was a *paradigm shift*: the established

95

system of racial meanings and identities, based in the ethnicity paradigm of race, experienced increasing strain and opposition. This opposition gradually took shape within the civil rights movement, as the challenge it had launched against segregation in the South was transformed into a national movement against racism.[1] The second change was the mobilization of *new social movements*, led by the black movement, as the primary means for contesting the nature of racial politics. These movements irreversibly expanded the terrain of political contest, and set the stage for the general reorganization of U.S. politics.

Paradigm Shift

The modern civil rights movement was initially organized *within* the dominant paradigm of ethnicity. The ethnicity perspective provided an analytic framework by which to assess the situation of blacks, and correspondingly shaped the movement's political agenda. The early movement leaders were racial moderates who sought to end "race-thinking" and assure "equality" to each individual. The movement initially focused its energies on the South, where the ethnicity paradigm remained a challenging ideology to the racist logic of segregation. Later, when demands for racial reforms attained national scope and expanded beyond the black movement to other racially defined minorities, the limited explanatory abilities and programmatic usefulness of the ethnicity paradigm were revealed. The "eclipse" of this perspective led to a period where competing paradigms—the class- and nation-based views—flourished and contested for hegemony.

New Social Movements

The upsurge of racially based movements which began in the 1950s was a contest over the *social meaning* of race. It was this process which created what we call "the great transformation"[2] of racial awareness, racial meaning, racial subjectivity. Race is not only a matter of politics, economics, or culture, but of all these "levels" of lived experience simultaneously. It is a pre-eminently *social* phenomenon, something which suffuses each individual identity, each family and community, yet equally penetrates state institutions and market relationships. The racial minority movements of the period were the first *new social movements*—the first to expand the concerns of politics to the social, to the terrain of everyday life. New social movement politics would later prove "contagious," leading to the mobilization of other racial minorities, as well as other groups whose concerns were principally social. As playwright David Edgar has noted, most of the new social movements of the 1960s—student, feminist, and gay—drew upon the black struggle "as a central organizational fact or as a defining political metaphor and inspiration."[3]

Taken together, these two interrelated dimensions—the eclipse of the ethnicity paradigm and the emergence of new social movement politics—constitute an alternative framework by which to assess the racial politics of the period. Our account suggests that racial identity, the racial state, and the very nature of racial politics as a whole were radically transformed during the 1960s—tranformed so profoundly that the racial meanings established during this period continue to shape politics, even in the current period of reaction.

While the 1960s witnessed the weakening of the ethnicity paradigm and the growth of perspectives within the class-based and nation-based paradigms of race, none of the challenging viewpoints could achieve hegemonic status. They suffered from serious deficiencies, largely because (as we have argued in Part One) of their reduction of race to other phenomena. The subsequent waning of the movements and specific organizations operating within these challenging paradigms left a vacuum in racial theory and politics. This created the political space for the resurgence of the ethnicity paradigm in the 1980s.

Despite this, the depth and breadth of "the great transformation" can hardly be exaggerated. The forging of new collective racial identities during the 1950s and 1960s has been the enduring legacy of the racial minority movements. Today, as gains won in the past are rolled back and most organizations prove unable to rally a mass constituency in racial minority communities, the persistence of the new racial identities developed during this period stands out as the single truly formidable obstacle to the consolidation of a newly repressive racial order. Apparently, the movements themselves could disintegrate, the policies for which they fought could be reversed, their leaders could be coopted or destroyed, but the racial subjectivity and self-awareness which they developed had taken permanent hold, and no amount of repression or cooptation could change that. The genie was out of the bottle.

The Emergence of the Civil Rights Movement

The moderate goals of the early civil rights movement did not challenge the nationally dominant paradigm of racial theory, the ethnicity perspective. Indeed, early movement rhetoric often explicitly appealed to the ideal of a "race-free" society, the centerpiece of the liberal ethnicity vision.[4] This was consistent with the call for integration framed by Gunnar Myrdal in 1944, or with Nathan Glazer's description of the "national consensus" which abolished Jim Crow in the mid-1960s.[5]

Although its political goals were moderate, the black movement had to adopt the radical tactics of disruption and "direct action" due to the "massive resistance" strategy of the South, a region which clung to the racist assumptions of an earlier paradigm. The modern civil rights movement came into being when southern black organizations, frustrated by southern intransigence and drawing on both national and indigenous support bases, moved to mobilize a *mass* constituency in the South. They thus augmented the tactics of judicial/legislative activism—used in the elite politics which had previously characterized the civil rights struggle[6]—with those of direct action, which required an active "grass-roots" constituency. This was the key shift of the mid-1950s.

What made this change possible? Traditionally studies of social movements have developed models of "collective behavior" or "resource mobilization" to explain the emergence of significant struggles for change. Analyses of the formation of the modern civil rights movement in the mid-1950s are often based on one of these models.[7] Clearly both these approaches have their merits: the essential conditions for each—inadequacy of "normal" political channels to process demands (collective behavior model), and availability of material and political resources for the mobilization of movement constituencies (resource mobilization model)—were both present. The monolithic southern resistance to desegregation is an instance of the failure of "normal" politics to respond to demands for change. The role of such organizations as the local NAACP chapters, and particularly the black churches, effectively documented by Aldon Morris,[8] exemplifies the centrality of resource mobilization issues.

Although both the resistance to change and the availability of economic and political resources in the black community were essential components of the civil rights movement's shift to a direct action strategy, neither of these conditions were sufficient to spark the transition. A third factor, perhaps the most central, was required. This was an ideological or cultural intervention, the politicization of black identity, the *rearticulation of black collective subjectivity*. It was this change which would eventually place radical objectives on the agenda of racial minority movements, facilitate the diffusion of racially based movement activity to other groups, and become anathema to the moderate advocates of civil rights operating within the ethnicity paradigm of race.

Origins of New Social Movement Politics:
Identity, Rearticulation, and Political Opposition

Before the modern black movement's appearance on the political stage, the U.S. political system had not significantly changed since the New Deal. The Democratic Party had served as a repository of consensus ever since Roosevelt led it to power in the 1930s. Compromise and pragmatic coalition-building among disparate interests, constituencies, and loyalties ("interest-group liberalism")[9] shaped national politics. "Interests" themselves were largely defined economically. Such a system had obvious limitations in its ability to respond to challenges which cut across class (or status) lines. It was limited by an inability to confront an unjust *social* system which had not only economic but also political and cultural causes and consequences.[10]

In its efforts to transform precisely that social system, the black movement sought to *expand* the concerns of politics, without abandoning the earlier economically centered logic. This expansion of "normal" politics to include racial issues—this "common sense" recognition of the political elements at the heart of racial identities and meanings—made possible the movement's greatest triumphs, its most permanent successes. These did not lie in its legislative accomplishments, but rather in its ability to create new racial "subjects." The black movement *redefined the meaning of racial identity*, and consequently of race *itself*, in American society.

Social movements create collective identity by offering their adherents a different view of themselves and their world; different, that is, from the worldview and self-concepts offered by the established social order. They do this by the process of *rearticulation*,[11] which produces new subjectivity by making use of information and knowledge already present in the subject's mind. They take elements and themes of her/his culture and traditions and infuse them with new meaning.

The civil rights movement linked traditional black cultural and religious themes with the ideas and strategies of social movements around the world. On this basis it could rearticulate black collective subjectivity—it could forge a new black politics.

The movement's "intellectuals" were largely preachers. They infused their activism with a well-known set of symbols and rhetorical tools.[12] The centuries-long black interrogation of biblical images of bondage and liberation—as embodied in the Exodus, for instance, or the theology of Christian redemption—had traditionally furnished a familiar vocabulary and textual reference-point for freedom struggle, a home-grown "liberation theology."[13]

The civil rights movement augmented this imagery with ideas, lessons, and strategies developed in India, Africa, Europe (in the experience of anti-

Nazi resistance),[14] and in the U.S. (in the sit-down strikes of the 1930s). Martin Luther King's application of the Gandhian philosophy of *satyagraha*, the adoption of the "sit-in" as a tactic for forcing integration, and the parallels drawn to African liberation movements, were examples of this borrowing from the repertorie of other political struggles.

The formation of the modern civil rights movement is a classsical illustration of rearticulation processes. In order to win mass black support for the tactics of direct action, it was necessary to replace the established cultural norms through which ordinary blacks, particularly in the South, had previously sought to ameliorate the impact of racial oppression: "shuckin and jivin," "putting on Whitey," feigning ignorance and humility, etc. These strategies had served in the past to limit the extent of white control, to insulate the black community and black institutions from white intrusion and surveillance, and to protect individual blacks who ran afoul of white authority. But they had also limited the extent and depth of black organization, organization that would be necessary to challenge the system of segregation. They had been pre-political responses, survival efforts carried out by blacks as *individuals* in the absence of a movement. They were, in effect, adaptations to powerlessness.[15]

The modern civil rights movement sought not to survive racial oppression, but to overthrow it. Thus the traditional ideological themes of liberation and redemption and the political tactics of protest derived from movements around the world were incorporated in the heat of political struggle as elements of a new *identity*, one of *collective* opposition. According to Robert Moses or Martin Luther King, Jr., blacks were, collectively, the moral, spiritual, and political leadership of American society. They represented not only their own centuries-long struggle for freedom, but the highest and noblest aspirations of white America as well.

Far from having to passively accept the "'bukes and scorns" of segregation and perhaps trying to outmaneuver "Whitey," blacks were now called upon to oppose the system with righteous and disciplined action:

> To accept passively an unjust system is to cooperate with that system; thereby the oppressed become as evil as the oppressor. Noncooperation with evil is as much a moral obligation as cooperation with good.[16]

The old linkages of religious and cultural themes—of the Christian virtues of humility, of "turning the other cheek"—were thus not negated, but dramatically captured by the movement. The "culture of resistance" with which these virtues had previously been identified was displaced from an emphasis on individual survival to one of collective action. This process of rearticulation made the movement's political agenda possible, especially its challenge to the existing racial state.

The Radicalization of the Black Movement: Black Power

In subsequent stages of the movement's history, rearticulation processes continued to function as radical perspectives filled the void created by the eclipse of the ethnicity paradigm. This is particularly true of the emergence of *black power*. After the moderate demands of the civil rights movement were met in 1964 with the passage of the Civil Rights Act, and in 1965 with the enactment of voting rights legislation, many black activists saw their underlying ideals as unfulfilled. Not only had they failed to create a "beloved community" (which they now admitted had been a utopian vision),[17] but they had failed to achieve significant change in the social conditions faced by blacks. Kenneth Clark echoed these sentiments in 1967:

> The masses of Negroes are now starkly aware that recent civil
> rights victories benefited a very small number of middle-class
> Negroes while their predicament remained the same or worsened.[18]

The radicalization of an important segment of the black movement took shape in the myriad disappointments and disillusionments that afflicted civil rights activists: the acrimonious division between SNCC (Student Nonviolent Coordinating Committee) and civil rights moderates at the August, 1963 March on Washington;[19] the ferocity of the Birmingham campaign of April–May, 1963, combined with the limited victory won there;[20] the experience of the Mississippi Freedom Democratic Party, a SNCC-organized project to unseat the segregationist "regular" delegation at the 1964 Democratic Party convention in Atlantic City;[21] the onset of rioting in many Northern cities during the summer of 1964, followed by hundreds of riots during the next four years;[22] and the development of a new "backlash" politics in the middle 1960s, after the "massive resistance" strategy of the South had been broken.[23]

By the time of the Selma campaign (February–March 1965), no more than limited tactical cooperation existed between the radicals, led by SNCC, and the moderate SCLC (Southern Christian Leadership Conference). Militants from SNCC were infuriated when King, maneuvering between Washington, the federal courts, and the marchers themselves, halted an attempt to march from Selma to Montgomery on March 10, 1965.[24] By June, 1966, when diverse civil rights groups came together to complete a march through Mississippi begun by James Meredith (who had been shot by a sniper), there was open competition between advocates of "black power" and supporters of integration.

Beginning with the Meredith march,[25] the more radical wing of the movement signalled its disillusionment with past emphases on civil rights and the transformative power of nonviolence. SNCC and CORE (Congress of Racial Equality), in particular, adopted the more militant positions associated with the slogan *black power*.

Black power was a flexible, even amorphous concept, but it was frequently interpreted to mean separatism. It was this connotation which the moderates, operating within the ethnicity paradigm, despised and strenously denounced:

> We of the NAACP [National Association for the Advancement of Colored People] will have none of this. It is the father of hatred and the mother of violence. Black power can mean in the end only black death.[26]

Ironically, the cry of "black power" was no more a complete break with the civil rights movement than that movement had been a break with the older "establishment" of civil rights organizations such as the NAACP and National Urban League. The concept of black power embraced a wide spectrum of political tendencies, extending from moderate "self-help" groups through reform-oriented advocates of "community control" to cultural and revolutionary nationalists. The concept's emergence as a rallying cry was an effort once more to rearticulate traditional themes of the black movement. It was an effort which, interestingly, drew upon the themes of the dominant ethnicity paradigm and the civil rights movement, while simultaneously rejecting their integrationist and assimilationist goals.

In the early 1960s, ethnicity theorists, mindful of their model's origins in the experiences of white ethnic groups of previous generations, suggested that blacks in the North should be organized as an interest group.[27] Much of the black power current could be understood as following this advice. The ideas that the black community should patronize businesses owned by blacks, that it should adopt cooperative forms of organization, that it should mobilize politically at the local level ("community control") were concepts which borrowed as much from the tradition of Booker T.

Washington as they did from those of Cyril Briggs, Marcus Garvey, or Malcolm X. Robert Allen notes that in many respects black power was "only another form of traditional ethnic group politics."[28]

Despite its many "moderate" elements, black power drew an important line of demarcation within the black movement and deeply disturbed the dominant (i.e., white) political culture. White liberals reacted in horror when their ethnic prescriptions were put into practice by black militants and quickly retreated into a fundamentalist individualism which would have embarrassed Adam Smith.[29]

While embracing aspects of the ethnicity paradigm, black power theorists also initiated a rupture with that perspective by drawing upon colonial analogies to analyze the plight of blacks in America, and by focusing attention on racially based intra-class conflict. The political implications of this paradigmatic shift represented a distinct departure from the "interest group" politics of the ethnicity paradigm. Some examples were Stokely Carmichael and Charles V. Hamilton's *Black Power: The Politics of Liberation in America*,[30] which addressed black conditions in the U.S. within a nationalist paradigm, and James Boggs's essays,[31] which focused on the role of black industrial workers and urban struggles from a perspective based in Marxism-Leninism.

A key figure in the transition from civil rights to black power was Malcolm X, who placed a radical nationalist position on the political agenda and attracted mass black support for that view. First as organizer and chief spokesperson for the Nation of Islam, and then, briefly, as founder of the Organization of Afro-American Unity, Malcolm played a role unparalleled in the black community since Garvey's time. Although he often derided the civil rights movement, referring to its organizations and leaders as "Uncle Toms," Malcolm also recognized the importance of raising civil rights demands, even while arguing that the U.S. could not meet them.[32] After his 1963 break with the Nation of Islam, Malcolm moved closer to the radical wing of the movement and influenced SNCC thinking. In late 1964 he met with SNCC leaders in Nairobi, Kenya, at which time he stressed the importance of Pan-Africanism for U.S. blacks. He also approached socialist positions in a number of respects.[33] Malcolm formulated a radical challenge to the moderate agenda of the civil rights movement and prefigured the themes of black power. In February, 1965 he was assassinated at the Audubon Ballroom in Harlem, under circumstances that remain mysterious.[34]

Black power advocates and adherents broke away from the earlier black movement's struggle for a "raceless society." Integration, they argued, could only be a *result* of political power and equality, never its cause. The radicalization of the black movement appropriated the legacy of civil rights, much as the earlier movement had appropriated the legacy of the Southern "culture of resistance" which had been nourished in the black church, in black music, in folklore and literature, even in food.[35]

In addition to the demand for social justice, the question of "self-determination" was raised. The prospect of having not only "rights" but "power" once again rearticulated black cultural and political traditions, reviving themes from black political history. The cultural nationalism and black Marxism of the late-1960s were restatements of positions which harked back to the 1920s and 1930s, the days of the Harlem Renaissance, the African Blood Brotherhood, the Garvey movement, and the "black nation" thesis of the Communist Party.[36] The nation-based paradigm was not, however, synonymous with radical politics. Less "progressive"—or, as Huey P. Newton once called them, "pork chop"—nationalists tended to dilute their vision of black power by ignoring its racial dimensions for a more limited, "ethnic" view of its meaning. These groups often adopted reformist orientations, embracing "black capitalism," for example.[37] Here the distinction between the two paradigms became muted.

Encountering and Reforming the Racial State

There were two phases to the minority encounter with the state in the 1950s and 1960s.[38] The first phase was shaped by the civil rights movement's mass mobilization in the South, a "direct action" political strategy which, as we have seen, already depended upon new social movement politics, on the "politics of identity." This first phase resulted in the civil rights reforms of the mid-1960s. Through desegregation campaigns the black movement set in motion a reform-oriented democratization process. The resulting concessions were limited but real: policy shifts through executive order and legislation, judicial action against specific racist practices, establishment of new state programs and agencies with "equal opportunity" mandates, and the hiring of many black activists by state institutions. These victories ended the exceptional situation in the South by forcing that region to accept the nationally dominant racial ideology, as defined by the ethnicity paradigm. The reforms of the 1960s also signalled the fulfillment of that paradigm's limited vision of racial equality.

The second phase of the movement/state encounter was marked by the fragmentation of the minority movements into competing currents during the institutionalization of the racial reforms of the mid-1960s. This took place as the new reforms took hold, gradually and partially transforming the movement into a constituency for the new programs its efforts had won.

The state was the chief movement target for several reasons. First, the state, as the "factor of cohesion in society,"[39] had historically maintained and organized racial practices. In the present too, it gave shape to the racial order. Second, the state was traversed by the same antagonisms which penetrated the entire society, antagonisms that were themselves the results of past cycles of racial struggle. The lukewarm commitments to desegregation in public employment and the armed forces extracted by A. Philip Randolph from Roosevelt and Truman, the use of the 14th Amendment by NAACP lawyer Thurgood Marshall to challenge school segregation, the freedom rides of the 1940s and 1960s (which probed the federal commitment to integration of interstate travel), and the voting rights drives in the South were all examples of the small but significant "openings" through which the existing racial state was susceptible to challenge. Movement tactics often sought to make use of the state's internal racial contradictions. For example, the voting rights drives sought to induce confrontations between different branches of the state: the courts vs. state legislatures, federal police vs. local or state police. The idea was to force the federal government to defend civil rights from infringement by racist local and state agencies.

By the latter stages of this process—the late 1960s—the reform-oriented program of the black movement had acquired a foothold in state institutions such as social service agencies, and in electorally based positions. At the same time, splits and divisions had surfaced in the movement, and in minority communities as well. These included inter-group rivalries, class divisions, controversies over strategy, and disputes over the meaning of race within the minority movements themselves (e.g., integration vs. black power).[40] Class polarization was deepening within minority communities as those who were able to do so took advantage of new jobs and educational opportunities, while the majority of ghetto and barrio dwellers remained locked in poverty. The war on poverty was lost, as King had warned, on the battlefields of Vietnam.[41] Some formerly integrated movement organizations now became all black (e.g., SNCC); others that formed in the mid-1960s were organized from the beginning as exclusively black, Mexican American, Asian American, etc.

In the racial minority movements of the period, the state confronted a new type of opposition. Racial minority movements challenged established racial practices simultaneously through direct action, through penetration of the mainstream political arena (electoral/institutional projects from voter registration to community organization), and through "ethical/political" tactics (taking the "moral initiative," developing "resistance cultures," etc.).[42] These movements were able to link spontaneity and mass participation on the one hand, with electoral/institutional politics on the other. The unifying element in this opposition was at first the burgeoning collective subjectivity of blacks—and later that of other minorities—which connected demands for access to the state with more radical demands for freedom, "self-determination," cultural and organizational autonomy, "community control," and a host of other issues.

By combining these different oppositional tactics, the racial minority movements of the 1960s initiated the reforms which eventually created a new racial state. This new state, however, was not the institutional fulfillment of the movements' ideals. Rather it held a cloudy mirror up to its antagonists, reflecting their demands (and indeed their rearticulated racial identities) in a distorted fashion.

The state responded to movement demands with tactics of *absorption* and *insulation*.[43] Absorption (or cooptation) reflected the recognition that movement demands were often greater threats as rallying cries for minority opposition than they were after they had been adopted in suitably moderate form. Furthermore, absorption resulted in a certain "ghettoization" within state institutions that transformed militancy into constituency.[44] A pluralist interest-group framework replaced "grass-roots" opposition as the main organizational dynamic.

For example, civil rights workers in the South during the 1960s were continually frustrated in their efforts to obtain Justice Department protection for their efforts, frequently asking why the U.S. government was so willing to "defend democracy" in Vietnam but so slow to do so in Mississippi.[45] In such a form the demand for federal protection was ominous, for it linked issues which state policy makers preferred to keep separate and thus "insulated" from movement demands. U.S. foreign and domestic policy, interventionism abroad and racial despotism at home, and the domestic and international "third worlds" were all articulated in a single oppositional demand for *state guarantees of democratic rights*. But once the demand for protection was absorbed, appearing in the creation of the Community Relations Service in the Justice Department under the Civil Rights Act of 1964, its challenge to the state was largely blunted.[46]

Insulation is a related process in which the state confines democratizing demands to areas that are, if not entirely symbolic, at least not crucial to its operation as a "factor of cohesion" in society. The federal system in the U.S. permits a degree of insulation of key state institutions from popular demands that is unequalled elsewhere in the capitalist democracies.[47] Thus whole areas of potential conflict, such as the operation of the Federal Reserve Board or the framing of tax policy, were defined as non-racial issues during the 1960s.

Challenging Paradigms and Strategic Divisions

By the late 1960s, the fragmentation within the racial minority movements was clearly visible and consolidated into discernible currents. New social movement politics had galvanized activists in their respective communities, but the lack of theoretical clarity about racial dynamics in the U.S. splintered political action. Although the ethnicity paradigm had been seriously challenged, it remained an important explanatory model, not only for academics, but also for movement activists. The challenging paradigms—the class- and nation-based views—gave rise to counterposed strategic orientations. Strategic divisions also flowed from class cleavages internal to minority communities, from state repression which marginalized radical tendencies, and from the very effectiveness of state strategies of reform, which tended to replace movement perspectives with the constituency-based viewpoints of "normal" politics.

Three broad political currents can be recognized within the racial minority movements of this period.[48] These were *electoral/institutional "entrism," socialism,* and *nationalism.*

Advocates of *electoral/institutional entrism* argued for greater movement participation in existing political organizations and processes, such as party politics, local government agencies, welfare state and poverty programs, etc. While this tendency was perhaps most closely associated with the reform orientation of moderate movement factions, more militant currents also adopted "entrist" perspectives, for example the La Raza Unida Party,[49] or the Georgia legislative campaigns of SNCC activist Julian Bond.[50] The necessity of "entering the mainstream" was advocated for the following reasons: to avoid marginalization, since no other historically continuous political terrain was available to minority activists; to achieve reforms that would allow for further movement-building, redistribution of income, goods, and services, and increased access to the racial state; and to educate and "raise consciousness," since electoral office and bureaucratic position confer opportunities to publicize one's views and to initiate policy.

A second tendency was the *socialist* tradition. Marxist-Leninist and internal colonialist perspectives were the main representatives of this current. Marxist-Leninist approaches pointed out the class dimensions of antiracist struggles. They argued that racism is an indispensable support to advanced capitalism; that class cleavages exist within minority communities (this served to curb excessive nationalism and point out the dangers of multiclass alliances); and that it was essential to base organizational efforts on the (traditionally defined) working class. Somewhat paradoxically, Marxist-Leninist groups often successfully recruited minority memberships, particularly among students, even as they became increasingly marginal on the U.S. political landscape.[51]

Internal colonialist perspectives saw racism as an ongoing historical process which contained *both* class- and nationally based elements. Racially defined communities within the U.S. were analogized to colonies, and said to face the same types of economic exploitation and cultural domination which the developed nations had visited on the underdeveloped ones. The internal colonialism rubric included a strategic spectrum running all the way from moderate reform initiatives to revolution and "national liberation." Demands for increases in the number of "natives" occupying key posts in businesses or state institutions (police, schools, social agencies), plans to achieve "community control" of the ghetto and barrio economies, and schemes for a two-stage revolutionary process[52] analogous to the Angolan or Vietnamese experiences, were all put forward based on the internal colonialism analysis.

Nationalism was a diverse current whose main strategic unity lay in rejection of the assimilationist and integrationist tendencies associated with the movement moderates. A tremendous diversity of political tendencies were understood in different minority communities under the "nationalist" label.

In the black community, for example, the term referred not only to a legacy of radical opposition to integration, but also to the "separate development" strategy associated with Booker T. Washington, and to various Pan-Africanist currents which passed through Garvey and Du Bois. It also encompassed black Marxism-Leninism and anticolonialist orientations (which straddle the nationalist and socialist categories), and even included a cultural nationalist current which was largely antipolitical.

In the Mexican American community, nationalism had its roots in Mexican revolutionary traditions, notably those of land struggles,[53] and in the proximity of the border. In the pre-1960s period, political activity aimed at improving conditions for Mexican Americans in the U.S. had been linked to an "entrist" perspective of civil rights/integration, such as that advocated by LULAC or the GI Forum. Nationalism in this context focused on Mexico, not the U.S., and was fueled by immigration, geographical proximity, and the regional particularities of the border area, on both the Mexican and U.S. sides.[54]

With the 1960s, though, an alternative *Chicano* nationalism appeared, which rearticulated many traditionally Mexican elements within a U.S.-based perspective, usually focused on the Southwest. In Chicano communities, new "anticolonial" struggles erupted, taking the form of land seizures as well as the community control struggles of the urban barrio.

The struggle for land was necessarily premised on the existence of substantial Mexican American populations which could constitute local majoritarian constituencies for radical political action. Such concentrations in turn reflected the long-standing semi-colonial conditions which existed in many rural areas of the Southwest. In these areas Mexican Americans were an impoverished agricultural labor force, exploited by agribusiness interests, victimized by immigration policies, and heir to a "colonial labor system."[55]

The urban manifestations of this new *Chicanismo* largely took shape among student and youth organizations, which flourished in the Mexican American community during the middle- and late-1960s, often adopting cultural nationalist orientations.[56] Many groups rejected the Mexican American identity, which they saw as assimilationist, in favor of a specifically Chicano identity which in their view reflected commitment to a new and higher level of political struggle.[57]

Asian American nationalism, for the most part, centered on community control issues. In many cities Asian Americans fought to prevent commercial transformation or obliteration of their communities. In many urban areas (such as San Francisco), Manilatowns and Japantowns had been destroyed by urban renewal schemes which had dispersed residents. Always a popular tourist attraction, Chinatowns have historically been the site of continual political battles over low-cost housing versus commercial development.[58] Within this context, Asian Americans sought to build alternative institutions which would more adequately address the needs of community residents than could the state or the existing conservative community leadership.

Cultural nationalism found expression in every minority community. This was an explicit critique of the dominant Eurocentric (i.e., white) culture, understood to pervade both everyday life and "high culture." Cultural nationalists sought to redefine and recapture the specificity of their minority cultures, an objective which they identified as "nationalist." Painting, theater, dance, music, language, even cars and clothes, all became media through which a new style could be developed, and through which "genuine" oppositional culture could be distinguished from assimilationist practices.

In the Chicano student movement, a variety of organizations sought to educate their members and communities about their heritage and the lost "nation" of *Aztlán*, to set up schools and cultural clubs (for folk dancing, mural painting, etc.), and to establish journals and newspapers.[59] In Native American communities there was a return to traditional religious and spiritual concerns. Cultural nationalism helped to link distinct groups who were racialized as one monolithic entity. The very term "Asian American" arose to express the similarity of experiences and treatment at the hands of various institutions which the specific "ethnicities" of Japanese, Chinese, Korean, and Filipino, among others, encountered in the U.S. Cultural and historical antagonisms which existed between these groups were muted among college students who became radicalized during the Vietnam War. The war was seen as a racist one in which Asian life as a whole was regarded as "cheap."[60]

Each of these tendencies—"entrism," socialism, and nationalism—rearticulated racial ideology and each responded to existing racial practices while initiating new ones.

The electoral/institutional *"entrists"* built political organizations that could win elections, penetrate and influence state bureaucracies, and either exercise power in the Democratic Party[61] or openly compete with it. By the 1970s forces such as the Congressional Black Caucus and the Joint Center for Political Studies had achieved real influence on the national political scene, while local political machines developed under victorious black and Chicano mayors in such cities as Atlanta, Birmingham, Denver, Detroit, Philadelphia, and San Antonio.[62] These instrumentalities were in turn linked to the many civil rights, lobbying, and local political groups, including those at the neighborhood, social agency, union, or church level. Thus, as a result of the 1960s movement victories, social programs and policies—with all their limitations—addressed the needs of minority communities as never before. The nascent influence of "entrist" minority activists made innovations not only in the obvious areas of policy, in employment, housing, education, health; but also established the less obvious racial content of such policy areas as foreign affairs, taxation, environment, science and arts support, etc. The network of "entrists" as a whole played a key long-term role in maintaining minority viewpoints and positions—for example the Congressional Black Caucus's annual alternative budget proposals—in the mainstream political process.

Among the *socialists.* Marxist-Leninists confronted the substantial class cleavages that exist in minority communities, as well as the conflicts that exist *among* minority groups (such as black/Asian American conflict or Chicano/black rivalries for electoral office), precisely by stressing the supposedly "fundamental" class conflict. This pointed to an alternative perspective which could allow people to understand that the sources of racial oppression lay in the broader society. The focus on class, it was felt, could permit communication across the chasms and gulfs that separate minority communities and racial minorities as a whole from the white working class.

Socialists or nationalists who adopted the internal colonialist approach offered a synthesis of cultural nationalism and the Marxist-Leninist analysis of class, arguing that cultural domination reinforced and shaped class domination, and that racial logic characterized the system as a whole. Strategies based on the internal colonialism perspective frequently focused on community control struggles, and on efforts to develop autonomous racial minority organizations.[63]

Nationalists called on minority communities to develop their unique histories, distinct collective identities, and separate political agendas. They opposed both integrationist political currents and the homogenizing, culturally dominant thematics of "mainstream" America. This generated the range of particularist racial movements we have described above—focused on Africa, *Aztlán*, or the ghetto/barrio as a locus of "community control."[64] Cultural nationalists in every minority community challenged the ubiquitous and at times forcible imposition of the dominant white culture.[65] They often formulated this challenge in terms which were explicitly antipolitical, focusing on the recreation (and creation!) of the cultural framework by which their group recognized and understood itself.

Considered critically, none of these political projects succeeded even remotely in forging an oppositional racial ideology or movement capable of radically transforming the U.S. racial order. The electoral/institutional "entrists" succumbed to illusions about the malleability of the racial state and were forced into a new version of ethnic group pluralism—the idea that racial minorities, like the white ethnics of the past, could claim their rights through "normal" political channels. The Marxist-Leninists could fight racism only by recourse to a futile dogma, and moreover one which consigned race to the terrain of "false consciousness." The internal colonialists, like an earlier generation of black (and other minority) nationalists, refused to recognize the particularities of the U.S. racial order and the limits of all analogies with revolutionary movements abroad.[66] The cultural nationalists ignored the political sphere, and indeed heaped scorn upon both reform-oriented "entrists" and minority socialists.[67]

All these tendencies were but partial assaults on the U.S. racial order; all failed to grasp the comprehensive manner by which race is structured into the U.S. social fabric. All *reduced* race: to interest group, class fraction, nationality, or cultural identity. Perhaps most importantly, all these approaches lacked adequate conceptions of the racial state. In their radical as much as in their moderate phases, minority movements neglected the state's role in the organization and enforcement of the U.S. racial order, not to mention its capacity for adaptation under political pressure.

The movement's limits also arose from the strategic divisions that befell it as a result of its own successes. Here the black movement's fate is illustrative. Only in the South, while fighting against a backward political structure and overt cultural oppression, had the black movement been able to maintain a *de*centered unity, even when internal debates were fierce. Once it moved north, the black movement began to split, because competing political projects, linked to different segments of the community, sought either integration in the (reformed) mainstream, or more radical transformation of the dominant racial order.

After initial victories against segregation were won, one sector of the movement was thus reconstituted as an interest group, seeking an end to racism understood as discrimination and prejudice, and turning its back on the oppositional "politics of identity." Once the organized black movement became a mere constituency, though, it found itself locked in a bear hug with the state institutions whose programs it had itself demanded, while simultaneously isolated from the core institutions of the modern state.

The radical sectors of the movement were marginalized in cultural arenas or on the left. Cultural nationalists disdained engagement with the racial state. Those who confronted the state from radical positions (SNCC, the Black Panther Party, the League of Revolutionary Black Workers, and others) were met with intense repression.

Beyond this, organizationally, the minority movements of the 1950s and 1960s nearly ceased to exist. Yet, as we have argued, the complex of racial meanings had been irrevocably altered by years of political activity, by intense campaigns for racial equality and democracy, by the transformed character of "blackness," "whiteness," and all other racial identities that the movements had initiated. The specter of racial equality, and beyond that, of an end to racial oppression itself, continued to haunt American dreams and nightmares.

7

Race and Reaction

Introduction

In March 1985, some 2500 people gathered in Alabama to commemorate a dramatic chapter in the history of the civil rights movement. Twenty years before, Martin Luther King, Jr. had led more than 4000 demonstrators on a fifty-mile march from Selma to Montgomery, a major turning point in the struggle for black voting rights. Twenty years later, Rev. Joseph E. Lowery, president of the Southern Christian Leadership Conference, told the crowd gathered at the commemoration, "We have kept the faith but the nation has not kept its promise." Political forces, including the Reagan administration itself, were trying to "turn back the clock of racial history."[1]

Lowery's comments were painfully accurate. The state of black America was worsening when measured by indicators such as unemployment rates, number of families falling below the poverty line, and the widening gap between white and black infant mortality rates.[2] Yet despite these continuing problems, the American populace remained callous about the situation of blacks and other racial minorities. A new mood of "social meanness" pervaded the U.S., and many Americans resented having to provide for the "underprivileged." Indeed many felt that far from being the victims of deprivation, racial minorities were unfairly receiving "preferential treatment" with respect to jobs and educational opportunities.

How, after several decades of attempts to eliminate racial inequality, had we arrived at this point? What political and ideological shifts had occurred to bring about such a tragic reversal?

Race and Reaction

Although much has been written about racial minority movements, little attention has been given to the way racial issues have shaped political movements on the right. Certainly there has been an explicit revitalization of the racist ideologies of the past, but there are also new currents which seek to reinterpret the meaning of race in the U.S., to *rearticulate* racial ideology once more, this time in a conservative direction. These currents have incubated and developed in the political space created by the racial minority movements of the past several decades. They include a wide range of perceptions about racial politics and the meaning of race in American life.

Among the welter of reactionary and conservative tendencies, we focus our attention on three main currents: the *far right*, the *new right*, and *neo-conservatism*. While varying widely in perspective, these currents share a similar ambition to discredit the key ideas and objectives of the 1960s minority movements. In attempting to do so by advancing their own vision of race, they have transformed the terrain of racial politics once again.

In this chapter, we first examine the historical context for racially based reaction; we then survey these three currents with an analytic focus on the processes of rearticulation they employ; we conclude with an examination of the Reagan administration's role in consolidating and abetting the racial reaction which these currents advocate.

The Context for Reaction

On the surface, the 1970s seemed relatively quiescent, a decade without a firm identity. In fact, those years ushered in a period of profound social transformation and dislocation in American life. During these years, many of the themes of racial reaction, of opposition to the egalitarian ideals of the 1960s, were developed and disseminated. For the first time in a sustained and programmatic way, setbacks in the domestic economy and U.S. reversals on the international level were "explained" by attacking the liberal interventionist state. Many of these criticisms had racial subtexts.

The 1970s were shaped by profound sectoral and regional economic dislocations. Jobs and industry fled the "frostbelt" (formerly the industrial center of U.S. prosperity and progress) for the conservative "sunbelt" of the South and West. The "sunset" industries of steel, rubber, and auto production of the Northeast gave way to the "sunrise" electronic and emergent technologies of the sunbelt. The issue of "deindustrialization" gradually moved to the center of economic debates, as workers faced plant shut-downs, redundancy, and limited hi-tech occupational opportunities.[3]

Inflation also surged to unprecedented levels, eroding consumer pur-chasing power and curtailing investment. The problem of "stagflation," which Keynesian policies were helpless to overcome, came to seem a per-manent feature of U.S. economic life.[4]

The state was the obvious target of criticism for the economy's poor performance. The state was apparently unable to act as its New Deal lin-eage obliged it to do, to solve or at least ameliorate economic problems. Indeed, the state was blamed for obstructing the economy's "natural" ten-dencies toward recovery. Once state programs had been seen as treatments for the disease of economic crisis; now they began to appear as the disease itself. Meanwhile, economic sluggishness persisted, state revenues remained low, and demands for state intervention were heard from every social and economic quarter.

Thus arose the "fiscal crisis of the state," which manifested itself on local, state, and national levels.[5] The near-bankruptcy of major cities, the property tax revolt (exemplified by California's Prop. 13 tax-cutting ini-tiative), and the soaring federal deficit provided further fuel both for the crisis and for growing antistatist sentiment.

In the international arena, the country suffered the humiliating "losses" of Vietnam, Nicaragua, and Iran in the 1970s. The formerly uncontested hegemony of the U.S. was slowly being eroded, not only on the world stage, but also in the American popular imagination. The Bretton Woods system, the structure which formerly dominated postwar international finance, had collapsed by 1973.[6] With it went the unique advantages which the U.S. had previously enjoyed in international trade. Suddenly, it seemed, the U.S. was being "held for ransom" by the OPEC nations, which con-trolled "our" vital energy resources—a thought not taken lightly by Amer-icans waiting in endless lines for gas. The Iranian revolution also came to typify this fall from grace. America was suddenly "held hostage" by politico-religious forces far beyond popular comprehension.

As the decade ended, no relief was in sight. U.S. manufacturers were losing their markets to foreign competitors and the trade deficit grew alarm-ingly. People in the U.S. painfully contemplated the idea that perhaps we were not "No. 1" anymore.

Many of these changes which began during the 1970s—and which con-tinued and deepened in the 1980s—have been discussed by other observers, but few have appreciated their implicit racial dimensions. Popular ideology often makes use of racial themes as a framework by which to comprehend major problems, be they the declining U.S. dominance in the world, dis-locations in the workforce, or the fiscal crisis of state. Some examples:

- Domestic economic woes are attributed to unfair foreign competition—with Japan receiving an inordinate amount of blame.[7] National polls show an increase in unfavorable attitudes toward Japan, while labor leaders and politicians employ racist cliches redolent of World War II propaganda in their demands for restrictions on Japanese imports.[8] Asian Americans are particularly sensitive to, and affected by, this shift in climate.[9]

- The current influx of immigrants and refugees from Mexico, Cambodia, Vietnam, Haiti, and Cuba (among other countries) has been met in a climate of scarcity with "fear and loathing." Many blame job loss and dislocation on the seemingly endless stream of "illegal aliens."[10] Rising unemployment, scarce housing, and social program cutbacks have contributed to demands for restriction, if not outright exclusion.[11]

The reversals of the 1970s called into question the scope and capacities of the so-called "welfare state." During the pre-crisis era, the Great Society had promised the elimination of poverty and of the invidious effects of racial discrimination. Yet the problems remained—indeed some had intensified throughout the 1970s. It was time, conservatives argued with increasing popular support, to stop "throwing good money after bad." In attempting to remedy problems of poverty and inequality, the state, they charged, only made them worse and instilled a parasitic dependency in its clients.[12] The tax revolt was but one popular indication of this sentiment. Taxes, it was argued, replenished and expanded the welfare state, and its stereotypically minority clientele, at the expense of "productive" (i.e., white) taxpayers.[13]

Another target was affirmative action policies. Through its reckless intervention, conservatives alleged, the state committed "reverse discrimination"—*whites* were now the victims of racial discrimination in education and the job market. The dislocations which began in the 1970s, then, were often understood *racially*. This racial connection has various implications; for example, it has fed into random acts of racial violence. But perhaps more importantly, "racial" issues became central to the agenda of those forces and projects seeking a rightward realignment in U.S. politics. The far right, the new right, and neoconservatism reopened the 1960s debates about racial identity and racial equality, and questioned once more the role of racial issues in the democratic political process. The effectiveness of a right-wing challenge to ideals promoted by the racial minority movements of the 1960s hinged on its ability to rearticulate the meaning of race in contemporary American society.

The Rearticulation of Racial Ideology

As we noted in Chapter 6, the racial minority movements of the post-war period dramatically reshaped the political and cultural landscape of the nation. They imparted new meaning to established traditions and ideas. Equality, group and individual rights, and the legitimate scope of state activity were reinterpreted, *rearticulated*, by these movements in a radical democratic discourse. Ironically, by challenging the racial verities of the past and revamping the old political terrain, the racial minority movements set the stage for the racial reaction which first appeared in the late-1960s, grew and developed in the 1970s, and reached maturity in the 1980s.

There were clear limits to any attempt to undo the effects of the "great transformation." In the aftermath of the 1960s, any effective challenge to the egalitarian ideals framed by the minority movements could no longer rely on the racism of the past. Racial equality had to be acknowledged as a desirable goal. But the *meaning* of equality, and the proper means for achieving it, remained matters of considerable debate.

With the exception of some on the far right, the racial reaction that developed in the last two decades claimed to favor racial equality. Its vision was that of a "color-blind" society where racial considerations were never entertained in the selection of leaders, in hiring decisions, and the distribution of goods and services in general. As the right understood them, racial problems from the 1970s on consisted of new forms of racial injustice which originated in the "great transformation." This new injustice conferred group rights on racial minority groups, thus granting a new form of privilege—that of "preferential treatment."

The culprit behind this new form of "racism" was the state itself. In attempting to eliminate racial discrimination, the state went too far. It legitimated group rights, established affirmative action mandates, and spent money on a range of social programs which, according to the right, debilitated, rather than uplifted, its target populations. In this scenario, the victims of racial discrimination had dramatically shifted from racial minorities to whites, particularly white males.

Beginning in the 1970s, the forces of racial reaction seized on the notion of racial equality advanced by the racial minority movements and *rearticulated* its meaning. Racial reaction repackaged the earlier themes—infusing them with new political meaning and linking them to other key elements of conservative ideology.

The different currents of reaction were not all equally successful in shifting the terms of racial politics. The far right for the most part revived the racist ideologies of previous periods. Yet even this current employed processes of rearticulation in its attempt to attack the liberal state as the

117

perpetrator of a racially unjust society. The new right's use of "code words" (non-racial rhetoric used to disguise racial issues) was a classic example of rearticulation, geared to mobilize a mass base threatened by minority gains, but disinclined to embrace overtly racist politics. Neoconservatism represented the most sophisticated effort to rearticulate racial ideology. It developed a limited but real coherence in challenging the underpinnings of the 1960s quest for social justice. It sketched out a vision of an "egalitarian" society where racial considerations were no longer the concern of state policy. We now turn our attention to each of these three currents.

The Far Right

In 1980, Tom Metzger, a television repairman from San Diego County, California, won nomination as the Democratic candidate for Congress in the 43rd Congressional District. His bid received national attention when it was revealed that Metzger, among other posts he held on the far right, was once Grand Dragon of the California branch of the Ku Klux Klan. An embarassed state central committee subsequently stripped him of his Democratic Party membership.[14]

Metzger was always civic-minded. He first garnered public attention when he offered to help the U.S. Border Patrol hunt down "illegal aliens." He also offered Klan members as a "goon squad" against the organizing efforts of the United Farm Workers union in the fields of California. He later dropped the Klan affiliation to found the White American Resistance (WAR) and he began to produce "Race and Reason," a "white man's talk show" which was broadcast on public access cable television in San Francisco, San Diego, Orange County in California, and in Austin, Texas.

Metzger was not alone in his efforts. A range of white supremacist groups appeared in the 1980s—Aryan Nations, the Silent Brotherhood, the Church of the Creator, the Order—joining forces with various sects of the Ku Klux Klan. Most were interconnected and constituted an underground network which embraced neo-Nazis, survivalists, and militant tax resisters, among others. These groups came to public attention through a series of dramatic crimes such as the killing of Jewish radio talk show host Alan Berg in Denver, a Brinks armored car robbery in Ukiah, California, and numerous shoot-outs with federal police.

Since the Civil War, white supremacist groups have periodically resurfaced on the American political scene. As D. W. Griffith's epic *Birth of a Nation* (1915) effectively conveyed, there was a "populist" impulse in such politics which resonated with whites who felt dislocated by the changes around them. In the view of such groups, racial "justice" (i.e., white supremacy) is perpetually threatened and the legitimate authorities are always too weak, naive, or corrupt to maintain America's "true" identity. Such logic has often inspired vigilante action as white supremacist groups sought to restore "white honor" and a "just" racial order.

In the past, the targets of such actions were racial minority groups themselves—groups which had to be terrorized into "knowing their place." In the 1980s, however, the target expanded to include the federal government. For example, to the neofascists of the shadowy Order, the "Zionist Occupied Government" (ZOG) was now the problem. To the Posse Comitatus, the federal income tax represented the opening wedge in the government's assault on white rights. Klansman Thomas Robb, publisher of *The Torch* newsletter, summarized the historic difference between previous and current far right thinking:

> The Klan in the '20s made a mistake thinking that evil resided in men who came home drunk or in Negroes who walked on the wrong side of the street. Today we see the evil is coming out of the government. To go out and shoot a Negro is foolish. It's not the Negro in the alley who's responsible for what's wrong with this country. It's the traitors in Washington.[15]

Targeting the federal government was a direct response to the racial activism of the state in the 1960s. Busing, affirmative action, and other egalitarian measures created, in the white supremacist view, a racially unjust society. The society became "polluted"[16] and the federal government, and liberalism in particular, were responsible. Pastor Richard G. Butler of the Aryan Nations preached such a view at his "Church of Jesus Christ Christian"[17] in Idaho:

> When the Declaration of Independence talks about 'one people,' it's not talking about a nation made for Asia, Africa, India [or] the Soviet Union. That's a document based on a Christian people. We have watched like frightened sheep as do-gooders sniveling about the underprivileged gleefully grabbed our children by the nape of the neck and rubbed their faces in filth to create equality.[18]

As some commentators noted, the economic dislocations of the 1980s had much to do with the revitalized presence of the far right.[19] In the midst of massive farm foreclosures and the crisis of the American farmer as a whole, the far right fed on rural despair and formed such groups as the Farmers Liberation Army, the Christian-Patriots Defense League, and the new Populist Party.[20]

But economic arguments are insufficient to explain the growth and popularity of far right and white supremacist organizations. The revitalized presence of such groups was also a political response to the liberal state and reflected a crisis of identity engendered by the 1960s. The far right was attempting to develop a new white identity, to reassert the very meaning of *whiteness*, which had been rendered unstable and unclear by the minority challlenges of the 1960s.[21] Nor was it clear what "rights" white people had in the wake of challenges to their formerly privileged status.

The appeal of the far right project extends, therefore, to people who would normally disagree with extreme racist views. More moderate sympathizers can naively view such politics as merely the expression of "white interest group" politics. As a supporter of Metzger's congressional bid told a television interviewer:

It's nice to have someone that represents the white people. It seems like nobody cares what the white people say anymore and all the candidates seem to run around and go out to all the minorities and never even once ask the white people how they feel so I guess we're turned around: the whites are now the minority and the minorities are the majority.[22]

Even as the far right gained a certain legitimacy with those more "mainstream" white conservatives who did not share its violence, the rightward drift of American politics as a whole also drew far right sympathizers into the newly emerging conservative consensus.[23] Conversely, as "moderate" right-wing demands against busing and affirmative action achieved success through legitimate political channels, hardcore extremists sometimes found themselves increasingly politically isolated. Observers feared that this isolation would push far right groups to adopt terrorist tactics.[24]

The effort to revive past white supremacist notions of race in the contemporary U.S., we think, has some serious limits. It would be difficult to attract a mass base to such an explicitly racist political project. The tenor of national debates about race—what we have called the *context for reaction*—precludes such a possibility. But if far right white supremacist politics remain marginal, this is not the case for more mainstream projects.

The right-wing initiatives which sought to overturn the minority achievements of the 1960s, therefore had to advance a new racial politics. Once again they had to *rearticulate*, and not merely reverse, the meaning of race and the fundamental issues arising from racial inequality. The far right is generally unable to do this and therefore represents a "failed" attempt at rearticulation. The far right has tried to reassert white identity and reaffirm the nation as "the white man's country." It has shifted the

b. ıme for racial injustice from individual racial minorities to the state. Buı it continues to cling to biological notions of race and racial purity which render it fairly similar to the racism prevalent at the turn of the century. Its inability to part with these basic racist assumptions dooms the far right to political marginality.

Though incapable of rearticulating the radical democratic racial ideologies of the 1960s, the far right is hardly vanishing. The far right can act as a "conscience" for other parts of the American right, or serve as their "shock troops."[25] If our analysis is correct, its inability to establish a broad political base may indeed force its degeneration into terrorism.[26] Its numbers may be small and its political impact minor, but the far right may remain a frightening and highly visible reminder of the violence which has often characterized the enforcement of the racial order.

The New Right: Origins

Walter Dean Burnham has noted that the political culture of the U.S. is highly influenced by the values of 17th-century dissenting Protestantism and that this has frequently become manifest in periods of transition and crisis:

> Whenever and wherever the pressures of "modernization"—secularity, urbanization, the growing importance of science—have become unusually intense, episodes of revivalism and culture-issue politics have swept over the American social landscape. In all such cases since at least the end of the Civil War, such movements have been more or less explicitly reactionary, and have frequently been linked with other kinds of reaction in explicitly political ways.[27]

The new right operates in this political space. It is a contemporary attempt to create an authoritarian, right-wing populism—a populism fuelled by resentment.

The appeal of the new right is based on the way many people experienced "the great transformation" and the transformations and dislocations of the 1970s and 1980s. These shocks inspired fear. They portended the collapse of the "American Dream"—the apolitical, perpetually prosperous, militarily invincible, and deeply self-absorbed and self-righteous "mainstream" American culture was, we think, shaken to its foundations by developments over this period. Commonly held concepts of nation, community, and family were transformed, and no new principle of cohesion,

121

no new cultural center, emerged to replace them. New collective identities, rooted in the "new social movements," remained fragmented and politically disunited.

In short, the U.S. was politically fragmented as differences of all sorts—regional, racial, sexual, religious—became more visible, while economic stability and global military supremacy seemed to vanish. A plethora of interest groups, it seemed, had suddenly emerged, invoking a bewildering array of new social and political values, creating unprecedented political disorientation, and leaving the "mainstream" with no clear notion of the "common good."[28]

In the face of these challenges, traditional conservatism seemed to have little to offer—society and politics, and the conventional way in which they were understood, had already been radically transformed. Only the appearance of the new right in the middle 1970s gave the millions of threatened members of the "silent majority" (Richard Nixon's phrase, let it be remembered, coined to steal some of George Wallace's thunder) any relief. The new right was a well-organized alternative to the moral and existential chaos of the preceding decades: a network of conservative organizations with an aggressive political style, an outspoken religious and cultural traditionalism, and a clear populist commitment.

Gillian Peele defines the new right as "a loose movement of conservative politicians and a collection of general-purpose political organizations which have developed independently of the political parties."[29] The main new right affiliates emerged in the 1970s: the American Conservative Union, the National Conservative Political Action Committee (NCPAC), the Conservative Caucus, the Young Americans for Freedom (whose origins were earlier), and a group of fundamentalist Protestant sects incorporating millions of adherents. Leading figures of the 1980s new right were fundraiser/publisher Richard A. Viguerie, Paul Weyrich (Committee for the Survival of a Free Congress), Howard Phillips (Conservative Caucus), and the late John T. Dolan (NCPAC), as well as activist Phyllis Schlafly (Eagle Forum, Stop-ERA) and fundamentalist evangelist Rev. Jerry Falwell (Moral Majority). Periodicals identified with the new right included the *Conservative Digest*, *Policy Review*, and *New Guard*. The key new right think tank is the Heritage Foundation, founded by brewer Joseph Coors and Paul Weyrich in 1973. Central to the new right's growth has been the use of direct-mail solicitation:

> Collecting millions of dollars in small contributions from blue-collar workers and housewives, the New Right feeds on discontent, anger, insecurity, and resentment, and flourishes on backlash politics.[30]

Much has been written about the new right's tendency to focus on controversial *social* issues as a means of rallying and organizing its constituency. Left and progressive analyses have argued that the defining project of the new right is the reassertion of "patriarchy" by attacking the limited gains of the feminist and gay movements.[31] While much of this is true, such analyses understate the crucial importance of *race* as a defining issue. Race was crucial in the initial reaction against the progressive gains of the 1960s (then known as "backlash"; e.g., anti-busing movements),[32] central to the electoral perspective of the new right (the "southern strategy"), and continues to be a major, if at times disguised, issue for the new right today.

In this respect the racial politics of the new right cannot be seen as a simple "backlash" against the gains of the 1960s movements for racial equality. In the early 1970s, there was little awareness among progressive analysts that behind the "backlash" was a potentially innovative political project: *authoritarian populism.*

New right populism combined such venerable American ideological themes as respect for authority, mistrust of "big government," and defense of traditional morality, with resistance to minority demands for group rights. The latter concern should hardly be surprising. A striking feature of America's populist tradition, reaching back to Andrew Jackson, is that it has been fuelled by heavy doses of nativism and racism.

The new right cannot simply defend patterns of racial inequality by demanding a return to segregation, for example, or by reviving simplistic notions of biological superiority/inferiority.[33] As we have previously noted, the racial upheavals of the 1960s precluded a direct return to this form of racial logic.

The new right objective, however, was to dismantle the political gains of racial minorities. Since these gains could not be easily reversed, they had to be *rearticulated.* The key device used by the new right in its effort to limit the political gains of racial minority movements was "code words." These are phrases and symbols which refer indirectly to racial themes, but do not directly challenge popular democratic or egalitarian ideals (e.g., justice, equal opportunity). Beginning with the Wallace campaign of 1968, we can trace the pattern of new right experimentation with these code words, and with the rearticulation of racial meanings they attempt.

The first rumblings of the present-day new right agenda were heard in George Wallace's 1968 presidential bid. Wallace's initial role on the national political stage had been that of die-hard segregationist.[34] His entry into the presidential race was first seen as a replay of the Dixiecrat strategy which had led to the candidacy of Strom Thurmond twenty years before.

Few analysts expected Wallace to have mass appeal outside the South, yet in northern blue collar strongholds like Milwaukee, Detroit, and Philadelphia, he demonstrated surprising strength.

Although Wallace's image as a racist politician had originally placed him in the national spotlight, it did not make good Presidential politics, and he was forced to incorporate his racial message as a subtext, implicit but "coded," in a populist appeal. Wallace thus struck certain chords that anticipated the new right agenda—defense of traditional values, opposition to "big government," and patriotic and militaristic themes. But the centerpiece of his appeal was his racial politics. Wallace was a law-and-order candidate, an antistatist, an inheritor of classical southern populist traditions. He called for the stepped-up use of force to repress ghetto rebellions, derided the black movement and the war on poverty, and attacked liberal politicians and intellectuals. Wallace departed from his early 1960s style, however, by avoiding direct race-baiting.

During the same campaign, political analyst Kevin Phillips submitted a lengthy and rather scholarly analysis of U.S. voting trends to Nixon headquarters, arguing that a Republican victory and long-term electoral realignment were possible on racial grounds. Published the following year as *The Emerging Republican Majority*, Phillips's book suggested a turn to the right and the use of "coded" antiblack campaign rhetoric (e.g., law and order).[35] Wallace's success, the disarray in Democratic ranks caused by the "Negro socioeconomic revolution," and polling data from blue-collar districts around the country convinced Phillips that a strategic approach of this kind (dubbed the "southern strategy") could fundamentally shift political alignments which had been in effect since 1932.

These innovations bore rich political fruit. They coincided with the fragmentation of the New Deal coalition, the "loss" of the war on poverty, and the decline of the black movement. They represented an apparent alternative to ghetto riots and white guilt, to the integration of northern schools and the onset of stagflation. They effortlessly, if demagogically, appealed to a majority of the electorate—something which the new social movements of minorities, antiwar activists, and feminists had not succeeded in doing.

Most important of all, the "coded" racial politics of the late 1960s and after did not repudiate the legacy of the minority movements; indeed, they adopted a conservative egalitarian version of their demands.[36] Nixon advocated "black capitalism" and on the advice of Daniel Patrick Moynihan drew up a welfare reform plan featuring a guaranteed annual income.[37] While not a new rightist himself, Nixon set the stage for the later new right ascendance by simultaneously coopting *both* Wallace and suitably moderate blacks (and other minorities), by espousing *both* law and order and a negative income tax, neighborhood schools *and* black capitalism.

Cultural Politics, Antistatism, and the "New Class"

By 1980 the new right agenda was far more advanced. There was no longer any flirtation with the sort of centrism Nixon represented. The new right dream seemed within reach: to consolidate a "new majority" which could dismantle the welfare state, legislate a return to "traditional morality," and stem the tide of political and cultural dislocation which the 1960s and 1970s represented.[38] This project linked the assault on liberalism and "secular humanism,"[39] the obsession with individual guilt and responsibility where social questions were concerned (crime, sex, education, poverty), with a fierce *antistatism*. The political strategy involved was populist: use of the initiative process, for example, served as an "end-run" around the courts, the bureaucracy, the Congress and state legislatures. Traditional conservatives such as Alan Crawford have labeled this channeling of popular rage through direct democratic channels "antipolitical":

> A near-constant theme of conservative thought, from Edmund Burke to William Buckley, has been that unrestrained expressions of popular will militate against the orderly processes of government on which stable societies depend. . . . The New Right, impatient for short-run results, has rejected this dominant theme of conservatism in favor of direct democracy, threatening to shatter the safeguards against political centralization and, therefore, freedom itself.[40]

Crawford believes that "the New Right exploits social protest and encourages class hostility by trying to fuel the hostilities of lower-middle-class Americans against those above and below them on the economic ladder."[41] Some analysts see the new right as a status revolt[42] by those who, according to Ben Wattenberg, are "unyoung, unpoor and unblack"[43]—those whose identities and interests were articulated *negatively* by the social movements of the 1960s and the crises of the 1970s. They resent any mobility on the part of lower-status groups, and demand that the political process recognize the traditional values to which they subscribe. Their anger is directed at those who are "not like themselves"; this involves a racial dimension which is experienced as a *cultural* threat as much as an economic one:

> . . . [T]he fear of black power, "reverse discrimination," at the community level—associated with fear of crime, property devaluation, dirtiness and noisiness—reflects not only the direct economic crunch on white working-class people but also a less tangible sense of cultural disintegration.[44]

The failure of the Great Society and other liberal experiments also focused attention on members of the *new class* (educators, administrators, planners, consultants, network journalists, etc.) and revived traditional themes of *antistatism*. The new right believes that "pointy-heads" control the state and are responsible for the current political, economic, and cultural malaise. During the 1960s and 1970s the state was recklessly allowed to expand and intervene in every aspect of social life; it came to dictate social policy with disastrous results. In particular, it acceded to racial minority demands and gave minorities privileged access to jobs and social services. Ed Davis, a new right cult figure and former Chief of the Los Angeles Police Department, put it this way: "I always felt that the government really was out to force me to hire 4-foot-11 transvestite morons."[45]

Critiques of liberal statism abound on the new right. The Supreme Court is criticized for liberal bias in matters of race relations. The electoral college system is opposed for restricting third-party efforts and, as Kevin Phillips has suggested, maximizing the influence of a "third world state"[46] such as California. While constantly calling for a return to the basics of the Constitution, new right activists also seem intent on revising it through amendents to stop busing, prohibit abortions, or encourage school prayer.

New right figures appeal to white racial anxieties. Spiro Agnew's acceptance by the new right was based on the way he "talked back" to black leaders. Sen. Jesse Helms built his reputation by refusing to pursue black votes in North Carolina and by his highly publicized smears of Martin Luther King, Jr. as a communist.[47] Years before his 1992 presidential bid, new right columnist Patrick J. Buchanan argued, as a headline put it, that the "GOP Vote Search Should Bypass Ghetto" since blacks have been ungrateful for Republican efforts to help and assist them.[48]

As we have suggested, race and class politics interface and overlap in the U.S. Individuals and groups interpret their conditions of existence and their subjective experiences in ways which draw upon both racially based and class-based meanings:

> On one side, threatening traditional values, are the feminists, the liberals, the university communities, minorities, residents of urban centers, and the media. On the other—the side of the angels—are the "pro-family" forces, the leadership of the New Right and its disguntled constituents, plus a growing political movement of fundamentalist evangelical ministers. . . . Both sides are competing for the soul of America.[49]

Thus the new right grafts together issues of race and issues of class. New right publisher William Rusher provides an apt illustration of the racial dimension "hidden" in much of the "new class" analysis on the right:

A new economic division pits the producers—businessmen, manufacturers, hard-hats, blue-collar workers, and farmers—against a new and powerful class of non-producers comprised of a liberal verbalist elite (the dominant media, the major foundations and research institutions, the educational establishment, the federal and state bureaucracies) and a semipermanent welfare constituency, all coexisting happily in a state of mutually sustaining symbiosis.[50]

The "semipermanent welfare constituency" is implicitly non-white in the popular political imagination.[51] Rusher's approach conjures up anti–big government sentiments by blaming unemployment among minorities for parasitism at the expense of "productive" workers. His *ressentiment* is racial, even though his vocabulary is that of class. This rearticulation of racial ideology is, we believe, crucial to recent new right advances.

The new right generally does not display *explicit* racism. It has gained political currency by rearticulating racial ideology. As we have argued, rearticulation does not require an explicitly racial discourse, and would in fact be severely limited by any direct advocacy of racial inequality. Some examples of this process:

Busing. The new right has opposed busing not as an overt effort to maintain residential or school segregation, but as an assault on "the community" and "the family." School integration, new right activists have argued, means that the state usurps the decision-making powers which should be vested in parents: deciding in what kind of communities their children will be raised and what kind of education their children will receive. A similar argument is made against busing on "pro-family" grounds. As Gordon and Hunter suggest, "The antibusing movement is nourished by . . . fears for the loss of the family. The loss of neighborhood schools is perceived as a threat to community, and therefore family stability, by many people, particularly in cities where ethnically homogenous communities remain."[52]

The formerly progressive themes of "community control" and "parental involvement" are thus harnessed to prevent race mixing in the schools, while charges of racism are blunted or avoided altogether. One measure of the success of this anti-integration strategy was the confusion it sowed even on the left during the Boston busing controversy of the 1970s.[53]

Textbook Censorship. The monitoring of books for public school adoption is another issue where a "hidden" racial dimension informs new right politics. As early as 1975, the Heritage Foundation formed the National Congress for Educational Excellence to coordinate the activities of roughly 200 textbook-protester organizations nationwide. This effort capitalized on the feelings of many whites that their values and lifestyles were being neglected by "multicultural" texts.[54] The new right, in this instance, can push a racial

127

agenda merely by arguing for "traditional" lifestyles and families, for the return to a more homogeneous image of everyday life, purged of "secular humanism" and the rest of the unsettling ambiguities of the 1960s and 1970s. Textbooks focusing on Dick and Jane and Spot, and avoiding any mention of Ahmad or Chabrika, Fernando or Nguyen, effectively *re*-marginalize minority cultures without ever having to invoke issues of race.

"Reverse Discrimination". On the issue of affirmative action, the right has made significant advances in rearticulating the meaning of racial equality. The strength of this argument is its specific appeal to equality and "fairness." What has become unfair, the right argues, is the state's accommodation to the demands of racial minorities and other "special interests" at the expense of whites. The new right's ability to mobilize resentment against the "group rights" demands of racial minorities dovetails with the neoconservative argument that only "equality of opportunity" can be a valid objective of state policy. The ability of the new right to mobilize "grass roots" opposition to residential and school desegregation, to preferential hiring and school admissions schemes, and to minority "set-asides" in government contracting provides a populist counterpoint to the more abstract and theoretically developed critique developed by ethnicity theorists such as Nathan Glazer and Michael Novak. It is to this current that we now turn our attention.

Neoconservatism

Perhaps worst of all from the ethnicity theory point of view, blacks and other racial minorities questioned the legitimacy of reforms based on the principle of equality of *individuals*, seeking instead a radical *collective* equality ("group rights") which ethnicity theory viewed as anathema to a democracy. Such a policy would break faith with the generations who had come before, break faith with the civic ideals which were the soul of American society. True, the ethnicity theorists had flirted briefly with the idea of "equality of result" during the early heady days of the Great Society. Moynihan, for example, was co-author of an important 1965 speech by Lyndon Johnson which contained these famous lines:

> . . . [F]reedom is not enough. You do not wipe away the scars of centuries by saying: Now you are free to go where you want, do as you desire, and choose the leaders you please.

> You do not take a person who, for years, has been hobbled by chains and liberate him (sic), bring him up to the starting line of a

race and then say, "you are free to compete with all the others," and still justly believe that you have been completely fair.

Thus it is not enough just to open the gates of opportunity. All our citizens must have the ability to walk through those gates.

This is the next and more profound stage of the battle for civil rights. We seek not just freedom but opportunity—not just legal equity but human ability—not just equality as a right and a theory but equality as a fact and as a result.[55]

Very quickly, though, they drew back from the larger implications of this position. Glazer wrote during the same year that "a new national interest" in "the final liquidation of Negro separation" was being defined, and that blacks themselves had best not oppose it, for "When an ethnic group interest has clashed with a national interest, we have been quite ruthless and even extreme in overriding the group interest."[56]

By the 1970s, opposition to minority demands for "group rights" had become a centerpiece of the neoconservative perspective. The ethnicity theorists associated with the current did not ground their arguments, as some in the new right did, on "white rights." They minimized references to "reverse discrimination" or "reverse racism," preferring to center their critique on the illegitimacy of state policies which engaged in "race-thinking." Thus Glazer's objections to affirmative action policies centered on their ineffectiveness and their challenge to the fundamental civic ideals which had made the "American ethnic pattern" possible: individualism, market-based opportunity, and the curtailment of excessive state interventionism. Affirmative action, he wrote,

... [H]as meant that we abandon the first principle of a liberal society, that the individual's interests and good and welfare are the test of a good society, for we now attach benefits and penalties to individuals simply on the basis of their race, color, and national origins. The implications of this new course are increasing consciousness of the significance of group membership, an increasing divisiveness on the basis of race, color, and national origin, and a spreading resentment among the disfavored groups against the favored ones. If the individual is the measure, however, our public concern is with the individual's capacity to work out an individual fate by means of education, work, and self-realization in the various spheres of life. Then how the figures add up on the basis of whatever measure of group we use may be interesting, but should be of no concern to public policy.[57]

He did not argue that white resentment against such programs was justified—in the manner of a William Rusher or a George Wallace—only that it was inevitable.[58] This distinguishes the neoconservative and new right oppositions to such policies: the neoconservatives fear the politics of *ressentiment* as an unwanted consequence of state over-involvement, while the new right mobilizes precisely such sentiments.

The power of the neoconservative critique of affirmative action is based on the ability of such authors as Glazer to present themselves as simultaneously opposed both to discrimination and to antidiscrimination measures based on "group rights" principles. The neoconservatives thus refocus the debate on the question of what *means* are best for achieving equality. Such an approach is attractive but misleading.

In the neoconservative view opposition to affirmative action is consistent with the goals of the civil rights movement; it is a challenge to "race-thinking."[59] According to this logic, only individual rights exist, only individual opportunity can be guaranteed by law, and only "merit" justifies the granting of privilege. Yet even the most cursory examination of such arguments reveals their deeper political subtexts. Glazer's concern about the resentments and heightened racial polarization any *abandonment* of traditional liberalism would inspire, for example, does not extend to the resentments and polarization which *adherence* to liberalism entails. Morris Abram, a former liberal partisan of civil rights who served on the U.S. Civil Rights Commission under Reagan, proposed the extension of unionization as a better remedy than affirmative action for alleviating minority poverty and powerlessness.[60] Thereby he merely indicated which groups he considered acceptable vehicles for political demands. Workers are apparently free to have collective interests, but racial minorities are not. Concepts of "individual merit," as Philip Green has shown, have the same shallowness. "Merit" is a political construct, by which employers, schools, state agencies, etc. legitimate the allocation of benefits to favored (i.e., organized) constituencies, and deny the validity of competing claims.[61]

Once we recognize that the attack on affirmative action is not simply about "fairness," but also about the maintenance of existing social positions and political stability, it becomes easier to explain its enormous appeal. The unpopularity of affirmative action by now extends far beyond the new right and the neoconservatives who originally authored the "reverse discrimination" critique. In our view the defeat of affirmative action testifies to two things: the subtlety and pervasiveness of the right's rearticulation of the meaning of racial equality as a matter of individual rather than group or collective concern, and the increasing convergence of the neoconservative and new right tendencies.

Rearticulating the Meaning of Racial Equality. The concept of "reverse discrimination" appropriated the demand for equality presented by the minority movements of the 1960s and stood it on its head. The neoconservative argument redefined racial meanings in such a way as to contain the more radical implications of the 1960s upsurge. Racial discrimination and racial equality—in the neoconservative model—were problems to be confronted *only* at an individual level, once legal systems of discrimination such as *de jure* segregation had been eliminated. Thus discrimination may be an illegitimate infringement on individual rights, but it can no longer be a legitimate source for group demands. What the neoconservatives opposed was therefore not racial equality, but racial collectivity.

By limiting themselves to considering discrimination against *individuals*, though, the neoconservatives trivialized the problem of racial equality, and of equality in general. Discrimination never derived its main strength from individual actions or prejudices, however great these might have been or might still be. Its most fundamental characteristic was always its roots in the racially organized *social* order. The minority movements of the 1950s and 1960s, even in their early, "moderate" incarnations, definitively questioned this social assignment of identities and racial meanings. It was this questioning, this challenge, that the neoconservatives sought to confine and reorganize in their assault on affirmative action. They did this by limiting the meaning of racial discrimination to the curtailment of individual rights, a distinction that could apply to whites and non-whites alike. The social logic of race was thus rendered opaque without any necessary recourse to explicit prejudice or institutionalized inequality à la the segregation laws of the past.

Convergence of Neoconservatism and the New Right. Neoconservatism incubated in the ever-widening division between liberals and radicals of the late 1960s and early 1970s, and drew further strength from the rise of the new right. In the eyes of the ethnicity theorists, not only were the black radicals and other new social movements upsetting the pluralist applecart of tolerance, individualism, accommodation of conflicting interests through established political processes, etc., but they were inspiring a right-wing intolerance equal to their own, and threatening to open a second breach in the body politic, this time to the liberals' right. As the 1960s drew to a close and the 1970s began, many ethnicity theorists felt they had to choose an alliance with the right in order to stem the tide of radical collectivism which the black movement had set in motion. They defined neoconservatism in the pages of *Commentary* and *The Public Interest*, and in editorials in *The Wall Street Journal*. In a series of publications emerging from Harvard, they spelled out the tragic implications of affirmative action.[62]

Race and Reaction

The neoconservatives originally polemicized against the politics of *ressentiment*, but by the 1980s they had made their peace with its chief practitioners, the forces of the new right. This was, in our view, largely a matter of political expedience. It must be remembered that the radical democratic demands (of "equality of result," etc.) typified by affirmative action particularly threatened certain vulnerable groups. Unionized workers benefiting from *de facto* segregated seniority systems, for example, or white ethnic residents of urban enclaves who felt themselves to be an "endangered species"—hemmed in by ghettos or barrios, fearful of crime—became potential conservative constituencies. These groups were certainly harmed by the implementation of affirmative action in employment, busing, and minority "set-asides," though the extent of the threat such programs represented remains a matter of debate.[63] By formulating a sophisticated counter-argument to minority calls for "equality of result," neoconservative scholars rationalized existing systems of racial inequality. They helped the beneficiaries of *de facto* occupational segregation, for example, to avoid confronting the disquieting implication of racism.[64] Thus the neoconservative scholars of ethnicity tacitly provided ammunition to the new right in its racially based mobilization of (ethnic, working-class, etc.) whites.

Having seen the radical challengers at home throw their support to communist revolutionaries fighting the U.S. in Vietnam and elsewhere, having experienced a series of threats to traditional values of family, the work ethic, and sexual discipline (in such new social movements as feminism, welfare rights, and gay liberation), the neoconservatives ultimately came to share many points of agreement with the new right. True, some divergent elements remained—for example some neoconservatives who had been associated with Hubert Humphrey and Henry "Scoop" Jackson continued to support certain welfare state programs and trade unionism, however much they detested affirmative action and were Cold War hawks—but in all the main points a new intellectual and policy-oriented realignment had occurred. Once more, the issue of race had played a crucial role in restructuring the central dynamics— political, cultural, and perhaps most important, intellectual—of U.S. society.

The Reagan "Revolution"

During the vice presidential debate in October 1984, George Bush was clearly overwhelmed by questions on minorities and racial discrimination. As Jack White of *Time Magazine* reminded Bush,

Many critics of your administration say that it is the most hostile to minorities in recent memory. Have you perhaps inadvertently encouraged that view by supporting tuition tax credits, the anti-busing amendment and siding with Bob Jones University in a case before the Supreme Court, your original opposition to the Voting Rights extension and so forth?[65]

Bush sidestepped some issues and made vague statements about others, but was clearly at a loss to justify the Reagan administration record.

Reagan's record on racial policy was not a particularly enlightened one. Since his emergence as a Republican leader, Reagan had opposed every major civil rights measure considered by Congress. He opposed the Civil Rights Act of 1964, denouncing it as a "bad piece of legislation," and the Voting Rights Act of 1965, opining that "The Constitution very specifically reserves control of voting to local governments. Additional legislation is unnecessary."[66] His consistency on racial issues extended through the 1980 and 1984 Presidential campaigns. On the campaign trail in 1980, Reagan told the South that he favored "state's rights" in the same Mississppi town where civil rights workers James Chaney, Andrew Goodman, and Michael Schwerner had been murdered by Klansmen in 1964.

During that same campaign, Nancy Reagan told a crowd in New Hampshire that she wished her husband could be with her to "see all these beautiful white people."[67] It was a revealing *faux pas*. President Reagan, more than any other President in recent memory, had cultivated an image as "the white people's president." In the 1984 election, Reagan took 74 percent of the white male vote in the South, 68 percent in the West, and 66 percent in the nation as a whole:

Reagan won every category of white males except white Jewish males. . . . He won rich and poor, Catholic and Protestant, young and old, North and South, Yuppie and blue collar. Generally he won them by overwhelming margins.[68]

The impact of Reagan's 1984 success among white men continues to resonate not only in the Republican but also in the Democratic Party. As Democratic pollster William Hamilton warned, the Democrats "can't very well lose [the white male vote] by 2 to 1 and expect to be serious players in a two-party system."[69] Many Democrats now argue that the Party has lost touch with a majoritarian constituency and needs to shed its image as the vehicle of "special interests." In such a context, racial minority demands are bound to be submerged. In February 1985, newly elected Democratic National Committee Chair Paul Kirk said that caucuses within the DNC (representing such groups as blacks, Hispanics, Asians/Pacific Islanders, women, and gays) were "political nonsense" and promised to abolish them.[70]

On the policy level, the Reagan administration took its cue from both the new right and neoconservatives, arguing that the important forms of racial discrimination had been eliminated. Thus most civil rights remedies and mechanisms for achieving racial equality were suddenly considered to discriminate *against whites.* In January 1985, Reagan remarked that some civil rights organizations are no longer needed because they have accomplished their goals.[71] School busing plans and affirmative action policies came under attack by the Reagan "revolutionaries." Former Attorney General William French Smith dropped desegregation appeals in cities such as Kansas City and Houston and slowed integration efforts in Chicago, Phoenix, Albuquerque, and Rochester. Former Secretary of Labor Raymond Donovan issued new regulations in 1981 which substantially weakened the affirmative action requirements attached to federal contracts.

In an important 1985 Supreme Court case, the Justice Department opposed the city of Indianapolis' efforts to use hiring quotas to help minorities get jobs in local government.[72] In the same year, the Department urged over fifty states, counties, and cities to voluntarily modify their affirmative action plans to remove numerical goals and quotas. It was hinted that failure to comply "voluntarily" might result in court action.

The Reagan administration also tried to alter the perception of racial discrimination by eliminating record-keeping. In March 1985, the Office of Management and Budget ordered the Department of Housing and Urban Development and the Veterans Administration to stop tracking the racial and ethnic characteristics of Americans who receive benefits from these two agencies. This policy would have severely hampered the administration of civil rights and fair housing programs. George D. Moerman, assistant director for loan policy for the VA, said that the lack of information "will put us in the position where, if abuse exists, we will not be able to find it."[73] During the same period, the administration opposed a bill (HR 1171) which would have required the FBI's uniform crime reports to include categories of offenses "involving the expression of racial, ethnic or religious prejudice." Reagan administration officials felt that it would be too difficult to include "hate crime" categories in national crime statistics. Hate crime legislation subsequently passed and soon became entangled in litigation.

While President Reagan departed from significant aspects of the new right agenda, he seemed in firm agreement with new right racial positions. He drastically reduced the welfare state with the rationale that such spending not only fails to ameliorate the problems of poverty, but actually exacerbates them.[74] These cuts disproportionately affected racial minorities.[75] Schemes such as urban "free enterprise zones" coupled with the attempt to deal with unemployment in the inner cities by instituting a sub-minimum wage echoed new right antistatism and arguments that only the "free market" can alleviate minority poverty.

Perhaps the Reagan administration's biggest policy shifts took place in the area of affirmative action. As we have argued, under the guise of creating a truly "color-blind" society, administration officials sought to define and eliminate the "new racism" *against whites*. As Reagan's U.S. Civil Rights Commission Chairman Clarence Pendleton, Jr. characterized it, the new racists were "supporters of civil rights" who "exhibit the classical behavior system of racism. They treat blacks differently than whites because of their race."[76] The tables had turned. It was now the liberals who were guilty of racism. Blacks, and other minorities, needed to be saved from liberal efforts to help them.

While Reagan incurred the wrath of some quarters of the right for his abandonment of, or slow-moving posture towards, some social issues (e.g, anti-abortion laws and prayer in public schools), his scorecard on racial issues remained nearly impeccable. Reagan harnessed the discontent which has been simmering among the large numbers of whites who have felt threatened by the racial politics of the past two decades. He opposed racial equality and civil rights for minorities in a manner which seemed on the surface "color-blind." After commenting on studies which suggest that racism motivates some people to become Republicans, political scientist Merle Black noted that:

> Reagan's kind of civilized the racial issue. He's taken what Wallace never could do and made it acceptable. It fits in with their [white students'] sense of perceived injustice, with what they see as the status of being a white person not being as high as it was 15, 20 or 30 years ago.[77]

Reagan "civilized" the race issue by being quite adept at rearticulating the issues of race and racial equality. Drawing on themes derived from both new right and neoconservative currents, Reagan successfully assaulted the racial policies initiated in response to "the great transformation." Under his leadership, the federal government reversed itself and switched sides on racial policy. This was accomplished by rewriting recent history to suggest that discrimination against racial minorities had been drastically curbed and by radically transforming the state institutions which were previously mandated to "protect" racial minority interests.

Race and Reaction

The racial reaction initiated in the late 1960s and early 1970s developed in the 1980s into a pervasive ideological effort to reinterpret once again the meaning of race in the U.S. As the Reagan administration adopted its major themes, the racial reaction achieved legitimate, if not hegemonic, status in "normal" politics. It attained maturity and power, operating behind a subtle and seductive veneer of opposition to "race-thinking."

Conclusion

At the end of World War II, Henry Luce's designation of the coming period as "the American century" hardly seemed an exaggerated vision of things to come. The U.S. apparently had limitless opportunities: to develop and extend its unparalleled economic and commercial position, to project its political and military power globally, and to institutionalize its vision of political democracy and social justice as a model for the world to emulate. Americans delighted in their country's unprecedented preeminence; they viewed themselves as the world's saviors.

The American century was short-lived. In the 1980s Americans had to contemplate the painful possibility that the dream was over. The U.S. did not appear to dominate world affairs, but instead to cope with a prevalent climate of disruption in the global arena. Once the world's creditor, it had become its chief debtor; once the chief exporter of manufactured goods, it was now their main importer. Once the model of democracy for the under-developed world, the U.S. was now wracked with doubt about the proper level of support for "authoritarian" regimes there. Once able to guarantee a prosperous and secure future to its citizens, the U.S. now contemplated a minimum unemployment rate (in periods of economic expansion, to say nothing of contraction) of 7 percent, and a national debt which by 1984 had reached the $200 billion per annum range. Since 1970 the U.S. had experienced defeat in war, the impeachment and resignation of a President, an inflationary peak of 22 percent, peacetime shortages of oil and gas, and the fall of Keynesianism and the political alignment which it sustained. It had also witnessed the election of a President whose chief commitment was to stem the tide of deterioration these events reflected.

Although no one factor, no single causative principle, could adequately account for the contemporary crisis, there was an aspect of recent U.S. history whose political importance in structuring the present situation had been systematically overlooked. We refer, of course, to the *racial* dimension of American life. In contrast to much of existing political and racial theory, the present work has emphasized the *centrality of race* in American society. We have sought to explain the process by which race has shaped, and been shaped by, U.S. politics.

We have approached race as a phenomenon whose meaning is contested throughout social life. Race is a constituent of the individual psyche and of relationships among individuals; it is also an irreducible component of collective identities and social structures. In American history, racial dynamics have been a traditional source, both of conflict and division, and of renewal and cultural awareness. Race has been a key determinant of mass movements, state policy, and even foreign policy in the U.S. Racial meaning-systems are contested and racial ideologies mobilized in *political* relationships.

Beginning in the 1950s and more intensively in the 1960s, racially based social movements initiated a "great transformation" of the American political universe, creating new organizations, new collective identities, and new political norms; challenging past racial practices and stereotypes; and ushering in a wave of democratizing social reform. The ability of racially based movements to *rearticulate* traditional political and cultural themes—first among blacks, and later among Latinos, Asian Americans, and Indians—permitted the entry of millions of racial minority group members into the political process. They initiated a trajectory of reform which exposed the limits of all previously existing political orientations—conservative, liberal, and radical. In transforming the meaning of race and the contours of racial politics, the racially-based movements transformed the meaning and contours of American politics itself. Political mobilization along racial lines resulted in the enactment of reforms which dramatically restructured the racial order, reorganized state institutions, and launched whole new realms of state activity.

In processing racial demands, the state demonstrated a tremendous flexibility and resilience. Using strategies of *absorption* and *insulation*, the state was able to accept moderate reforms while simultaneously containing the more radical potentialities of the minority upsurge.

In the effort to adapt to the new racial politics they themselves had created, racial movements lost their decentered political unity. Working within the newly reformed racial state was more possible, and confronting it more difficult, than during the preceding period. Opposition to the backward and coercive racial order of the South had permitted a tenuous alliance between moderate and radical currents of the movement, an alliance which the winning of civil rights reforms ruptured. The "triumph" of liberal democracy failed to placate radicals who sought not only *rights*, but power and resources as well. The conferring of rights did not appreciably change the circumstances of a black youth in Harlem or a *vato loco* in East Los Angeles. What was heralded as a great victory by liberals appeared to the radicals as merely a more streamlined version of racial oppression.

The dominant paradigm of ethnicity, the centerpiece of liberal racial politics, fell into disrepute among radicals. Radical theories of race—the class-based and nation-based paradigms—challenged the explanatory power and political efficacy of the ethnicity perspective. Embracing these new paradigmatic conceptions, radical movement tendencies advanced their demands for a more throughgoing restructuring of the social order—one which would recognize the pervasiveness of racial oppression not only in "normal" politics, but in the organization of the labor market, in the geography of living space, and in the forms of cultural life.

Yet these challengers failed to consolidate a new political project of "radical democracy" which could expand beyond the issue of race and aspire to majoritarian status. This failure was due to factors both "internal" and "external" to the movement itself. Internally, the radical currents were increasingly plagued by fragmentation along class and political lines. Tensions developed between (and among) those engaged in electoral work, workplace organizing, "antipoverty" projects, and the "long march through the institutions"; activists politicized on the university and college campuses; and those, like the Black Panther Party, who sought to mobilize the "lumpenproletariat."[1] Some organizations became romantically fascinated by third world revolutionary movements whose "lessons" were largely irrelevant to U.S. conditions. This fragmentation resulted in an absence of unified radical politics and an inability to define a coherent political subject. Externally, the racially based movements were, by the 1970s, largely outmaneuvered by the new racial state which had responded to moderate demands and marginalized radical ones.

The 1980s bore ironic witness to the impact of the racial minority upsurge on the overall political terrain in the U.S. While failing to consolidate a new radical democratic politics with majoritarian aspirations, "the great transformation" provided the political space in which a right-wing reaction could incubate and develop its political agenda.

The new social movements inspired a profound reaction, even revulsion, in those whose political and cultural reference points they challenged. Intellectuals decried a "crisis of democracy"[2] in which the political system was becoming "overloaded." The self-identification of the majority of Americans as "conservative" (as opposed to "liberal") emerged as people came to perceive the racial minority, women's, and peace movements as opposed to the "traditional" values they upheld. The new social movements were held responsible for the decline and dislocations Americans had experienced in the later 1960s and after. According to Jonathan Rieder, liberalism came to be associated with "profligacy, spinelessness, malevolence, masochism, elitism, fantasy, idealism, softness, irresponsibility, and sanctimoniousness," while conservatism acquired "connotations of pragmatism, character, reciprocity, truthfulness, stoicism, manliness, realism, hardness, vengeance, strictness, and responsibility."[3] Liberalism was seen as beholden to minorities, for whom it provided "handouts," while conservatism was thought to embrace traditional individualist (and thus "colorblind") values of hard work and sacrifice.

Amid a general decline of U.S. economic and political hegemony around the globe, the resurgent right adopted an "authoritarian populist"[4] character which sharply contrasted with traditional conservatism. The primary objectives of the right-wing were the containment of the demands and political vision of the new social movements, the restoration of "governability" to democracy, and the reassertion of traditional cultural and social values.

By the 1980s, the right-wing reaction had captured the popular political imagination. Its analysis of the ills which beset the nation and its prescription for reclaiming the "American century" had resonated with large parts of the American public. Popular support for the Reagan administration, reflected in Reagan's "landslide" electoral victory in 1984, testified to the eclipse of New Deal liberalism and provided political justification for the rightward trend in social policy. Racial policy was dramatically affected. The Reagan administration demonstrated its opposition to affirmative action, reconstituted the U.S. Civil Rights Commission in order to fight "reverse discrimination," relaxed or eliminated government action against racist practices and institutions, and in general attempted to reverse the political consequences of the "great transformation."

Yet right-wing initiatives could not really dismiss racial history. The accomplishments of the 1960s could not simply be reversed. Since 1965, for example, it has been impossible to argue *for* segregation or *against* racial equality. Any "legitimate" politics must claim to favor racial equality *in the abstract,* even if specific egalitarian measures are condemned. To argue for a return to the explicitly racist ideology of pre-civil rights movement days is to move to the proto-fascist fringes of the far right. An unabashedly "white man's government" would face severe opposition and would bring about an immediate crisis of legitimacy—at the very least it would have to be presented as a state of emergency requiring the suspension of democratic rights.[5]

Racial reaction, therefore, also encountered clear limits in the wake of the political and ideological transformations of the 1960s. Both because of the successes of "the great transformation" and because the minority movements could not be consolidated as a permanent radical democratic political force, the right had been able to rearticulate racial meanings once again. This time, though, it was not the justice but the very *meaning* of racial equality which was at stake. The right, especially the neoconservatives, had institutionalized their interpretation—focused on "equality of opportunity" and explicitly oblivious to "equality of result"—as the national "common sense."

From the standpoint of racial theory, the 1980s witnessed the resurrection of the ethnicity paradigm in a new form. The theory which once justified state racial interventionism now presented itself in far more market-oriented terms.[6] The theory which once encouraged racial minorities (seen, of course as "ethnic groups") to organize along interest-group lines, in pursuit of greater political power and distributional equity in the allocation of public resources, now shrank from such prospects.

Of course, neoconservatism was but one of several tendencies on the right. If the far right could in general be characterized by an explicit racism, the new right could be located somewhere between these two tendencies. Unlike the far right, the new right was adroit enough to avoid overt appeals to white supremacy. Unlike the neoconservatives, though, the new right has not renounced the use of racial "code words," and continues political mobilization on the basis of an implicit racial agenda. This is not conscious manipulation for the most part, but rather a consequence of the "great transformation," which brought to light the ubiquity of race. Given that racial meaning inheres in every social relationship, given the "threat" to "traditional" values posed by the new social movements, and given the correspondence between the racial upsurge of the 1960s and America's seeming fall from divine grace, is it all that surprising that a "racial reaction" can be found on the new right? Our study suggests that no post-1960s political initiative can avoid being interpreted, to some degree, through the lens of racial ideology.

Given the atmosphere of economic, political, and cultural change that characterized the 1980s, then, the options for racial policy are rather bleak. The climate of anti-statism severely limited the expansion of state activity to deal with impoverishment and the invidious effects of racism in housing, education, and welfare. On the other hand, even Reaganism was unable to liquidate the gains achieved by racial minority movements during the

1950s and 1960s. In the contemporary period such a rollback would be unimaginable short of a "proto-fascist" policy.[7] Such an alternative, besides being abhorrent, is obviously untenable, since it would have to contend not only with constitutional and institutionalized opposition, but also with the enormous disruptive powers of racial minorities, particularly those of the underclass.

Jesse Jackson's two presidential bids suggested some lessons that those on the left would have to learn well if they were to seek a new rearticulation of racial politics.[8] Although Jackson's messianism and refusal to build a grassroots base were not promising, between 1984 and 1988 his strategic orientation developed dramatically. His 1984 run was largely a black campaign, and a beleaguered one at that. Jackson lacked black elite support to run, and was seen by many established black leaders as a spoiler who would drive a wedge between their local political machines and civil rights organizations on the one hand, and the mainstream Democratic Party on the other. Paradoxically, this division within the black Democratic establishment forced Jackson to adopt a more grass-roots message, and to develop a more populist/progressive political orientation than he otherwise might have taken. Jackson was hardly a stranger to the black political elite or the inner circles of the Democratic Party, and under other conditions could easily have transformed himself into a very moderate, almost Urban League style black capitalism spokesperson.[9]

Having entered the 1984 campaign under these circumstances, though, Jackson was inevitably marginalized beyond the black community, and embattled within it. He was constantly on the defensive in the mainstream media, in part because of his own errors and weaknesses (his anti-semitic "Hymietown" remark being the most egregious of these), and he only occasionally achieved any access to the national political audience. Thus his 1984 support was preponderantly drawn from the black community and the less than numerous remnants of the new left. The concept of the "rainbow coalition," the campaign's central theme, had at least a dual significance: first, it expressed—to be sure, in a positive and historically grounded fashion—the enduring significance of race in the Democratic Party[10] and U.S. society; second, in the theme of the "rainbow" the Jackson campaign sought to expand beyond its black constituents to address the mainstream of national politics, but this approach was *still based on the primary ground of race*. The 1984 campaign was, then, limited by a central contradiction: organized along racial lines, it had to transcend race in order to achieve tangible political gains. The media and the electorate perceived this problem in terms of the campaign's racial meaning: was Jackson the black candidate, or was the the candidate as well of other sectors of the "rainbow"?

By 1988 many of these questions had been resolved. In strategic depth, program, message, and style Jackson was able steadily to address a national political audience in 1988, something which could occur only fitfully four years earlier. He was largely able to overcome the defensive posture his errors and weaknesses had created for him in 1984. Most importantly, Jackson confounded his detractors by clearly enunciating a left alternative current within the Democratic Party.[11]

While in 1984 he had lacked mainstream black political support, in 1988 Jackson could count on a very solid black base, both "elite" and "mass." The black mayors, congresspeople, and civil rights organizations were generally behind him now. The midterm elections of 1986 were testimony to Jackson's centrality as a Democratic player, for his registration efforts in the South proved crucial in returning the Senate to the Democratic column. In preparation for the 1988 race, Jackson consulted with old hands on the Democratic left, and worked out a fairly detailed social democratic agenda, tame stuff for other countries, but radical in the U.S. context. He pulled in southern moderates (e.g., Bert Lance), who recognized the importance of black voters to any hopes of breaking what had become the Republican solid South. With a nearly monolithic black base, a formidable political style, and a message of realignment, Jackson's project could by 1988 continue to discuss race explicitly while addressing the mainstream American electorate from the left. The beginnings of the articulation of race and class, which had appeared in the "rainbow" of 1984, now were presented in terms that were far more class-centered and class-conscious: "common ground."

By no means do we wish to suggest that Jackson downplayed race in 1988; indeed it is instructive to compare his analysis of racial issues—South Africa, ghetto poverty, etc.—with those of his Democratic competitors. Jackson was the only candidate who could securely discuss racism in 1988, but the program and message of his campaign went far beyond that.

The Jackson campaigns displayed a refreshingly explicit racial awareness by emphasizing the "multicultural" nature of U.S. society. Yet the campaigns also faced the necessity of submerging overt racial appeals. The legacy of the "great transformation," which as we have seen limits the racial logic of the right, also limits the possibilities for the left.

By the end of the 1980s it was clear that a period of racially based mobilization such as "the great transformation" would not recur. The conjuncture in which the 1960s racial upsurge took place was almost certainly unique. The sophistication of the contemporary racial state and the transformed political landscape as a whole seemed to thwart any short-term radical political initiative based in opposition to the racial order. Rather, a sustained period of reconceptualization and regrouping appeared to be in order.

Conclusion

Racial minority communities underwent huge changes in the post–civil rights era. Ferocious debates took place about the dramatic class cleavages which have arisen *within* these communities, and about their consequences for political action.[12] For Asian American and Latino communities, the liberalization of immigration laws in the mid-1960s led to a vast influx of both "old" and "new" groups. Koreans, Vietnamese, Laotians, and Filipinos are distinct in ethnic and class composition from each other and from more "established" groups such as Japanese Americans. Salvadorans, Guatemaltecos, Dominicans, and even Brazilians now represent substantial and distinct minorities within the Latino population. An increasingly variegated "community" made it difficult to speak of a shared experience, common sensibility, or unified political outlook. In the face of these realities, political mobilization along presumed "racial" lines became an ambiguous project, even though state policy, and the majority of the American public, continued to identify the groups mentioned along racial lines (i.e., as "Asians").

While widespread racially based mobilization did not seem likely to arise, it was equally unlikely that the right-wing reaction could consolidate itself on racial grounds. The Reagan administration's attempt to create a "color-blind society" certainly exacerbated already wide disparities between whites and non-whites in economic and political terms. The neoconservative theorists who endorsed the Reagan strategy (and indeed helped to fashion it) continued to cling to a deterministic model of race which vastly overemphasized America's capacity for incorporating "difference." While such trends do exist, very powerful countertendencies toward permanent racial division simply cannot be ignored. The central argument of this work, the central issue in racial policy—that U.S. racial dynamics are the subject of permanent political contestation—cannot be addressed by "color-blind" theory or policy.

Thus, as the Reagan era ended, racial dynamics were adrift in the unsettled waters of an overall crisis in U.S. politics and culture. From the 1960s to the 1980s, racial politics profoundly transformed personal identity, collective action, the state, and American society as a whole. What would the contours and battlelines of racial contest be the next time around? This question remained open.

Epilogue

Closing Pandora's Box—
Race and the "New Democrats"

In the 1960s, the liberals were widely seen as having failed to deal with major questions of law enforcement, taxation, fiscal management and the role of government, as well as race. They were repudiated, and the Republicans moved into a 25-year period of executive hegemony.

Twelve years of Reagan and Bush has not cured the problems, either. It hasn't given us morning in America. It's produced more columns of smoke rising from our inner cities.

—Kevin Phillips[1]

Introduction

The Los Angeles riot of 1992 marked the beginning of a new period in U.S. racial politics.[2] It served as a dramatic reminder for much of the nation of the continuing economic marginality, social decay, and human despair of the inner cities. Thanks to amateur cameraman George Holliday's videotape of the beating of black motorist Rodney King, police coercion and harassment were revealed in detail more graphic than mainstream America had witnessed in years.

Epilogue

Occurring as it did in the final stretch of an important presidential campaign, the L.A. riot threatened to recast the election into a debate about race, social inequality, and urban decay.[3] These topics, though, were none of the leading contenders' strongest suit. A renewed debate on racial issues could easily have polarized the electorate. It could have revealed the fundamental lack of vision on racial issues plaguing the entire political spectrum. Political leaders—who had by and large determined that the road to victory and influence did not pass through the inner city—were unnerved by the riot.[4] They scrambled to find appropriate individuals, groups, policies, and priorities to blame for the tragic events in L.A.

In early May 1992, toward the conclusion of his 38-hour tour of Los Angeles in the wake of the riot, George Bush stated:

> Things aren't right in too many cities across our country, and we must not return to the status quo. Not here, not in any city where the system perpetuates failure and hatred and poverty and despair.[5]

"The system" to which Bush referred was not the one which disenfranchised minority voters, shipped industrial jobs overseas, and systematically underfunded inner city schools and hospitals. Rather, he claimed, liberal social welfare policies were to blame for the riot. Not only had they consumed many billions of federal dollars, but even worse, they had fostered state dependency, nurtured irresponsible personal behavior, and facilitated the overall deterioration of inner city communities. In place of such programs, Bush called for "policies that foster personal responsibility."[6]

Bush's remarks underscored the dramatic shift in racial "common sense" which had occurred over the past twenty-five years. In the wake of the urban riots of the 1960s, a range of liberal social programs were implemented to deal with the invidious effects of racial discrimination and poverty. In the wake of the L.A. riots, those same programs were being blamed for causing them. The nation had come full circle.

Centrist Democrats who were grouped around Bill Clinton wanted to address some of these issues, but in a manner which would not make their party vulnerable to charges of merely refashioning 1960s-style liberal initiatives. At stake was an important part of the electorate. In order to win the election and reinvigorate the once-powerful Democratic coalition, Bill Clinton believed he needed to attract white working class voters—the "Reagan Democrats." His appeal was based on lessons learned from the right, lessons about race. Pragmatic liberals in the Democratic camp proposed a more activist social policy emphasizing greater state investment in job creation, education, and infrastructural development. But they conspicuously avoided discussing racial matters such as residential segregation or discrimination. The Democrats' approach, which harked back to Kennedy's remark that "A rising tide lifts all boats," aspired to "universalistic" rather than "group-specific" reforms.

Thus the surprising shift in U.S. racial politics which took shape around 1992 was not the riot itself, nor was it the Republican analysis which placed the blame on the racially defined minority poor and the welfare policies which had supposedly taught them irresponsibility and dependency. The "surprise" was rather the Democratic retreat from race and the party's limited but real adoption of Republican racial politics, with their support for "universalism" and their rejection of "race-specific" policies. With their appeals firmly directed toward white surburban voters, and their emphasis on economic stagnation ("It's the economy, stupid," was the Clinton staff's famous motto) rather than social and racial inequality, the Democrats went on to retake the presidency.

In this brief epilogue we discuss U.S. racial politics in the 1990s. We are, of course, concerned with the racial dimensions of Clinton's victory in 1992 and of his self-definition as a "new Democrat." But these should be understood as aspects of a broader phenomenon: the emerging hegemony of the racial project of *neoliberalism*.[7] This developing neoliberal project seeks to rearticulate the neoconservative and new right racial projects of the Reagan-Bush years in a centrist framework of moderate redistribution and cultural universalism. Neoliberals deliberately try to avoid racial themes, both because they fear the divisiveness and polarization which characterized the racial reaction, and because they mistrust the "identity politics" whose origins lie in the 1960s. They want to close the Pandora's box of race.

It is still too early fully to analyze the liberal project which, as of this writing (July 1993), is still slouching toward Washington to be born. Yet some of the basic contours of racial neoliberalism can already be discerned. It is to these that we now turn our attention.

Neoliberalism and Race

Although on balance Clinton's racial politics are still better than those of Bush, the price of his election was paid by racially defined minorities who were forced to accept relegation of their issues to the electoral—and presumably governmental—back burner. The Clinton political formula reflected, not only the pragmatic politics of winning a presidential election in the aftermath of twelve years of Republican rule, but also the judgment that racial politics were divisive. The U.S., many influential thinkers argued, had to abandon the "disuniting" tendencies of a "politics of difference" in favor of a unifying and universalistic politics of common culture and national identity.

The furor over "multiculturalism" and "political correctness," which erupted in the late-1980s/early-1990s, particularly embodied these concerns. It was a moral panic about the continuing disruptive effects of racial divisions (and polarization around gender and sexuality as well) in American society. It generated various best-sellers,[8] attracted serious media attention, and even prompted a presidential scolding in an address at the University of Michigan.[9] The multiculturalism and political correctness debates confronted proponents of identity politics, especially those based in the universities, with a difficult dilemma. These struggles permitted the reappropriation of "universalism" and the values of a supposedly "common culture" by the right; they induced not only many conservatives, but also liberals and ex-leftists, to enlist in the defense of "standards" and "values" which served as stalking horses for quite authoritarian politics.[10]

Both as political strategy and as cultural initiative, the neoliberal racial project is consolidating as the new form of racial hegemony in the 1990s. In its *structural* dimension it is designed to rearticulate the neoconservative and new right racial politics of the Reagan-Bush years in a more benign, mildly progressive politics of redistribution. Unlike the neoconservative project, the racial neoliberalism of the 1990s does not claim to be color-blind; indeed it argues that any effort to reduce overall inequality in employment, income, education, health care access, etc., will disproportionately benefit those concentrated at the bottom of the socioeconomic ladder, where racial discrimination has its most damaging effects.

In its *signifying* or representational dimension, the neoliberal project avoids (as far as possible) framing issues or identities racially. Neoliberals argue that addressing social policy or political discourse overtly to matters of race simply serves to distract, or even hinder, the kinds of reforms which could most directly benefit racially defined minorities. To focus too much attention on race tends to fuel demagogy and separatism, and thus exacerbates the very difficulties which much racial discourse has ostensibly been intended to solve. To speak of *race* is to enter a terrain where *racism* is hard to avoid. Better to address racism by ignoring race, at least publically.

In his 1992 campaign, Bill Clinton was endorsed and advised by sociologist William Julius Wilson. Wilson argued that Clinton had assembled a "remarkable biracial coalition" by promoting programs which unite rather than divide racial minorities and whites. Clinton's strategy, Wilson declared, had destroyed the myth that blacks respond only to race-specific issues and that whites, particularly the poor and working class, will not support a candidate heavily favored by blacks:

[I]f the message emphasizes issues and programs that concern the families of all racial and ethnic groups, whites will see their mutual interests and join in a coalition with minorities to elect a progressive candidate.[11]

This belief flows from Wilson's analysis in *The Truly Disadvantaged* (1987).[12] There he argued that the impersonal forces of the market economy explain more about the current impoverishment of the inner city African American poor than any analysis relying on notions of racial discrimination. While he does not dismiss the effects of historical racial discrimination, his conclusion is that capital is "color-blind," and that the large-scale demographic, economic, and political changes which have negatively affected the ghetto have little to do with race. In this situation, race-specific policies, whose origins lie in the civil rights movement's drive for integration, can do little for the African American "underclass." Programs based on equality of individual opportunity on the one hand, or organized in terms of group preferential treatment on the other, are equally ineffective. Wilson ends his book with a call for *universal* programs, rather than group-targeted ones, to halt the deterioration of inner city communities:

The hidden agenda is to improve the life chances of groups such as the ghetto underclass by emphasizing programs in which the more advantaged groups of all races can positively relate.[13]

Wilson's policy prescription of universal programs, though obviously important, remains at best partial, since significant evidence exists that the racial discrimination which civil rights era legislation was designed to outlaw remains ubiquitous.[14] But as a recipe for electing a Democrat after twelve years of the Reagan and Bush administrations' manipulation of white racial fears, Wilson's formula surely proved useful to the Clinton forces. Indeed, Wilson's "hidden agenda" was undoubtedly more effective as campaign strategy than it ever would be as social policy.

Another key analysis shaping the Clinton campaign was that of Thomas and Mary Edsall. Their book *Chain Reaction*[15] argued that race has become a powerful wedge issue, fracturing what had been, since the New Deal, the majoritarian economic interests of the poor, working, and lower-middle classes in the traditional liberal coalition. Since 1965, whites have found less and less reason to carry the burden of redressing social grievances. Working-class and middle-class whites were directly affected, the Edsalls claim, by school integration, affirmative action programs of various sorts, and higher taxes to fund group-specific programs. The result of all this has been massive defections from the Democratic Party and the consolidation of a conservative Republican majority.

The Edsalls documented dramatic new patterns of segregation which have emerged as whites have moved to the suburbs and abandoned the declining cities. As a result, urban areas have become reservations, with majority black and Latino populations and declining tax bases. Their local governments are less and less capable of addressing the basic needs of their citizens. The nation as a whole is moving steadily toward a politics that will be dominated by the suburban vote.[16] The suburbs allow white middle-class voters to fulfill communitarian impulses by taxing themselves for direct services (e.g., schools, libraries, police), while both ignoring urban decay and remaining fiscally conservative about federal spending. Thus whites shield their tax dollars from going into programs to benefit racial minorities and the poor. The Edsalls argue:

> What all this suggests is that a politics of suburban hegemony
> will come to characterize presidential elections. With a majority
> of the electorate equipped to address its own needs through local
> government, not only will urban blacks become increasingly iso-
> lated by city-county boundaries, but support for the federal gov-
> ernment, a primary driving force behind black advancement, is
> likely to diminish.[17]

The "new Democrats" sought a way out of this pessimistic scenario by simultaneously advocating universalistic reforms and blunting the wedge issue of race. The call for more jobs, better education, and increased social investment was especially well-suited for the benefits it offered to suburban, middle-class, white voters who had been battered—though not on the scale of inner city residents—by recession. To dismiss charges of catering to minorities, Clinton adopted the rhetoric of "personal responsibility" and "family values" which was so successfully utilized by the right. In order to win back white suburbanites, liberals too claimed the right to "blame the victim," to disparage the "dependence" of welfare mothers, and bemoan the disintegration of the family. In their use of racially coded language, the "new Democrats" chose to remain silent on any explicit discussion of race and its overall meaning for politics.

This shift is apparent in the Clinton-Gore campaign document *Putting People First*.[18] In this book the Democratic candidates list a host of proposals and policy initiatives they supported, many in areas where racial justice and inequality are particularly sensitive issues. For example, they propose expanding the Head Start program, insuring a minimum income for all working households through tax rate adjustments, and addressing unemployment through public sector job creation. These ideas are presented, however, without any mention of their impact on specific racial groups, indeed with as little reference to race as possible. Beyond pledging to enforce existing civil rights laws and to oppose discrimination in such areas as immigration,[19] *Putting People First* consistently downplays racial themes. It makes no mention of affirmative action, preferring to argue, along the lines suggested by Wilson, for universal programs. Thus Clinton and Gore make the familiar argument that "For too long we've been told about 'us' and 'them'.... But there can be no 'them' in America. There's only us ... " (pp. 64–65), and pledge to

> ... fight for civil rights, not just by protecting individual liberties, but by providing *equal economic opportunity*; support new anti-poverty initiatives that move beyond the outdated answers of both major parties and instead reflect the values most Americans share: work, family, individual responsibility, community.[20]

This is neoliberal racial coding at its finest. Very little of this formula would seem out of place in a Republican campaign document or neoconservative policy paper. And what are those outdated antipoverty initiatives, one wonders? Presumably, they include such items as affirmative action, minority set-asides, and support for school desegregation. In fact, the one clear statement about race in the civil rights section of *Putting People First* is a pledge to oppose racial quotas!

While on the campaign trail, Clinton very rarely brought up race in a direct way—and then often made his point at the expense of racial minorities, as in the case of his rebuke of rap artist Sister Souljah for supposedly making racist remarks. Here his underlying racial message was that blacks were as guilty of racism as whites, and that black racism needed to be confronted and challenged as vigorously as any other form. This was an important symbolic issue for many whites. It relieved them of the onus of being the sole "oppressors" of the nation, took attention away from the structural manifestations of racism, ignored the continuity of racial hegemony and white supremacy across the decades, and reduced the issue of racism to a matter of group prejudice. Such an intervention could only have been designed to demonstrate "new Democrat" Clinton's independence from the traditional party deference to civil rights issues and organizations. In 1992, for the first time in almost half a century, the Democratic Party platform made no specific pledge to address racial injustices and inequalities.[21]

The Clinton administration seeks to establish a new consensus with respect to race, a framework based on universal reforms and a rejection of group-specific demands. In many respects this neoliberal agenda has rearticulated the right-wing racial logic which gained currency during the racial reaction of the 1970s and 1980s. It is in fact an effort to steal the racial "thunder on the right."

But in its quest to avoid the potentially divisive aspects of racial politics by rearticulation, by learning from the enemy, neoliberalism has quite deliberately fostered neglect of issues of race. It has, in effect, buried race as a significant dimension of its politics. It has attempted to close the Pandora's box first opened—in contemporary terms—during the 1960s. At best it advances a "hidden agenda" which seeks to improve the lot of racial minorities while avoiding race-baiting from the right. But such a perspective, although ostensibly premised on creating community and avoiding divisive political conflicts, misses the depth and degree to which competing definitions of race continue to structure and signify politics in the U.S.

What's Wrong with the Neoliberal Racial Project?

U.S. society is racially both more diverse and more complex today than at any previous time in its history. Racial theory must address this reality; that is the purpose of this book. Racial policy and politics must address it as well. Does the emergent neoliberal racial project, the "new Democratic" strategy employed by Clinton in his successful run for the presidency, fill this bill? We think not.

In our view, the neoliberal racial project has two basic flaws. First, it continues to conceive race in narrowly bipolar terms: black-white, city-suburb, etc. It thus neglects the increasing complexity of racial politics and racial identity today. Second, neoliberalism seeks to downplay the continuing significance of race in American society; indeed it promotes a false universalism which can only serve to mask underlying racial conflicts. Let us address these two issues in turn.

Dichotomizing Race

The lessons of the Los Angeles riot are instructive as a starting point to criticize bipolar conceptions of race. Journalist Tim Rutten described the devastation in the immediate wake of the Rodney King verdict as

> . . . the nation's first multi-ethnic urban riot, one that involved not simply the traditional antagonism of one race toward another, but

the mutual hostility, indifference, and willingness to loot of several different racial and ethnic groups.[22]

Indeed if only for a fleeting moment, the Los Angeles riot served to focus media attention on generally neglected racial/ethnic subjects—Koreans, Central Americans, Chicanos—who were both victims and victimizers.

Unfortunately, this perspective on the riot was not sustained and explored by the mass media. Nor, as we have seen, were these issues tackled by the presidential candidates. Naturally the neoconservative candidate—George Bush—focused his response to the riot on welfare bashing and denunciations of the irresponsibility of the rioters. But for reasons we have already described, it proved expedient for "new Democrat" Bill Clinton to do something quite similar, to avoid any explicit discussion of racial injustice, to emphasize the necessity of a growing economy to solve social ills, and to invoke the rhetoric of hard work and personal responsibility in his response to the riot. Neither grappled with the growing racial diversity of the nation, and the meaning of a situation in which a wide range of different "racialized" groups find themselves both in conflict and accommodation with one another.[23]

Of course, the candidates were not the only ones guilty of making the facts of the riot fit the prevailing bipolar black/white model of race relations. But in doing so, they emphasized once more the condition and consciousness of the black "underclass," while paying little or no attention to the widespread and multiracial discontent which crystallized in the riot. Nor did they concern themselves with the devastation's victims: principally Korean storeowners, but also businesses of every racial and ethnic provenance. Nor did the candidates, or the mass media, seem to notice or care that more Latinos were arrested during the riot than were blacks, or that substantial numbers of whites were also engaged in looting and burning.

Racial dichotomizing—focusing analysis and discussion of race solely on black-white relationships—is endemic in the U.S. As much as the politicians or mainstream media, academic analyses reproduce this distorted model of race as a largely black-white dichotomy. A list of the most recent popular books on race, works by such noted authors as Andrew Hacker, Thomas and Mary Edsall, Derrick Bell, and Studs Terkel,[24] includes not one work with a perspective broader than the bipolar, exclusively black-white view. Too often, today as in the past, when scholars and journalists talk about race relations, they mean relations between African Americans and whites.

There are several obvious problems with this situation. First, if the complex nature of race relations in the post–civil rights era is not analyzed and theorized, if it is not the subject of media attention, neither politicians nor ordinary citizens will be able to grasp emerging trends. Antagonisms and alliances *among* racially defined minority groups, differentiation *within* these groups, and the changing dynamics of white racial identity, to pick but a few central issues, are examples of the crucial developments which such approaches miss almost entirely.

Second, the dominant mode of biracial theorizing ignores the fact that a range of specific issues—involving access to education, patterns of residential segregation, and stratification in labor markets—cannot be adequately addressed by narrowly assessing the relative situations of whites and blacks. In his analysis of race and higher education, for example, Andrew Hacker covers Asian Americans at some length in order to address race-based admissions policies.[25] But his research unfortunately does not lead him to consider that America, in this area as well as in many others, may be more than simply "two nations."[26]

A third and related problem of this racially bipolar vision is that policies such as affirmative action, immigration, welfare, bilingual education, and community economic development have different consequences for different racially defined minority groups. The meaning of affirmative action for Latinos, for example, may be quite distinct from its meaning for Asian Americans. Even as it affects different ethnic groups within a single racial category—say, Cubans and Salvadorans within the overall boundaries described by the term "Latino"—the implications of a particular social policy may vary widely. Policies and politics which are framed in black-white terms miss the ways in which specific initiatives structure the possibilities of conflict or accommodation among different racial minority groups.

Fourth, employing an exclusively black-white model ignores many particularities of contemporary racial politics. For example it neglects the increasingly racial scapegoating of particular minorities who are seen as somehow responsible for U.S. cultural and economic decline. Examples here include Japan-bashing and anti-Asian violence, and rising anti-immigrant sentiment directed particularly toward Asians and Latinos.

Fifth and finally, bipolar racial discourse tends at best to marginalize and at worst to eliminate other positions and voices in the ongoing dialogue about race in the U.S. A recent example of this was the critical exchanges in the media over the Hughes brothers' film *Menace II Society* (1993). When called upon to assess the film's impact on target audiences, both white and black cultural commentators interpreted and debated the meaning of a crucial scene in which a Korean shopkeeper and his wife are shot and killed. No one, however, asked Korean Americans what they thought.[27]

The enormous task for racial theory is to begin to address these issues and developments in a way which would decisively break with the bipolar model of race that has informed, indeed structured, not only popular and academic discourse but also political initiatives in the area of race.

Universalism and Its Discontents

We have already discussed Bill Clinton's avoidance, as far as possible, of racial issues while on the road to the White House. Was this merely a campaign tactic, or is Clinton committed to downplaying discussion of race in favor of a supposedly more universalistic position—the neoliberal discourse—whose primary target audience is the white and suburban middle class, the "Reagan democrats"? Although the final verdict is not in, the early money is on the latter hypothesis.

Clinton sent a key signal when he withdrew the nomination of law professor Lani Guinier as head of the Justice Department's Civil Rights Division. Although by no means a radical, Guinier was portrayed as such in a right-wing media campaign led by Clint Bolick, Litigation Director of the conservative Institute for Justice in Washington and close associate of Supreme Court Justice Clarence Thomas. Bolick dubbed Guinier a "quota queen" in a *Wall Street Journal* op-ed piece, and the racist label (redolent of Ronald Reagan's remarks about "welfare queens") spread across the battlefields of Washington and the pages of the press, while the administration hardly lifted a finger to correct the record or defend its nominee.[28] After allowing Guinier to twist in the wind for more than a month, Clinton withdrew her nomination, stating that her ideas on race were contrary to his own. His vision of an inclusive society, he argued, conflicted with that of his nominee, whose writing supported different political mechanisms and rules for minorities.[29] Incredibly, Clinton claimed he had been unaware of Guinier's views when he first selected her. Those views, however, were not particularly extreme. The most radical thing Guinier had advocated, in a series of law review articles on the limits of voting rights remedies for electoral discrimination, was extension of electoral formulas for increasing minority electoral influence. These schemes—proportional voting in particular—were already in place in various (mostly southern) localities, and had been endorsed by the Reagan-Bush Justice Department and the Supreme Court. Guinier had also criticized some of the redistricting arrangements developed after 1990, deals in which leading civil rights organizations, black politicians, and Republicans had cooperated to gerrymander various (again southern) legislative districts in order to guarantee black "safe seats" and, not incidentally, conservative white majorities in adjacent jurisdictions.

Guinier's sin, it is clear in retrospect, was not her supposed radicalism, but her willingness, indeed her eagerness, to discuss the changing dimensions of race in contemporary U.S. politics. She sought an open and democratic dialogue, to be held in legislative, academic, journalistic, and judicial fora, on the meaning of race in the post–civil rights era. This flew in the face of Clinton's political strategy of downplaying race. Had Clinton been willing to support Guinier—whether or not he associated himself with all her views—there would have been a contentious but ultimately productive debate in the Senate about the new contours of race. This in itself would have been an important advance. As Harlon Dalton, a law professor at Yale, commented:

> Her Senate hearings would have been a conversation about what democracy looks like in a multicultural society in the 1990's, and I think that's a conversation we need to have. Instead, the Senate and President ran away from it.[30]

Clinton's performance in the Guinier affair, and more broadly his claim that he supports a "single society," rather than a "we and they" orientation to race, place him firmly in the camp of racial universalism.[31] It is but a small distance from Clinton's neoliberal position to the neoconservative "color blind" position—from which, indeed, it was fashioned. In contrast, Guinier's recognition that, in the post–civil rights era as previously, racial injustice still operates, that it has taken on new forms, and that it needs to be opposed if democracy is to advance, in our view located her in a far more realistic position. Guinier understood the flexibility of racial identities and politics, but also affirmed that racism still shapes the U.S. social structure in a widespread fashion. She resisted the idea of closing Pandora's box; in fact she denied the possibility of closing it, arguing that the racial dimensions of U.S. politics are too complex, too basic, and too subtle to be downplayed for long.

We predict that this conflict will continue to plague the "new Democrats," and that it will set clear limits on the neoliberal racial project which has been central to their resurgence. The universalist view of race does not recognize the instability inherent in racial politics and identity. It treats race as something we can "get beyond." Paradoxically, this position shares with racial essentialism—as displayed, for example, in both white and black racial nationalisms—the belief that race is something fixed and permanent. It conceives of the choices posed by racial politics in a rigid "either-or" scenario. One must either become "color blind" or adopt the particularism supposedly inherent in one's racial identity.

From a racial formation perspective, this rigidly dichtomous model is absurd. Racial difference and racial identity are unstable. They are continuously being disputed, transformed, and eroded. The true challenge for both racial theory and racial politics is to find ways of disrupting the relationship and presumed fixity of both the universalist and the particularist positions.

We have suggested that the neoliberal project, with its deliberate neglect of racial politics, will reveal its ineffectiveness fairly quickly in the Clinton era. But if that judgment is proved correct, what opposing view can we propose, what strategic orientation do we recommend for the current and immediate future of U.S. racial politics? Obviously it would be presumptuous to prescribe some sweeping alternative approach. We can offer no simple formulas, and we recognize that it takes courage and insight to resist the various herd mentalities which characterize racial politics today. But despite the difficulties, we are firmly convinced that it is still quite possible to distinguish the main features of the racial formation processes, as well as of the racism, that characterize our time.

We conclude by suggesting three general precepts which can guide analysis of the present situation. We do this not in an effort to exhaust, but simply to orient, understanding and action in respect to race and racism today. Our three precepts are the following: 1. Old fashioned racism still exists; 2. The traditional victimology of racism is moribund; and 3. To oppose racism one must remain conscious of race.

Old-Fashioned Racism Still Exists

The legacy of the past—of conquest, slavery, racial dictatorship and exclusion—may no longer weigh like a nightmare on the brain of the living, but it still lingers like a hangover or a sleepless night that has left us badly out of sorts. Without question, there has been significant progress toward racial democracy in the years since 1965, yet it is implausible to believe that racism is a thing of the past. To assert such a position today requires either that one deny the ubiquitous evidence of everyday life—its continuing segregation, its racially assigned poverty and privilege, its bigotry, fear, and nihilism—or that one engage in wholesale victim-blaming, a procedure that merely updates the racial prejudices of days gone by. So David Wellman's argument that "racism is a structural relationship based on the subordination of one racial group by another,"[32] continues to reflect some basic realities. But only some, since today the multipolarity of racial identities (not just black and white, but also red, brown, and yellow), the crosscutting divisions of race, gender, and sexuality, and the tangible if still limited effects of egalitarian struggles have greatly complicated this picture.

The Traditional Victimology of Racism Has Become Moribund

In the past white supremacy was so thorough that it located all nonwhites in positions of comprehensive subordination. Racially defined minorities at one time lacked even victim status, which at least implies guilt or conflict among the victimizers.[33] Under the heel of conquest, in the face of "Indian removal," and under the regime of slavery, racial minorities simply got what their oppressors felt they deserved. This is the meaning of genocide and racial dictatorship. Thus the achievement of victim status, beginning in earnest around the turn of the century, was a challenge to white supremacy in some ways as serious as the civil rights and egalitarian challenges of the post–World War II period.

Today, however, the legacy of this achievement continues as *victimology*: the essentializing attribution of minority misfortunes *tout court* to victimization by whites. The tenacity of this viewpoint is indicated by the difficulty minority groups encounter when one of their own strays from the fold, exposing conflicts and inequalities within the community itself.[34] The more heavily committed one is to a view based on the status of one's group as victim, the more difficult it is to accept the possibility that one's group may also contain victimizers.

Today less than ever does minority status correlate with victim status, yet because old-fashioned racism and white supremacy are far from dead, this linkage is not yet dead either. It is, however, somewhat moribund, doubtful, suspect, particularly when it is afforded *prima facie*—and thus essentializing—validity.

To Oppose Racism One Must Notice Race

In the U.S., race is present in every institution, every relationship, every individual. This is the case not only for the way society is organized—spatially, culturally, in terms of stratification, etc.—but also for our perceptions and understandings of personal experience. Thus as we watch the videotape of Rodney King being beaten, compare real estate prices in different neighborhoods, select a radio channel to enjoy while we drive to work, size up a potential client, customer, neighbor, or teacher, stand in line at the unemployment office, or carry out a thousand other normal tasks, we are compelled to think racially, to use the racial categories and meaning systems into which we have been socialized. Despite exhortations both sincere and hypocritical, it is not possible or even desirable to be "color-blind."

So today more than ever, opposing racism requires that we notice race, not ignore it, that we afford it the recognition it deserves and the subtlety it embodies. By noticing race we can begin to challenge racism, with its ever-more-absurd reduction of human experience to an essence attributed to all without regard for historical or social context. By noticing race we can challenge the state, the institutions of civil society, and ourselves as individuals to combat the legacy of inequality and injustice inherited from the past. By noticing race we can develop the political insight and mobilization necessary to make the U.S. a more racially just and egalitarian society.

Notes

Preface to the 1994 Edition

1. To acknowledge all the work which we feel parallels our own would be both impossible and unnecessary. Some important contributions are Patricia Hill Collins, *Black Feminist Thought: Knowledge, Consciousness, and the Politics of Empowerment* (New York: Routledge, 1991); Yen Le Espiritu, *Asian American Panethnicity: Bridging Institutions and Identities* (Philadelphia: Temple University Press, 1992); Ann Ferguson, *Sexual Democracy: Women, Oppression, and Revolution* (Boulder: Westview Press, 1991); Ruth Frankenberg, *White Women, Race Matters: The Social Construction of Whiteness* (Minneapolis: University of Minnesota Press, 1993); Christopher Newfield, "What Was Political Correctness? Race, the Right, and Managerial Democracy in the Humanities," *Critical Inquiry* 19 (Winter 1993); Suzanne Oboler, *Labeling Hispanics: The Dynamics of Race, Class, Language, and National Origins* (Minneapolis: University of Minnesota Press, forthcoming); Lucius Outlaw, "Toward a Critical Theory of 'Race,'" in David Theo Goldberg, ed., *Anatomy of Racism* (Minneapolis: University of Minnesota Press, 1990); David R. Roediger, *The Wages of Whiteness: Race and the Making of the American Working Class* (New York: Verso, 1991); E. San Juan Jr., *Racial Formations, Critical Transformations: Articulations of Power in Ethnic and Racial Studies in the United States* (Atlantic Highlands, NJ: Humanities Press, 1992); John Solomos, *Race and Racism in Contemporary Britain* (London: MacMillan, 1989); Stephen Small, *Still Catchin' Hell: The Black Experience in the USA and England* (London: Routledge, forthcoming); Iris Marion Young, *Justice and the Politics of Difference* (Princeton: Princeton University Press, 1990).

2. Thomas Byrne Edsall and Mary D. Edsall, *Chain Reaction: The Impact of Race, Rights, and Taxes on American Politics* (New York: W.W. Norton & Co., 1991).

3. *The Truly Disadvantaged: The Inner City, The Underclass, and Public Policy* (Chicago: University of Chicago Press, 1987).

Introduction

1. Cited in J.K. Yamamoto, "Civil Rights Commission Under Fire," *Pacific Citizen*, 5 April 1985.
2. We define racism as a fundamental characteristic of social projects which create or reproduce structures of domination based on essentialist categories of race. See Chapter 4.
3. This is an introductory formulation. We shall have more to say later about the numerous variations (ethnic, national, class-based, etc.) possible within racial identity. Among Latinos, for example, the Puerto Rican, Central American, and Cuban cases all retain distinct aspects; among Asians, Vietnamese and other Southeast Asians, South Asians and Filipinos all have particular histories in the U.S. There are those whose racial category is ambiguous at present (e.g., Arabs). Further still, racial classification, as we shall argue below, is always flexible, a process without an end point or finality of any kind.
4. Concepts such as "internal colonialism" might offer important insights into U.S. racial conditions, but because they ultimately reason by analogy, they cannot range over the uniqueness and complexities of American racial ideology or politics.
5. In a letter to the *New York Times*, Mr. Ko Yung Tung made these comments on the 1980 census:

> I was somewhat puzzled and disturbed by the question relating to race/national origin on my census form. The categories were 'white, black, Japanese, Chinese, Korean,' etc.
>
> If the question is intended to get statistics on race, why is there a distinction between, say, Chinese and Japanese? They are both of the same race. If it is intended to elicit answers as to national origin, why are all whites undifferentiated? Why not German, French, Irish, etc.? Moreover, if this is to be an accurate study, it should allow for 'mixed' people. I myself am half Manchu and half Chinese (Han). My wife is 'white' (part Dutch, English, German, and Irish). What does that make my children?
>
> I had hoped that by 1980 the U.S. government was more enlightened. The question reflects at best ignorance, at worst racism."
> (Cited in Lewis M. Killian, "Black Power and White Reactions: The Revitalization of Race-Thinking in the United States," *Annals of The American Academy of Social and Political Sciences* 454 (March 1981) p. 50.)

6. The inclusion of the categories of "Hispanic" and "Asian and Pacific Islanders" in the 1980 U.S. census, for example, was the result of lobbying efforts and Congressional debate.

7. We employ this term with reservations to distinguish the popular movements of the postwar period from their earlier antecedents (where applicable), and from movements of class- or status-based groups understood in the traditional Marxian or Weberian sense.

    The black movement was hardly "new." It was the oldest and probably the most vital popular movement in U.S. history. Why, then, do we characterize it as the founding "new" social movement in the postwar period? The postwar black movement was different from its predecessors in *its ability to confront racial oppression simultaneously as an individually experienced and as a collectively organized phenomenon*. This is what it imparted to other new social movements. They have all interpreted politically the "immediate experience" of their members, adding the range of issues this engendered to the older grievances their predecessors had lodged, such as (in the case of the black movement) discrimination and prejudice. This "politics of identity" which spilled over into arenas not traditional defined as "political" is what made the new social movements "new." See Chapter 7.

8. Rearticulation is the process of redefinition of political interests and identities, through a process of recombination of familiar ideas and values in hitherto unrecognized ways. This concept is more fully elaborated in Chapters 5 and 6.

9. It should be noted that while many of the class- and nation-based studies of race challenged the ethnicity perspective from a radical position, by no means all of these analyses entertained such views.

Part I

Paradigms of Race

1. Blauner writes: " . . . [T]he general conceptual frame of European theory implicitly assumed the decline and disappearance of ethnicity in the modern world; it offered no hints in the other direction. Without significant alteration, American sociology synthesized this framework into its models of social structure and change." Robert Blauner, *Racial Oppression in America* (New York: Harper & Row, 1972), p. 4. See also Herman Schwendinger and Julia R. Schwendinger, *The Sociologists of the Chair: A Radical Analysis of the Formative Years of North American Sociology (1883–1922)* (New York: Basic Books, Inc., 1974), p. 39.

2. "After a promising start in the early period, the study of race and ethnic relations suffered. . . . With little room for ethnic and racial phenomena in the macroscopic models of social structure and process, the field was iso-

lated from general sociological theory and particularly from those leading conceptual themes that might have provided coherence and useful lines of inquiry: stratification, culture, community. The study of race relations developed in a kind of vacuum; no overall theoretical framework guided its research and development." Blauner, *Racial Oppression in America*, p. 5.

3. Lyman notes: "It [the race-relations cycle] was ideology too, for Park believed that once the racial cycle was completed, the social arena would be cleared of those racial impediments interfering with the inevitable class struggle." Lyman, Stanford M. *The Black American in Sociological Thought: A Failure of Perspective* (New York: Capricorn Books, 1972) p. 27.

4. Blauner, *Racial Oppression in America*, p. 2.

5. This alternative perspective rooted in a notion of institutional racism is elaborated in Louis L. Knowles & Kenneth Prewitt, eds., *Institutional Racism in America* (Englewood Cliffs, N.J.: Prentice-Hall, Inc., 1969).

6. Van den Berghe in a section critiquing the dominant trends in the study of race relations notes that " . . . in spite of the claim of many social scientists that detachment and objectivity are possible and that they can dissociate their roles as scientists and as private citizens, much of the work done by North Americans in the area of race has, until the last three or four years, been strongly flavored with a great deal of optimism and complacency about the basic 'goodness' of American society and with the cautious, slightly left-of-center, reformist, meliorative, gradualist approach of 'liberal' intellectuals." He goes on to say: "The field has been dominated by a functionalist view of society and a definition of the race problem as one of integration and assimilation of minorities into the mainstream of a consensus-based society." Pierre L. van den Berghe, *Race and Racism: A Comparative Perspective* (New York: Wiley, 1967), p. 7.

7. The concept of a *paradigm* in scientific or scholarly investigation gained currency with the publication of Thomas S. Kuhn's *The Structure of Scientific Revolutions* (Chicago: The University of Chicago Press, 1970, 2nd edition). Our usage of the term is slightly at variance with Kuhn's. A racial paradigm, in our view, is an assumed theoretical category which classifies racial phenomena. In our epoch there has been a strong reluctance in social scientific circles to indulge in "race-thinking" (undoubtedly due to the legacy of biologism with which pre–World War II scholarship encountered issues of race). Thus existing theories understand race in terms of other, supposedly more fundamental or objective, social scientific categories. These are the three paradigms of ethnicity, class, and nation-based racial theories.

1. Ethnicity

1. William Peterson, "Concepts of Ethnicity," in W. Peterson, M. Novak, and P. Gleason, *Concepts of Ethnicity: Selections from the Harvard Encyclopedia*

of American Ethnic Groups (Cambridge, MA: Harvard University Press, 1982), p. 2.

2. The biologistic view of race, of course, predated slavery's abolition. For example, in 1792 Dr. Benjamin Rush, one of the "Founding Fathers," presented a paper before the American Philosophical Society which argued that the "color" and "figure" of blacks were derived from a form of leprosy. He was convinced that with proper treatment, blacks could be cured (i.e., become white) and eventually assimilated into the general population. See Ronald T. Takaki, *Iron Cages: Race and Culture in 19th-Century America* (Seattle: University of Washington Press, 1979), pp. 28–35. For present purposes, it is not terribly important whether a single dominant current of race-thinking spanned the pre– and post–civil war period, or whether, starting in the later 19th century, a new biologistic paradigm emerged.

3. For the definitive intellectual history, see Thomas F. Gossett, *Race: The History of an Idea in America* (Dallas: Southern Methodist University Press, 1963); See also Peter I. Rose, *The Subject is Race* (New York: Oxford University Press, 1968), esp. pp. 11–66. A great deal of inflammatory "theoretical" material appeared during this time within the biologistic paradigm, e.g., Madison Grant, *The Passing of the Great Race* (New York: Scribners, 1916). Two good recent histories of eugenics are Allen Chase, *The Legacy of Malthus* (New York: Knopf, 1977); and Daniel J. Kevles, *In the Name of Eugenics: Genetics and the Uses of Human Heredity* (New York: Knopf, 1985).

4. Kallen's *Culture and Democracy in America* (New York: Boni and Liveright, 1924) first appeared in *The Nation* in 1915; For Park's contributions see Everett Hughes, et al, eds., *Race and Culture*, Vol. 1 of *The Collected Papers of Robert E. Park* (Glencoe, IL: The Free Press, 1950). A direct line runs through Park from the pioneering black struggles of the post-Reconstruction epoch and the modern ethnicity-based approaches of Frazier, Myrdal, and Hughes. The Marxist racial theorist Oliver C. Cox was also a student of Park. A good general account of the early days of modern racial (i.e., ethnicity) theory can be found in Rose, *The Subject Is Race*.

5. See William Peterson, "Concepts of Ethnicity"; N. Glazer and Daniel P. Moynihan, "Introduction," in Glazer and Moynihan, eds., *Ethnicity: Theory and Experience* (Cambridge, MA: Harvard University Press, 1975) p. 4.

6. Nathan Glazer, "Blacks and Ethnic Groups: The Difference and the Political Difference It Makes," in idem, *Ethnic Dilemmas, 1964–1982* (Cambridge, MA: Harvard University Press, 1983) p. 74, offers a slightly different laundry list of the cultural determinants of ethnicity.

7. Park's "race relations cycle," for example, typifies this assumption, not because it is biologistic (Park is clear in thinking about race in social terms), but because the origins of groups which first come into "culture contact"

with one another is not theorized. See Robert E. Park, "Our Racial Frontier on the Pacific" [1926], in *Race and Culture*, op. cit.

8. See for example Clifford Geertz, "The Integrative Revolution: Primordial Sentiments and Civil Politics in New States," in idem, ed., *Old Societies and New States* (Glencoe, IL: The Free Press, 1963); Orlando Patterson, *Ethnic Chauvinism: The Reactionary Response* (New York: Stein and Day, 1977). Gerald Berreman has argued that ethnic identities are "partial," representing a range of options in self-presentation that is essentially politically determined. See his "Bazaar Behavior: Social Identity and Social Interaction in Urban India," in G. DeVos and L. Romanucci-Ross, eds., *Ethnic Identity* (Palo Alto, CA: Mayfield, 1975).

9. Early work includes Park, "Our Racial Frontier"; see also his "Introduction," to Louis Wirth, *The Ghetto* (Chicago: University of Chicago Press, 1928); Horace Kallen, *Culture and Democracy in America* first took the "cultural pluralist" position and thus was first to argue from within ethnicity theory against assimilationism. Kallen's framework is explicitly Atlanticist. See also W. Lloyd Warner and Leo Srole, *The Social Systems of American Ethnic Groups* (New Haven: Yale University Press, 1945) for a caste-oriented approach which contrasts the prospects for assimilation (or "mobility") of white and non-white "ethnic groups"; this book thus straddles our ethnicity and class paradigms. Some representative modern work includes Milton M. Gordon, *Assimilation in American Life* (New York: Oxford University Press, 1964); Glazer and Moynihan, eds., *Ethnicity*; M. Walzer, E. T. Kantowicz, J. Higham, and M. Harrington, *The Politics of Ethnicity: Selections from the Harvard Encyclopedia of American Ethnic Groups* (Cambridge, MA: Harvard University Press, 1982.

10. For two contrasting views of New Deal policies toward blacks, see Harvard Sitkoff, *A New Deal For Blacks: The Emergence of Civil Rights as a National Issue* (New York: Hill and Wang, 1978); Nancy J. Weiss, *Farewell to the Party of Lincoln: Black Politics in the Age of FDR* (Princeton: Princeton University Press, 1983).

11. Milton M. Gordon, *Assimilation in American Life*, pp. 88–114.

12. Robert E. Park, "Introduction" to Louis Wirth, *The Ghetto*, p. vii.

13. Gunnar Myrdal, *An American Dilemma: The Negro Problem and Modern Democracy*, Twentieth Anniversary Edition (New York: Harper and Row, 1962 [1944]).

14. The study's collaborators included, among many others, Arnold Rose and Richard Sterner (Myrdal's principal associates), Ralph Bunche, Doxey Wilkerson, Sterling A. Brown, St. Clair Drake, E. Franklin Frazier, Melville J. Herskovits, Otto Klineberg, Edward Shils, and Louis Wirth; consultants included W. E. B. Du Bois, Horace Cayton, Robert E. Park, W. I. Thomas,

Hortense Powdermaker, John Dollard, Alain Locke, Walter White, Abram L. Harris, Ruth Benedict, and numerous others.

15. See for example Myrdal, *An American Dilemma*, p. 929. This version of the ethnicity paradigm was thus not the only one possible; indeed, cultural pluralist versions were left in the ambiguous status of competing accounts within the dominant approach.

16. Ibid., pp. 1021–1022; emphasis original.

17. Ibid., p. 927ff. Frazier later asserted this position as a supposed support to integration efforts:

> Since the institutions, the social stratification, and the culture of the Negro community are essentially the same as those of the larger community, it is not strange that the Negro minority belongs among the assimilationist rather than the pluralist, secessionist, or militant minorities. It is seldom that one finds Negroes who think of themselves as possessing a different culture from whites and that their culture should be preserved. (E. Franklin Frazier, *The Negro in the United States*, rev. ed. (New York: Macmillan, 1957) p. 681).

This argument, of course, is part of a larger controversy concerning black cultural heritage, the survival of African elements in slave culture, etc., with which we cannot engage here.

18. Nathan Glazer and Daniel Patrick Moynihan, *Beyond the Melting Pot* 2nd. ed (Cambridge, MA: MIT Press, 1970).

19. Ibid., p. 17.

20. Ibid., emphasis original.

21. Blacks are, for ethnicity theory, the great exception among racial minorities to the immigrant pattern, for they had experienced the formal and legal discrimination of slavery and its aftermath. Other racially defined groups were seen as fitting more easily into the immigrant/ethnic model. See Nathan Glazer, "The Peoples of America," in *Ethnic Dilemmas*, pp. 25–27.

22. See for example Gordon, *Assimilation in American Life*, p. 249:

> [Government] . . . must not use racial criteria positively in order to impose desgregation upon public facilities in an institutional area where such segregation is not a function of racial discrimination directly [i.e., there is no explicit effort to discriminate-MO/HW] but results from discrimination operating in another institutional area, or from other causes.

23. The support offered by ethnicity theory to the civil rights movement's struggles in the South was not a mere matter of some professors signing petitions

or advertisements. As the dominant racial paradigm, ethnicity theory represented racial "common sense" and informed state policy. The movement's substantial moderate support was thus vouchsafed it, so long as its target remained the "backward" South. See Chapter 6, below.

24. Nathan Glazer and Daniel P. Moynihan, *Beyond the Melting Pot*, p. x.

25. See note 20, above. Glazer's treatment of the question may be found in "Blacks and Ethnic Groups: The Difference and the Political Difference It Makes," in Glazer, *Ethnic Dilemmas*.

26. Any attempt at a definitive marking of the split between the dominant racial theory—based on the ethnicity paradigm—and the black movement will inevitably be arbitrary.

27. The neoconservative position is reviewed in depth in Chapter 7, below. We offer only the briefest of remarks here.

28. See "The Negro Family: The Case For National Action," in L. Rainwater and W. Yancey, *The Moynihan Report and the Politics of Controversy* (Cambridge, MA: MIT Press, 1967), p. 49. See also, in the same volume, the speech of President Lyndon Johnson "To Fulfill These Rights," delivered June 4, 1965 at Howard University, and drafted in part by Moynihan.

29. Glazer argued, also in 1965, that a "new national interest" in "the final liquidation of Negro separation" was being defined, and that blacks themselves had best not oppose it, for "When an ethnic group interest has clashed with a national interest, we have been quite ruthless and even extreme in overriding the group interest." ("The Peoples of America," *in Ethnic Dilemmas*, p. 27)

30. See for example, Robert Blauner, *Racial Oppression in America* (New York: Harper and Row, 1972), pp. 88–89n, 125; Stanley Lieberson, *A Piece of The Pie: Blacks and White Immigrants Since 1880* (Berkeley: University of California Press, 1980); Alexander Saxton, "Nathan Glazer, Daniel Moynihan, and the Cult of Ethnicity," *Amerasia Journal* Vol. 4, no. 2 (1977); William P. Ryan, *Blaming The Victim*, rev. ed. (New York: Vintage, 1976).

31. Glazer and Moynihan, "Introduction," in idem, eds., *Ethnicity: Theory and Experience* (Cambridge, MA: Harvard University Press, 1975), p. 7.

32. It also brings to mind Moynihan's earlier "tangle of pathology" thesis, contained in his "The Negro Family."

33. Milton Gordon, *Assimilation in American Life*, p. 70.

34. See, among a welter of possible sources, Kenneth Clark, *Dark Ghetto* (New York: Harper and Row, 1965); Carol B. Stack, *All Our Kin: Strategies for Survival in a Black Community* (New York: Harper and Row, 1974); John Langston Gwaltney, *Drylongso: A Self-Portrait of Black America* (New York: Vintage, 1980).

35. We discuss the process of "racialization" in Chapter 5 below.

2. Class

1. Stuart Hall, "Race, Articulation, and Societies Structured in Dominance," in *Sociological Theories: Race and Colonialism* (Paris: UNESCO, 1980) p. 306.
2. H. Gerth and C. Wright Mills, eds., *From Max Weber: Essays in Sociology* (New York: Oxford University Press, 1958) pp. 181–183.
3. Currently, much theoretical debate has arisen over the nature of "the economic." Is there a particular kind of real relationship, for example market exchange or immediate production (the "transformation of nature" through labor) that can be understood as purely or quintessentially "economic"? Or, to the contrary, is "the economic" a merely analytically distinct aspect of most, if not all, social relationships, in which various forms of "appropriation," "exchange," etc. are practiced, "power" is exercised, and "meaning" produced. This is not the place to examine these issues in depth, although we believe that all social relationships, including those of material production, are inherently structured politically and ideologically, as well as by "market rationality" (a category which also has noneconomic aspects). See Samuel Bowles and Herbert Gintis, "Structure and Practice in the Labor Theory of Value," in *Review of Radical Political Economics* Vol. 12, no. 4. (Winter, 1981); and idem, "On the Heterogeneity of Power," unpublished ms., 1983. In regard to the implications of this perspective for Marxian theory, Ernesto Laclau's remarks are provocative:

> I think the critique of economism should have a much wider deconstructive effect on traditional Marxist theory. That is, we should no longer conceive the economy as a homogeneous milieu that follows its own endogenous laws of development. . . . Today we can see that the space which traditional Marxism designated 'the economy' is in fact the terrain of a proliferation of discourses. We have discourses of authority, technical discourses, discourses of accountancy, discourses of information. Even categories such as profit can no longer be accepted as unequivocal. For instance, a multinational corporation today develops complex political and economic strategies within which the search for profit certainly plays a fundamental role, but does so within a whole policy of investment which can often require sacrificing immediate profits to wider strategic aims. The functioning of the economy itself is a political functioning, and cannot be understood in terms of a single logic. What we need today . . . is a non-economistic understanding of the economy, one which introduces the primacy of politics at the level of the 'infrastructure' itself.

(Ernesto Laclau and Chantal Mouffe, "Recasting Marxism: Hegemony and New Political Movements," *Socialist Review* 66 [November-December,

1982], p. 92.) See also Chantal Mouffe, "Working-Class Hegemony and the Struggle for Socialism," *Studies in Political Economy* 12 (Fall 1983).

4. Therefore, in the broad terms we have employed to describe the paradigm, these are class theories, even if the authors assume the existence of a totally free market An early and influential example was Gary Becker, *The Economics of Discrimination* (Chicago: University of Chicago Press, 1957), which analogizes racial relationships to international trade. Such "institutional" economists as Lester Thurow, who have subjected these approaches to critical readings, have understood the "idealistic" side of the neoclassicists very well. See Lester Thurow, *Poverty and Discrimination* (Washington, DC: Brookings, 1969).

5. Each approach is dealt with as an "ideal type." Just as there is no "pure" case of a class-, ethnic group-, or nation-based theory of race, so there is no "pure" stratification approach to race.

6. Milton Friedman, *Capitalism and Freedom* (Chicago: University of Chicago Press, 1962) pp. 108–110). Assuming for the moment an orthodox and unproblematic neoclassical theory, race may only appear in two ways: there may be efforts to explain the origins of racial inequality, and there may be debates about the efficiency of market forces in ending it.

7. Cf respectively, Becker, *The Economics of Discrimination*; Thurow, *Poverty and Discrimination*; Walter E. Williams, *The State Against Blacks* (New York: McGraw-Hill, 1982).

8. Most market-based analyses (and many other treatments as well), think of race in black-white terms. We consider such frameworks, where not required by the study's content (e.g., in studies of slavery), to be distorted and limited accounts of the range of racial phenomena. Our practice is to indicate that an author frames discussion of race in terms of blacks and whites, making no reference to other groups, by ourselves employing this terminology. Where the full range of racial minorities is being considered, we attempt to reflect this in our terminology as well.

9. Michael Reich, *Racial Inequality* (Princeton: Princeton University Press, 1981) pp. 86–88.

10. Williams, *The State Against Blacks*; Thomas Sowell, "Racism, Quotas, and the Front Door," *The Wall Street Journal*, 28 July 1979, p. 8.

11. Some Marxian theories, for example split labor market perspectives, also entertain a version of this idea. The reliance on labor market dualisms to explain racial inequality is prevalent in Marxist analysis of all sorts. See "Class Conflict Theory," below.

12. William Julius Wilson, *The Declining Significance of Race*, 2nd ed. (Chicago: University of Chicago Press, 1978) p. 17.

13. S. Shulman, "Race, Class, and Occupational Stratification: A Critique of William Julius Wilson's *The Declining Significance of Race*," in *Review of*

Radical Political Economics Vol. 13, no. 3 (Fall 1981); Paul Joseph, "An Implicit Marxist Theory of Race? A Review Essay of William Julius Wilson's *The Declining Significance of Race*" (unpublished ms, n.d.); Alfonso Pinkney, *The Myth of Black Progress* (New York: Cambridge University Press, 1984). See also Michael Omi's more balanced review in *The Insurgent Sociologist*, Vol. 10, no. 2 (Fall 1980).

14. See Wilson, *The Declining Significance of Race*, p. 161.

15. See for example, Thomas Sowell, ed., *The Fairmont Papers* (San Francisco: Institute for Contemporary Society, 1981). There is nothing particularly new in these phenomena. It is instructive to compare the new ethos of "black conservatism" to the classical works on the subject, such as E. Franklin Frazier, *Black Bourgeoisie* (New York: The Free Press, 1957), and W. E. B. Du Bois, *The Philadelphia Negro* (New York: Schocken, 1967 [1899]).

16. Many civil rights activists moved into government service during the 1960s; see Frances Fox Piven and Richard A. Cloward, *Poor People's Movements: Why They Succeed, How They Fail* (New York: Pantheon, 1977) pp. 254–255. Black attendance in college soared dramatically from the mid-1960s onward; the increase derived from numerous sources: the passage of equal opportunity legislation and federal efforts to improve secondary schooling for minorities, demands made upon colleges and universities by minority students and communities, etc. This in turn affected the production of skilled black professionals; see Institute for the Study of Educational Policy, *Equal Educational Opportunity: An Assessment* (Washington, D.C.: Howard University Press, 1976). See also Richard B. Freeman, *Black Elite: The New Market for Highly Educated Black Americans* (New York: McGraw Hill, 1976), pp. 290–291.

17. Neoconservative writers and new rightists have been quite clear about their abhorrence for the "new class" and its "dependents." Wilson argues that blacks continue to constitute disproportionate numbers of the latter category, but he neglects the fact that the new "privileged" black stratum is very much a "new class" phenomenon. On the relationship between the "new class" and the "underclass," see Peter Steinfels, *The Neoconservatives: The Men Who Are Changing America's Politics* (New York: Simon and Schuster, 1979), pp. 290–291.

18. The classic studies of race as a "caste" phenomenon in the U.S. are John Dollard, *Caste and Class in a Southern Town* (New York: Harper and Row, 1937); W. Lloyd Warner and Leo Srole, *The Social Systems of American Ethnic Groups* (New Haven: Yale University Press, 1945) esp. pp. 295–296.

19. Cf Hubert M. Blalock, *Toward a Theory of Minority-Group Relations* (New York: Wiley, 1967); Michael Banton, "Ethnic Groups and the Theory of Rational Choice," in *Sociological Theories: Race and Colonialism* (Paris: UNESCO, 1980).

20. The problems of the class-based view do not originate so much, we argue,

from assertions of the "primacy" of class as much as they do from the contention that class is an "objective" relationship. See the conclusion of this chapter.

21. John Roemer, "Divide and Conquer: Microfoundations of a Marxian Theory of Wage Discrimination," *Bell Journal of Economics* (Autumn 1979), provides an interesting new version of this neo-Marxist approach. Roemer's effort is to establish a microeconomic logic for capitalists' "divide and rule" strategies within particular enterprises, thus resolving a question which has been debated between "segmentation" and "split" labor market theorists of the class conflict school. The political orientation that informs Roemer's concept of interests is thus more micro-level as well.

22. Alexander Saxton, *The Indispensable Enemy* (Berkeley: University of California Press, 1971).

23. For example, Bowles and Gintis have recently suggested that

> [B]lacks and whites share a common form of exploitation *as workers*, but clearly a distinct form *as races*. Moreover, this system of racial exploitation is directly incorporated into the site of capitalist production itself.(Samuel Bowles and Herbert Gintis, "On the Heterogeneity of Power," p. 29.)

While the first sentence appears true, the second seems much more problematic. Queried on the point, Bowles has said that what is intended here is " . . . capitalist production broadly construed to mean production (narrowly construed) and distribution." (Samuel Bowles, personal communication, October 16, 1984.) This implies stratification within classes along racial lines—segmentation of the working class—which in turn can be identified with labor-*market* segmentation.

There is one possible exception: the assignment of workers to different jobs on a racial basis. See Martin Oppenheimer, "The Sub-Proletariat: Dark Skins and Dirty Work," *The Insurgent Sociologist* No. 4 (1974).

24. Oliver C. Cox, *Caste, Class, and Race* (New York: Monthly Review Press, 1970 [1948]); Reich, *Racial Inequality.*

25. Edna Bonacich,"A Theory of Ethnic Antagonism: the Split Labor Market," *American Sociological Review* 37 (1972); idem, "Advanced Capitalism and Black/White Relations in the United States: A Split Labor Market Interpretation," *American Sociological Review* 41 (1976); Jeffrey Prager, "White Racial Privilege and Social Change: An Examination of Theories of Racism," *Berkeley Journal of Sociology*, 1972–1973. Prager's approach is based on "internal colonialism" categories, but overlaps significantly with "split labor market" arguments as well.

26. Since our main interest here is the class conflict perspective we have found it useful to concentrate on Reich et al. With respect to Piore and Doeringer's

valuable contributions, though, it is important to note that as institution-alists, they are under less compulsion to insert every aspect of "segmenta-tion" in a unified class theory. Their procedure is more "middle range," and therefore often more convincing, than the more schematic Marxian approaches. For example, in studying so-called "internal labor markets" (within large firms) they find evidence of several different, and shifting, "class alliances" among management, elite labor, and secondary labor. Indeed, they recognize significant discontinuities in the patterns of "seg-mentation" itself. Race is thus seen as cutting more than one way. Such an ostensibly "Weberian" analysis is in many ways more in harmony with a "class formation" perspective (see this chapter's conclusion) than is the over-arching segmentation theory of Reich et al. P. Doeringer and M. Piore, *Internal Labor Markets and Manpower Analysis* (Lexington, MA: Heath, 1971) p. 136; see also M. Piore, *Birds of Passage: Migrant Labor and Indus-trial Societies* (New York: Cambridge University Press, 1979).

27. Reich, *Racial Inequality.*

28. David M. Gordon, Richard Edwards, and Michael Reich, *Segmented Work, Divided Workers; The Historical Transformation of Labor in the United States* (New York: Cambridge University Press, 1982).

29. Reich, *Racial Inequality*, p. 269. Another recent example of this line of argu-ment may be found in Erik Olin Wright: " . . . [I]n spite of the divisive char-acter of racism and in spite of the material differences between white and black workers which racism generates, workers of all races nevertheless share a fundamental class situation and thus share fundamental class inter-ests." ("Race, Class and Income Inequality," *American Journal of Sociol-ogy* Vol. 83, no. 6 (1978), p. 1397).

30. Gordon, Edwards, Reich, *Segmented Work*, p. 16.

31. Reich, Gordon, and Edwards, "A Theory of Labor Market Segmentation," in *American Economic Review* 63 (May 1973).

32. Gordon, Edwards, Reich, *Segmented Work*, p. 209.

33. Gordon, Edwards, Reich, *Segmented Work*, p. 220.

34. Bonacich, "A Theory of Ethnic Antagonism"; "Advanced Capitalism and Black/White Relations," idem, "The Past, Present, and Future of Split Labor Market Theory," in C. B. Marrett and C. Leggon, eds., *Research in Racial and Ethnic Relations* (Greenwich, CT: JAI Press, 1979); idem, "Class Approaches to Ethnicity and Race," *The Insurgent Sociologist* Vol. X, no. 2 (Fall 1980).

35. Bonacich, "Class Approaches," p. 14.

36. Split labor market approaches correlate well to the nation-based paradigm of race, especially in certain of its more Marxian variants which stress the "privileges" of "metropolitan" over "colonial" or "peripheral" labor forces. Cf Prager, "White Racial Privilege."

37. Bonacich, "Advanced Capitalism and Black/White Relations," p. 44.
38. Ibid. This critique has occasioned notable silence from Reich et al. Roemer's reformulation is the most serious attempt to address these issues by a "segmentation" theorist; see Roemer op. cit. Michael Burawoy has suggested that the debate confuses capitalist class with individual capitalist interests; see Burawoy, "The Capitalist State in South Africa: Marxist and Sociological Perspectives on Race and Class," in M. Zeitlin, ed., *Political Power and Social Theory*, Vol. 2 (Greenwich, CT: JAI Press, 1981) p. 283. Roemer addresses this point in part with his notion of "divide and rule in a single firm."
39. Doeringer and Piore, *Internal Labor Markets*.
40. James O'Connor, *The Fiscal Crisis of the State* (New York: St. Martin's, 1973).
41. For an interesting critique of dual labor market theory, particularly directed at the segmentation approach, see Constance Lever-Tracy, "The Paradigm Crisis of Dualism: Decay or Regeneration?" in *Politics and Society* Vol. 13, no. 1 (1984).
42. Ibid., p. 83.
43. The U.S. differs in this respect from the few societies which are even more racially divided, e.g., South Africa, although even there, as class formation processes are affected by the political imperative of black *embourgeoisement*, the lines of contiguity between race and class are beginning to blur. In respect to the U.S. case, this point should not be interpreted to mean that racial *stratification* does not exist. Our point is rather that segmentation/split models of the labor market are unable to specify with any certainty or comprehensiveness the locations and defining characteristics of their "segments" and "splits," and that, contrary to appearances, race does not furnish an adequate guidepost to these lines of demarcation. For an excellent comparative study of racial dynamics in the U.S. and South Africa, see George Frederickson, *White Supremacy* (New York: Oxford University Press, 1982).
44. See for example, Adam Przeworski, "Proletariat Into a Class: The Processes of Class Formation from Karl Kautsky's *The Class Struggle* to Recent Controversies," *Politics and Society*, Vol. 7, no. 4 (1977).
45. For an exemplary effort to analyze the politics of production in terms similar to these, see Michael Burawoy, "Terrains of Contest: Factory and State Under Capitalism and Socialism," *Socialist Review* 58 (July-August 1981).
46. Two useful attempts which focus on earlier historical conjunctures are David Montgomery, *Workers' Control in America* (New York: Cambridge University Press, 1979) and Herbert Gutman, "The Negro and the United Mine Workers of America: The Career and Letters of Richard L. Davis and Something of Their Meaning, 1890–1900," in idem, *Work, Culture, and Society in Industrializing America* (New York: Knopf, 1976).

3. Nation

1. In 1854, for example, a National Emigration Convention was held at Pittsburgh, with Delany in the leadership, which called for emigration " . . . towards those places where the black and colored man comprise, by population . . . the ruling element of the body politic." J. H. Bracey, Jr., A. Meier, and E. Rudwick, eds., *Black Nationalism in America* (Indianapolis and New York: Bobbs-Merrill, 1970), p. 93. A good historical account of black nationalism's development from slavery times through the early 20th century is Wilson Jeremiah Moses, *The Golden Age of Black Nationalism: 1850–1925* (New York: Oxford University Press, 1978).

2. (Greenwich, CT: Fawcett, 1961 [1903]). See also Robert L. Allen, *Black Awakening in Capitalist America: An Analytic History* (Garden City, NY: Doubleday, 1969), p. 97.

3. *Rebellion or Revolution?* (New York: William Morrow, 1968); *The Crisis of the Negro Intellectual* (New York: William Morrow, 1967).

4. The phrase, of course, is Immanuel Wallerstein's. See his *The Modern World System* Vols. I and II (New York: Academic Press, 1974, 1980). Other interesting observations by Wallerstein on race and colonialism, to which we cannot address ourselves here, may be found in "Social Conflict in Post-Indepedence Black Africa: The Concepts of Race and Status-Group Reconsidered," in Ernest Q. Campbell, ed., *Racial Tensions and National Identity* (Nashville, TN: Vanderbilt University Press, 1972); "The Rise and Future Demise of the World Capitalist System: Concepts for Comparative Analysis," in Wallerstein, *The Capitalist World-Economy* (New York: Cambridge University Press, 1979); and "Class Formation in the Capitalist World-Economy," in ibid.

5. The vestiges of colonialism extend to a wide variety of contemporary global arrangements. For example: although the introduction of high-tech satellite communications systems have allowed many Third World countries to break the monopoly of international communications traffic held by many of their former European rulers, examples of "communications colonialism" still exist. Gregory C. Staple notes that "A.T.& T. routes U.S. telephone calls to Angola via Portugal, which receives a twenty percent cut of the toll charges; U.S. calls to Benin are routed via France, which receives roughly three dollars for a routine three-minute call." Gregory C. Staple, "Satellite Politics: The Assault on Intelsat," *The Nation*, Vol. 239, No. 21 (22 December 1984).

6. See Alfonso Pinkney, *Red, Black, and Green: Black Nationalism in the United States* (New York: Cambridge University Press, 1976) ; J. H. Bracey, A. Meier, and E. Rudwick, *Black Nationalism.*

7. See for example E. Rudwick, "Du Bois vs. Garvey: Racial Propagandists at War," *Journal of Negro Education* XXVII (Fall 1959); J. H. Clarke, ed.,

Marcus Garvey and the Vision of Africa (New York: Vintage, 1974), esp. pp. 195–255.

8. A sixth (or seventh, depending on which events are counted) Pan-African Congress was held in Tanzania in 1974.

9. Some general sources on the Garvey movement: Clarke, *Marcus Garvey*; T. H. Vincent, *Black Power and the Garvey Movement* (Berkeley: Ramparts Press, 1971); and the recently begun series of volumes containing Garvey's complete papers, being edited by R. A. Hill, which represents the first systematic effort to present and interpret the movement's written legacy. (The first volume has appeared as Hill, ed., *The Marcus Garvey and Universal Negro Improvement Association Papers* (Berkeley: University of California Press, 1983); additional volumes are forthcoming.

10. See among many statements his "Speech at Royal Albert Hall," in Clarke, ed., *Marcus Garvey*, pp. 284–299.

11. E. U. Essien-Udom, *Black Nationalism: A Search for Identity in America* (Chicago: University of Chicago Press, 1962) p. 50.

12. Garvey visited Ku Klux Klan headquarters in June, 1922, and subsequently declared his agreement with the Klan that "this is a white man's country." He also flirted with the Anglo-Saxon Clubs of America, a white supremacist group led by one John Powell. His connection with such groups was certainly ill-advised, but his motivation in making these contacts has never been sufficiently explained. He was obviously not in agreement with such groups on white supremacy itself. See Richard B. Moore, "The Critics and Opponents of Marcus Garvey," in Clarke, ed., *Marcus Garvey*, pp. 225, 233–234.

13. Much important work must go without mention here, and Garveyism is thus afforded a pride of place which, in scholarly terms, it perhaps does not deserve. At the least, the contributions of such Pan-Africanist writers as Du Bois, Padmore, or James (all of whom fused Pan-Africanism with Marxism to greater or lesser extent, and who found Garvey politically misguided if not vulgar), should be mentioned.

14. Even opposing tendencies of black nationalism were so influenced. For example, it is unlikely that the Communist Party would have adopted its "black nation" approach in 1928 had not Party leaders both in the U.S. and in Moscow become alarmed at Garvey's successes. See below.

15. Two good general sources on Pan-Africanist theory are Colin Legum, *Pan Africanism: A Short Political Guide* (New York: Praeger, 1965), and R. Chrisman and N. Hare, *Pan-Africanism* (Indianapolis and New York: Bobbs-Merrill, 1974).

16. On Carmichael's 1967 meetings with Sekou Toure and Kwame Nkrumah in Guinea, see Clayborne Carson, In *Struggle: SNCC and the Black Awakening of the 1960s* (Cambridge, MA: Harvard University Press, 1981) p. 276.

Carmichael later founded a small Pan-Africanist party in the U.S., the All African Peoples Revolutionary Party.

17. See Manning Marable, "Black Nationalism in the 1970s: Through the Prism of Race and Class," *Socialist Review* No. 50–51 (March-June, 1980) pp. 86–88. Of course, we do not argue that such issues as apartheid have no relevance for black politics in the U.S.; we simply suggest that they cannot be *substituted* for domestic concerns. Recent successful actions undertaken in the U.S. in opposition to apartheid suggest that it may present an important rallying point for a broader black agenda that also includes coalition-building.

18. See Alain Locke, *The New Negro* (New York: Atheneum, 1968).

19. Some examples: "low-rider" youth culture and the mural movement in the Chicano barrios of the Southwest; the re-emphasis currently being given to Native American customs, religious, and spiritual traditions by Native activists. See Roxanne Dunbar Ortiz, "Land and Nationhood: The American Indian Struggle for Self-Determination and Survival," *Socialist Review* 63–64 (May–August 1982).

20. *The Crisis of the Negro Intellectual.*

21. *Rebellion or Revolution*, op. cit., p. 111.

22. See his "Revolutionary Nationalism and the Afro-American," *Studies on the Left* Vol. 2, No. 3 (1962).

23. *Rebellion or Revolution*, op. cit., pp. 111–112.

24. Ibid.

25. Ibid., p. 117.

26. Ibid., p. 112.

27. Cruse's contention that the demand for "public ownership" of the cultural apparatus formed the basis for a new revolutionary nationalist politics must be doubted. As he presented it, his program was utopian. The *integration* of the U.S. cultural apparatus, on the other hand, proved rather easy, demonstrating, as Robert Allen has pointed out, how far the co-optation of cultural nationalism was possible. See Allen, *Black Awakening*, p. 179).

28. Both Karenga and Baraka abandoned their cultural nationalist positions in the 1970s. Compare Baraka, *Raise, Race, Rays, Raze* (New York: Random House, 1971) and idem, "Needed: A Black Revolutionary Strategy," *The Black Scholar* (October, 1975); Pinkney, *Red, Black, and Green*, pp. 127–143, treats Karenga and Baraka in their cultural nationalist periods.

29. A good example is Baraka's essay on "A Black Value System," *The Black Scholar*, November, 1969, which *ascribes* to African traditions Baraka's culturally oriented agenda of the period.

30. See Gonzales' poem, *Yo Soy Joaquin/ I Am Joaquin* (New York: Bantam, 1972); see also idem, "El Plan de Aztlan," in Richard A. Garcia, ed., *The Chicanos in America, 1540–1974* (Dobbs Ferry, NY: Oceana Press, 1977).

Notes

31. Adolph L. Reed, Jr., "Black Particularity Reconsidered," *Telos* No. 39 (Spring 1979), p. 86.

32. Karl Marx and Frederick Engels, *Manifesto of the Communist Party* (Peking: Foreign Language Press, 1968), p. 55.

33. This point is elaborated by Michael Lowy, "Marxists and the National Question," *New Left Review*, no. 96 (March-April 1976). For specific references see Karl Marx and Frederick Engels, *On Colonialism: Articles from the New York Tribune and Other Writings* (New York: International Publishers, 1972) and *Ireland and the Irish Question: A Collection of Writings by Karl Marx and Frederick Engels* (New York: International Publishers, 1972).

34. V. I. Lenin, *Questions of National Policy and Proletarian Internationalism* (Moscow: Progress Publishers, 1970). Lenin sought to place these "national" conflicts in their international "class" context: the relationship between the proletariat of the "oppressor" nation and the proletariat of the "oppressed" nation (the so-called "aristocracy of labor") was also one of exploitation.

35. Horace B. Davis, ed., *The National Question: Selected Writings by Rosa Luxemburg* (New York: Monthly Review Press, 1976).

36. Joseph Stalin, *Marxism and the National-Colonial Question* (San Francisco: Proletarian Publishers, 1975), p. 22. We cannot dwell on the mechanical nature of this approach here.

37. See, for example, Revolutionary Union, *Red Papers 5: National Liberation and Proletarian Revolution in the U.S.* (Chicago: Revolutionary Union, n.d.) and October League, *The Struggle for Black Liberation and Socialist Revolution* (Chicago: October League, 1976).

38. Some of these analyses are tragically humorous. The Communist Labor Party understood the black nation in the following manner:

> Owing to the specifics of the rise of USNA [United States of North America] imperialism and the history of the Black Belt of the South, there arose a nation, oppressed by USNA [United States North American] imperialism, whose social root and base was the aforementioned Negro people. . . . Now, when referring to the nation, we use the term Negro and mean national and not color. . . . In the sense of national, Negroes are both the 'black' majority and 'white' minority.

(Nelson Peery, *The Negro National Colonial Question* (Chicago: Workers Press, 1975), p. 11.) One can well imagine the success of efforts to organize both blacks and whites in the South on the basis of their common identity as "Negroes."

39. For a critique of this literature and an analysis of its application see Racism Research Project, *Critique of the Black Nation Thesis* (Berkeley: Racism Research Project, 1975).

40. S. Berger, *Peasants Against Politics: Rural Organization in Brittany, 1907–1967* (Cambridge, MA: Harvard University Press, 1972).

41. Julio Cotler, "The Mechanics of Internal Domination and Social Change in Peru," in I. L. Horowitz, ed., *Masses in Latin America* (New York: Oxford University Press, 1970).

42. Harold Wolpe, "The Theory of Internal Colonialism," in I. Oxall et al, eds., *Beyond The Sociology of Development* (London: Routledge and Kegan Paul, 1975).

43. M. Hechter, *Internal Colonialism: The Celtic Fringe in British National Development* (Berkeley: University of California Press, 1975).

44. S. Carmichael and C. V. Hamilton, *Black Power* (New York: Random House, 1967); Robert L. Allen, *Black Awakening*).

45. Joan W. Moore, *Mexican Americans* (Englewood Cliffs, NJ: Prentice-Hall, 1970); M. Barrera, C. Muñoz, and G. Ornelas, "The Barrio as Internal Colony," in H. Hahn, ed., *People and Politics in Urban Society* (Beverly Hills, CA: Sage, 1972); see also M. Barrera, *Race and Class in the Southwest* (Notre Dame: University of Notre Dame Press, 1979); G. Flores, "Internal Colonialism and Racial Minorities in the U.S.: An Overview," in F. Bonilla and R. Girling, eds., *Structures of Dependency* (Stanford, CA: Stanford University Press, 1973).

46. Robert Blauner, *Racial Oppression in America* (New York: Harper and Row, 1972); Blauner's approach, like other "internal colonialism" analyses, can be faulted for deviating significantly from the original meaning of the term "colonialism." Burawoy, for example, offers a definition of colonialism that reasserts the criterion of territoriality in terms which no "internal" application can satisfy: "Colonialism may be defined as the conquest and administration by a 'metropolitan country' of a geographically separate territory in order to utilize available resources (usually human or natural) for the creation of surplus which is repatriated to the metropolis." Michael Burawoy, "Race, Class, and Colonialism," *Social and Economic Studies* Vol. 24, no. 4 (December, 1974) p. 546. Blauner's version of internal colonialism may be at variance with this more traditional notion, but it does not differ substantially from other "internal" approaches in this respect and is thus useful as a typical example.

47. Compare Blauner, *Racial Oppression in America*, pp. 88–89, and Glazer, *Ethnic Dilemmas 1964–1982* (Cambridge, MA: Harvard University Press), pp. 79–88.

48. "My own developing framework," Blauner writes, "probably owes more to the social movements of the oppressed than to standard sociology." Blauner, *Racial Oppression in America,* p. viii.

49. Ibid., p. 55. Blauner is not unaware that economic suffering and political per-

secution in their countries of origin impelled much immigration to the U.S., but he notes that these problems, however dire, did not force their victims to come to the U.S. *specifically*. Many European emigrants headed for South America, for example. For these and other reasons, we are in accord with Blauner's distinction here.

50. Ibid. p. 89.
51. See Piven and Cloward, *Poor Peoples' Movements*; P. Bachrach and M. Baratz, *Power and Poverty* (New York: Oxford University Press, 1971).
52. See M. Omi's review of William Julius Wilson's *The Declining Significance of Race*, in *Insurgent Sociologist*, Vol. 10, no. 2 (Fall 1980), p. 119.
53. See Chapter 7, below.
54. Internal colonialist approaches have tended to see the ghetto and barrio as colonized territory. See for example James Boggs, "The City is the Black Man's Land," in idem, *Racism and Class Struggle* (New York: Monthly Review Press, 1970); Barrera, Munoz, and Ornelas, "The Barrio as Internal Colony."
55. Burawoy, "Race, Class, and Colonialism," pp. 526–527.
56. See Seymour Martin Lipset, *The First New Nation* (New York: Basic Books, 1963). There is plenty of room for conservative nationalism, though, of the jingoistic sort, and credulity beyond bounds for it as well.

Toward a Racial Formation Perspective

1. In particular this is true of William Julius Wilson, *The Declining Significance of Race* 2nd ed. (Chicago: University of Chicago Press, 1978).

4. Racial Formation

1. *San Francisco Chronicle*, 14 September 1982, 19 May 1983. Ironically, the 1970 Louisiana law was enacted to supersede an old Jim Crow statute which relied on the idea of "common report" in determining an infant's race. Following Phipps' unsuccessful attempt to change her classification and have the law declared unconstitutional, a legislative effort arose which culminated in the repeal of the law. See *San Francisco Chronicle*, 23 June 1983.
2. Compare the Phipps case to Andrew Hacker's well-known "parable" in which a white person is informed by a mysterious official that "the organization he represents has made a mistake" and that " . . . [a]ccording to their records . . . , you were to have been born black: to another set of parents, far from where you were raised." How much compensation, Hacker's official asks, would "you" require to undo the damage of this unfortunate error? See Hacker, *Two Nations: Black and White, Separate, Hostile, Unequal* (New York: Charles Scribner's Sons, 1992) pp. 31–32.
3. On the evolution of Louisiana's racial classification system, see Virginia

Dominguez, *White By Definition: Social Classification in Creole Louisiana* (New Brunswick: Rutgers University Press, 1986).

4. This is not to suggest that gender is a biological category while race is not. Gender, like race, is a social construct. However, the biological division of humans into sexes—two at least, and possibly intermediate ones as well—is not in dispute. This provides a basis for argument over gender divisions—how "natural," etc.—which does not exist with regard to race. To ground an argument for the "natural" existence of race, one must resort to philosophical anthropology.

5. "The truth is that there are no races, there is nothing in the world that can do all we ask race to do for us. . . . The evil that is done is done by the concept, and by easy—yet impossible—assumptions as to its application." (Kwame Anthony Appiah, *In My Father's House: Africa in the Philosophy of Culture* [New York: Oxford University Press, 1992].) Appiah's eloquent and learned book fails, in our view, to dispense with the race concept, despite its anguished attempt to do so; this indeed is the source of its author's anguish. We agree with him as to the non-objective character of race, but fail to see how this recognition justifies its abandonment. This argument is developed below.

6. We understand essentialism as *belief in real, true human, essences, existing outside or impervious to social and historical context.* We draw this definition, with some small modifications, from Diana Fuss, *Essentially Speaking: Feminism, Nature, & Difference* (New York: Routledge, 1989) p. xi.

7. Michael Omi and Howard Winant, "On the Theoretical Status of the Concept of Race" in Warren Crichlow and Cameron McCarthy, eds., *Race, Identity, and Representation in Education* (New York: Routledge, 1993).

8. Charles Murray, *Losing Ground: American Social Policy, 1950–1980* (New York: Basic Books, 1984), p. 223.

9. Justice Thurgood Marshall, dissenting in *City of Richmond v. J. A. Croson Co.*, 488 U.S. 469 (1989).

10. See, for example, Derrick Bell, "Remembrances of Racism Past: Getting Past the Civil Rights Decline." in Herbert Hill and James E. Jones, Jr., eds., *Race in America: The Struggle for Equality* (Madison: The University of Wisconsin Press, 1993) pp. 75–76; Gertrude Ezorsky, *Racism and Justice: The Case for Affirmative Action* (Ithaca: Cornell University Press, 1991) pp. 109–111; David Kairys, *With Liberty and Justice for Some: A Critique of the Conservative Supreme Court* (New York: The New Press, 1993) pp. 138–41.

11. Howard Winant has developed a tentative "map" of the system of racial hegemony in the U.S. circa 1990, which focuses on the spectrum of racial projects running from the political right to the political left. See Winant, "Where Culture Meets Structure: Race in the 1990s," in idem, *Racial Conditions: Politics, Theory, Comparisons* (Minneapolis: University of Minnesota Press, 1994).

12. A familiar example is use of racial "code words." Recall George Bush's manipulations of racial fear in the 1988 "Willie Horton" ads, or Jesse Helms's use of the coded term "quota" in his 1990 campaign against Harvey Gantt.

13. From this perspective, far right racial projects can also be interpreted as "nationalist." See Ronald Walters, "White Racial Nationalism in the United States," *Without Prejudice* Vol. 1, no. 1 (Fall 1987).

14. To be sure, any effort to divide racial formation patterns according to social structural location—"macro" vs. "micro," for example—is necessarily an analytic device. In the concrete, there is no such dividing line. See Winant, "Where Culture Meets Structure."

15. We are not unaware, for example, that publishing this work is in itself a racial project.

16. Antisemitism only began to be racialized in the 18th century, as George L. Mosse clearly shows in his important *Toward the Final Solution: A History of European Racism* (New York: Howard Fertig, 1978).

17. As Marx put it:

    The discovery of gold and silver in America, the extirpation, enslavement, and entombment in mines of the aboriginal population, the beginning of the conquest and looting of the East Indies, the turning of Africa into a warren for the commercial hunting of blackskins, signalized the rosy dawn of the era of capitalist production. These idyllic proceedings are the chief momenta of primitive accumulation. (Karl Marx, *Capital*, Vol. I (New York: International Publishers, 1967) p. 751.)

    David E. Stannard argues that the wholesale slaughter perpetrated upon the native peoples of the Western hemisphere is unequalled in history, even in our own bloody century. See his *American Holocaust: Columbus and the Conquest of the New World* (New York: Oxford University Press, 1992).

18. Winthrop Jordan provides a detailed account of the sources of European attitudes about color and race in *White Over Black: American Attitudes Toward the Negro, 1550–1812* (New York: Norton, 1977 [1968]) pp. 3–43.

19. In a famous instance, a 1550 debate in Valladolid pitted the philosopher and translator of Aristotle, Ginés de Sepúlveda, against the Dominican Bishop of the Mexican state of Chiapas, Bartolomé de Las Casas. Discussing the native peoples, Sepúlveda argued that:

    In wisdom, skill, virtue and humanity, these people are as inferior to the Spaniards as children are to adults and women to men; there is as great a difference between them as there is between savagery and forbearance, between violence and moderation, almost—I am inclined to say, as between monkeys and men (Sepúlveda, *Democrates Alter,* quoted in Tsvetan Todorov, *The Conquest of America: The Question of the Other* (New York: Harper and Row, 1984), p. 153).

In contrast, Las Casas defended the humanity and equality of the native peoples, both in terms of their way of life—which he idealized as one of innocence, gentleness, and generosity—and in terms of their readiness for conversion to Catholicism, which for him as for Sepúlveda was the true and universal religion (Las Casas, "Letter to the Council of the Indies," quoted ibid, p. 163). William E. Connolly interrogates the linkages proposed by Todorov between early Spanish colonialism and contemporary conceptions of identity and difference in *Identity/Difference: Democratic Negotiations of Political Paradox* (Ithaca: Cornell University Press, 1991) pp. 40–48.

20. In Virginia, for example, it took about two decades after the establishment of European colonies to extirpate the indigenous people of the greater vicinity; fifty years after the establishment of the first colonies, the elaboration of slave codes establishing race as *prima facie* evidence for enslaved status was well under way. See Jordan, *White Over Black*.

21. Marx, *Capital*, p. 751.

22. Edward W. Said, *Culture and Imperialism* (New York: Alfred A. Knopf, 1993).

23. David Brion Davis, *The Problem of Slavery in The Age of Revolution* (Ithaca: Cornell University Press, 1975).

24. Quoted in Thomas F. Gossett, *Race: The History of an Idea in America* (New York: Schocken Books, 1965) p. 45.

25. Thomas *Jefferson, Notes on Virginia* [1787], in Merrill D. Peterson, *Writings of Thomas Jefferson* (New York: The Library of America, 1984) pp. 264–66, 270. Thanks to Kimberly Benston for drawing our attention to this passage.

26. Proslavery physician Samuel George Morton (1799–1851) compiled a collection of 800 crania from all parts of the world which formed the sample for his studies of race. Assuming that the larger the size of the cranium translated into greater intelligence, Morton established a relationship between race and skull capacity. Gossett reports that "In 1849, one of his studies included the following results: the English skulls in his collection proved to be the largest, with an average cranial capacity of 96 cubic inches. The Americans and Germans were rather poor seconds, both with cranial capacities of 90 cubic inches. At the bottom of the list were the Negroes with 83 cubic inches, the Chinese with 82, and the Indians with 79." Gossett, *Race*, p. 74. More recently, Steven Jay Gould has reexamined Morton's data, and shown that his research data were deeply, though unconsciously, manipulated to agree with his "a priori conviction about racial ranking." (Gould, *The Mismeasure of Man* (New York: W. W. Norton, 1981) pp. 50–69).

27. Definitions of race founded upon a common pool of genes have not held up when confronted by scientific research which suggests that the differences *within* a given human population are every bit as great as those *between*

populations. See L. L. Cavalli-Sforza, "The Genetics of Human Populations," *Scientific American* (September 1974) pp. 81–89.

28. A fascinating summary critique of Gobineau is provided in Tsvetan Todorov,
On Human Diversity: Nationalism, Racism, and Exoticism in French Thought,
trans. Catherine Porter (Cambridge, MA: Harvard University Press, 1993),
esp. pp. 129–40.

29. Two recent histories of eugenics are Allen Chase, *The Legacy of Malthus*
(New York: Knopf, 1977); Daniel J. Kevles, *In the Name of Eugenics: Genetics and the Uses of Human Heredity* (New York: Knopf, 1985).

30. Arthur Jensen, "How Much Can We Boost IQ and Scholastic Achievement?" *Harvard Educational Review* 39 (1969) pp. 1–123.

31. See Weber, *Economy and Society*, Vol. I (Berkeley: University of California
Press, 1978), pp. 385–87; Ernst Moritz Manasse, "Max Weber on Race,"
Social Research, Vol. 14 (1947) pp. 191–221.

32. Du Bois, *The Souls of Black Folk* (New York: Penguin, 1989 [1903]), p. 13.
Du Bois himself wrestled heavily with the conflict between a fully sociohistorical conception of race, and the more essentialized and deterministic
vision he encountered as a student in Berlin. In "The Conservation of Races"
(1897) we can see his first mature effort to resolve this conflict in a vision
which combined racial solidarity and a commitment to social equality. See
Du Bois, "The Conservation of Races," in Dan S. Green and Edwin D.
Driver, eds., *W. E. B. Du Bois On Sociology and the Black Community*
(Chicago: University of Chicago Press, 1978) pp. 238–49; Manning Marable,
W. E. B. Du Bois: Black Radical Democrat (Boston: Twayne, 1986) pp. 35–38.
For a contrary, and we believe incorrect reading, see Appiah, *In My Father's
House*, pp. 28–46.

33. A good collection of Boas's work is George W. Stocking, ed., *The Shaping
of American Anthropology, 1883–1911: A Franz Boas Reader* (Chicago: University of Chicago Press, 1974).

34. Robert E. Park's *Race and Culture* (Glencoe, IL: Free Press, 1950) can still
provide insight; see also Stanford H. Lyman, *Militarism, Imperialism, and
Racial Accommodation: An Analysis and Interpretation of the Early Writ-
ings of Robert E. Park* (Fayetteville: University of Arkansas Press, 1992);
Locke's views are concisely expressed in Alain Leroy Locke, *Race Con-
tacts and Interracial Relations,* ed. Jeffrey C. Stewart (Washington, DC:
Howard University Press, 1992), originally a series of lectures given at
Howard University.

35. Japanese, for example, could not become naturalized citizens until passage
of the 1952 McCarran-Walter Act. It took over 160 years, since the passage
of the Law of 1790, to allow all "races" to be eligible for naturalization.

36. Especially when we recall that until around 1960, the majority of blacks,
the largest racially defined minority group, lived in the South.

37. Toni Morrison, *Playing in the Dark: Whiteness and the Literary Imagination* (Cambridge, MA: Harvard University Press, 1992); Richard Drinnon, *Facing West: The Metaphysics of Indian-Hating and Empire-Building* (Minneapolis: University of Minnesota Press, 1980); Michael Paul Rogin, *Fathers and Children: Andrew Jackson and the Subjugation of the American Indian* (New York: Knopf, 1975).

38. This term refers to the practice, widespread throughout the Americas, whereby runaway slaves formed communities in remote areas, such as swamps, mountains, or forests, often in alliance with dispossessed indigenous peoples.

39. Antonio Gramsci, *Selections from the Prison Notebooks,* edited and translated by Quintin Hoare and Geoffrey Nowell Smith (New York: International Publishers, 1971) p. 182.

40. Anne Showstack Sassoon, *Gramsci's Politics,* 2nd ed. (London: Hutchinson, 1987); Sue Golding, *Gramsci's Democratic Theory: Contributions to Post-Liberal Democracy* (Toronto: University of Toronto Press, 1992).

41. Ralph Ellison, *Shadow and Act* (New York: New American Library, 1966) p. xiv.

42. Chantal Mouffe makes a related argument in "Radical Democracy: Modern or Postmodern?" in Andrew Ross, ed., *Universal Abandon: The Politics of Postmodernism* (Minneapolis: University of Minnesota Press, 1988).

43. Patricia Hill Collins, *Black Feminist Thought: Knowledge, Consciousness, and the Politics of Empowerment* (New York and London: Routledge, 1991).

44. Evelyn Nakano Glenn, "From Servitude to Service Work: Historical Continuities in the Racial Division of Paid Reproductive Labor," *Signs: Journal of Women in Culture & Society,* Vol. 18, no. 1 (Autumn 1992).

45. Toni Morrison, ed., *Race-ing Justice, En-gendering Power: Essays on Anita Hill, Clarence Thomas, and the Construction of Social Reality* (New York: Pantheon, 1992)

46. For example, in Magnus Hirschfeld's prescient book, *Racism* (London: Victor Gollancz, 1938).

47. This was the framework, employed in the crucial study of Myrdal and his associates; see Gunnar Myrdal, *An American Dilemma: The Negro Problem and Modern Democracy*, 20th Anniversary Edition (New York: Harper and Row, 1962 [1944]). See also the articles by Thomas F. Pettigrew and George Fredrickson in Pettigrew et al., *Prejudice: Selections from The Harvard Encyclopedia of American Ethnic Groups* (Cambridge, MA: The Belknap Press of Harvard University, 1982).

48. On discrimination, see Frederickson in ibid. In an early essay which explicitly sought to modify the framework of the Myrdal study, Robert K. Merton recognized that prejudice and discrimination need not coincide, and indeed could combine in a variety of ways. See Merton, "Discrimination and the

American Creed," in R. M. McIver, ed., *Discrimination and National Welfare* (New York: Harper and Row, 1949).

49. Gordon W. Allport, *The Nature of Prejudice* (Cambridge, MA: Addison-Wesley, 1954) remains a classic work in the field; see also Philomena Essed, *Understanding Everyday Racism: An Interdisciplinary Theory* (Newbury Park, CA: Sage, 1991). A good overview of black attitudes toward black identities is provided in William E. Cross, Jr., *Shades of Black: Diversity in African-American Identity* (Philadelphia: Temple University Press, 1991).

50. Stokely Carmichael and Charles V. Hamilton first popularized the notion of "institutional" forms of discrimination in *Black Power: The Politics of Liberation in America* (New York: Vintage, 1967), although the basic concept certainly predated that work. Indeed, President Lyndon Johnson made a similar argument in his 1965 speech at Howard University:

> But freedom is not enough. You do not wipe away the scars of centuries by saying: Now you are free to go where you want, do as you desire, and choose the leaders you please.
>
> You do not take a person who, for years, has been hobbled by chains and liberate him (sic), bring him up to the starting line of a race and then say, "You are free to compete with all the others," and still justly believe that you have been completely fair.
>
> Thus it is not enough just to open the gates of opportunity. All our citizens must have the opportunity to walk through those gates.
>
> This is the next and more profound stage of the battle for civil rights. We seek not just freedom but opportunity—not just legal equity but human ability—not just equality as a right but equality as a fact and as a result. (Lyndon B. Johnson, "To Fulfill These Rights," reprinted in Lee Rainwater and William L. Yancey, *The Moynihan Report and the Politics of Controversy* [Cambridge, MA: MIT Press, 1967, p. 125].)

This speech, delivered at Howard University on June 4, 1965, was written in part by Daniel Patrick Moynihan. A more systematic treatment of the institutional racism approach is David T. Wellman, *Portraits of White Racism* (New York: Cambridge University Press, 1977).

51. From the vantage point of the 1990s, it is possible to question whether discrimination was ever effectively outlawed. The federal retreat from the agenda of integration began almost immediately after the passage of civil rights legislation, and has culminated today in a series of Supreme Court decisions making violation of these laws almost impossible to prove. See Ezorsky, *Racism and Justice*; Kairys, *With Liberty and Justice for Some*. As we write, the Supreme Court has further restricted antidiscrimination laws in the case of *St. Mary's Honor Center v. Hicks*. See Linda Greenhouse,

"Justices Increase Workers' Burden in Job-Bias Cases," *The New York Times*, 26 June 1993, p. 1.

52. Robert Miles, *Racism* (New York and London: Routledge, 1989), esp. chap. 2.

53. The *locus classicus* of this position is Nathan Glazer, *Affirmative Discrimination: Ethnic Inequality and Public Policy*, 2nd ed. (New York: Basic Books, 1978); for more recent formulations, see Murray, *Losing Ground*; Arthur M. Schlesinger, *The Disuniting of America: Reflections on a Multicultural Society* (New York: W. W. Norton, 1992).

54. See Chapter 1.

55. Thomas Sowell, for example, has argued that one's "human capital" is to a large extent culturally determined. Therefore the state cannot create a false equality which runs counter to the magnitude and persistence of cultural differences. Such attempts at social engineering are likely to produce negative and unintended results: "If social processes are transmitting real differences—in productivity, reliability, cleanliness, sobriety, peacefulness [!]—then attempts to impose politically a very different set of beliefs will necessarily backfire. . . ." (Thomas Sowell, *The Economics and Politics of Race: An International Perspective* (New York: Quill, 1983) p. 252).

56. Bob Blauner "Racism, Race, and Ethnicity: Some Reflections on the Language of Race" (unpublished manuscript, 1991).

57. Essentialism, it will be recalled, is understood as belief in real, true human essences, existing outside or impervious to social and historical context.

58. An example would be the "singling out" of members of racially defined minority groups for harsh treatment by authorities, as when police harass and beat randomly chosen ghetto youth, a practice they do not pursue with white suburban youth.

59. For example, the biologistic theories found in Michael Anderson Bradley, *The Iceman Inheritance: Prehistoric Sources of Western Man's Racism, Sexism' and Aggression* (Toronto: Dorset, 1978), and in Frances Cress Welsing, *The Isis (Yssis) Papers* (Chicago: Third World Press, 1991).

60. "These remarks should not be interpreted as simply an effort to move the gaze of African-American studies to a different site. I do not want to alter one hierarchy in order to institute another. It is true that I do not want to encourage those totalizing approaches to African-American scholarship which have no drive other than the exchange of dominations—dominant Eurocentric scholarship replaced by dominant Afrocentric scholarship. More interesting is what makes intellectual domination possible; how knowledge is transformed from invasion and conquest to revelation and choice; what ignites and informs the literary imagination, and what forces help establish the parameters of criticism." (Toni Morrison, *Playing in the Dark*, p. 8; emphasis original.)

Notes

61. Lisa Lowe states: "The concept of 'strategic essentialism' suggests that it is possible to utilize specific signifiers of ethnic identity, such as Asian American, for the purpose of contesting and disrupting the discourses that exclude Asian Americans, while simultaneously revealing the internal contradictions and slippages of Asian Americans so as to insure that such essentialisms will not be reproduced and proliferated by the very apparatuses we seek to disempower." Lisa Lowe, "Heterogeneity, Hybridity, Multiplicity: Marking Asian American Differences," *Diaspora*, Vol. 1, no. 1 (Spring 1991) p. 39.

62. This view supports Supreme Court decisions taken in the late 1960s and early 1970s, for example in *Griggs v. Duke Power,* 401 U.S. 424 (1971). We agree with Kairys that only " . . . [F]or that brief period in our history, it could accurately be said that governmental discrimination was prohibited by law" (Kairys, *With Liberty and Justice For Some*, p. 144).

63. This analysis draws on Ezorsky, *Racism and Justice.*

64. See for example, Judy H. Katz, *White Awareness: Handbook for Anti-Racism Training* (Norman: University of Oklahoma Press, 1978).

65. The formula "racism equals prejudice plus power" is frequently invoked by our students to argue that only whites can be racist. We have been able to uncover little written analysis to support this view (apart from Katz, ibid., p. 10), but consider that it is itself an example of the essentializing approach we have identified as central to racism. In the modern world, "power" cannot be reified as a thing which some possess and other's don't, but instead constitutes a relational field. The minority student who boldly asserts in class that minorities cannot be racist is surely not entirely powerless. In all but the most absolutist of regimes, resistance to rule itself implies power.

66. To pick but one example among many: writing before the successes of the civil rights movement, E. Franklin Frazier bitterly castigated the collaboration of black elites with white supremacy. See Frazier, *Black Bourgeoisie: The Rise of a New Middle Class in the United States* (New York: The Free Press, 1957).

67. Interestingly, what they share most centrally seems to be their antisemitism.

68. Having made a similar argument, Lani Guinier, Clinton's nominee to head the Justice Department's Civil Rights Division was savagely attacked and her nomination ultimately blocked. See Guinier, "The Triumph of Tokenism: The Voting Rights Act and the Theory of Black Electoral Success," *Michigan Law Review* (March 1991). We discuss these events in greater detail in this book's Epilogue, below.

69. See Miles, *Racism*, p. 77. Much of the current debate over the advisability and legality of banning racist hate speech seems to us to adopt the dubious position that racism is primarily an ideological phenomenon. See Mari J. Matsuda et al., *Words That Wound: Critical Race Theory, Assaultive Speech, and the First Amendment* (Boulder, CO: Westview Press, 1993).

70. Or ideologies which mask privilege by falsely claiming that inequality and injustice have been eliminated. See Wellman, *Portraits of White Racism*.

71. Racial teachings of the Nation of Islam, for example, maintain that whites are the product of a failed experiment by a mad scientist.

72. Elinor Langer, "The American Neo-Nazi Movement Today," *The Nation*, July 16/23, 1990.

73. Such arguments can be found in Nathan Glazer, *Affirmative Discrimination*, Charles Murray, *Losing Ground*, and Arthur M. Schlesinger, Jr., *The Disuniting of America*, among others.

5. The Racial State

1. Thomas Byrne Edsall and Mary D. Edsall, *Chain Reaction: The Impact of Race, Rights, and Taxes on American Politics* (New York: W. W. Norton & Co., 1991) p. 270.

2. Dana Y. Takagi, *The Retreat from Race: Asian American Admissions and Racial Politics* (New Brunswick: Rutgers University Press, 1992) pp. 103–105.

3. Note that such movements can be egalitarian or counter-egalitarian, depending on the concepts of justice, equality, discrimination, etc., to which they adhere. For a theory of political change focused on this issue (drawing on German reference points), see Barrington Moore, *Injustice: The Social Bases of Obedience and Revolt* (White Plains, NY: Sharpe, 1978).

4. This does not mean that these channels are the sole province of reform-oriented movements or democratizing currents. They are also open to other uses, other interests, including those of reaction.

5. There are important continuities between present-day and past versions of racial ideology. Often in the past, the dominant viewpoint about what race was and what race meant has been believed to represent the culmination of a long struggle to eliminate pre-existing "unenlightened" racial beliefs. Religious and scientific exponents of the dominant racial ideology, for example, have often made such claims. Thus it is all too easy to believe that in the present ("finally") the U.S. has reached a stage at which racial oppression is largely a thing of the past, and that in the future race will play an ever-smaller role in determining the course of U.S. political and social history. We obviously do not share that view.

6. A brief selection of sources: Eugene Genovese, *Roll, Jordan, Roll: The World the Slaves Made* (New York: Pantheon, 1974); Julius Lester, *To Be a Slave* (New York: Dial, 1968); Vincent Harding, "Religion and Resistance Among Antebellum Negroes, 1800–1860," in A. Meier and E. Rudwick, eds., *The Making of Black America*, 2 Vol.s (New York: Atheneum, 1969); George Rawick, *From Sundown to Sunup: The Making of the Black Community* (Westport, CT: Greenwood, 1972); Herbert C. Gutman, *The Black Family in Slavery and Freedom, 1750–1925* (New York: Vintage, 1976); Robert Farris

Notes

Thompson, *Flash of the Spirit: African and Afro-American Art and Philosophy* (New York: Random House, 1983).

7. Roxanne Dunbar Ortiz, "Land and Nationhood: The American Indian Struggle for Self-Determination and Survival," *Socialist Review* 63–64 (May–August 1982).

8. Rodolfo Acuña, *Occupied America: A History of Chicanos*, 2nd ed. (New York: Harper and Row, 1981); see also Leonard Pitt, *The Decline of the Californios* (Berkeley: University of California Press, 1966).

9. Our treatment here is necessarily very brief. The contemporary configuration of racial politics is a major subject later on in this work.

10. The ideological residue of these restrictions in naturalization and citizenship is the popular equation of the term "American" with "white." Other "Americans" are seen as black, Mexican, Oriental, etc.

11. For a comprehesive discussion of racial minorities in 19th-century California, see Tomas Almaguer, *Class, Race, and Capitalist Development: The Social Transformation of a Southern California County, 1848–1903*, (unpublished doctoral dissertation, University of California, Berkeley, 1979).

12. Harry P. Pachon and Joan W. Moore, "Mexican Americans," *Annals of the American Academy of Political and Social Science*, Vol. 454 (March 1981).

13. They also set the stage for tragicomic attempts to manipulate this incomprehension. In 1979, for example, an Anglo named Robert E. Lee changed his name to Roberto E. Leon in order to qualify for affirmative action porgrams available to those with Spanish surnames. See David Hayes-Bautista, "Identifying 'Hispanic' Populations: The Influence of Research Methodology Upon Public Policy," *American Journal of Public Health* Vol. 70, no. 4 (April 1980) p. 355.

14. See note 17, below.

15. State theory is undergoing something of a renaissance, especially in its Marxist (or neo-Marxist) variants. We have been influenced by Bob Jessop, *The Capitalist State* (New York: NYU Press, 1982); Theda Skocpol, "Bringing the State Back In: A Report on Current Comparative Research on the Relationship Between States and Social Structures," *Items* Vol. 36, nos. 1–2 (New York: Social Science Research Council, 1982).

16. Consider the conflicting 1960s activities of the federal courts and federal urban policies: the courts ordered school desegregation while urban renewal ("Negro removal") programs exacerbated residential segregation. Many similar conflicts in policy could be cited, not only at a given level of the state (i.e., federal, regional, local, etc. agencies), but also between different levels.

17. Nobel laureate William Shockley, inventor of the transistor, has advocated a biologistic theory of race, and argues that blacks are genetically inferior to whites in intelligence.

18. For a provocative treatment of the evolution of these "micro-political" measures, see Michel Foucault, *Discipline and Punish* (New York: Vintage, 1979), esp. pp. 135–136.

19. On "hegemonic projects," see Bob Jessop, Accumulation Strategies, State Forms, and Hegemonic Projects," *Kapitalistate*, No. 10–11 (1983).

20. On "rules of the game," see Herbert Gintis and Samuel Bowles, "Structure and Practice in the Labor Theory of Value," *Review of Radical Political Economics* Vol. 12, no. 4 (Winter 1981) p. 4. See also Chapter 4, above.

21. Thus in agriculture, for example, farm lobbying groups, the Agriculture Department, and the House and Senate agriculture committees together constitute the dominant policy-making mechanism. This concept has its origins in the work of Grant McConnell, and has been further refined by Gordon Adams. See Grant McConnell, *Private Power and American Democracy* (New York: Vintage, 1966); Gordon Adams, *The Politics of Defense Contracting: The Iron Triangle* (New Brunswick, NJ: Transaction, 1981).

22. The concept of civil society has a complex intellectual history, which originates in classical political economy, and comes via Hegel and Marx to Gramsci. In Hegel's political philosophy, and still in the work of the early Marx, civil society is seen as the realm of "private" social relationships, and distinguished from that of the state. Economic relationships, understood in the classical sense of the "free market," are also located within civil society. Gramsci's conception is considerably more complicated, though built on these premises. Civil society for him is the terrain upon which hegemony is secured, the complex of social relationships whose existence depends upon the "consent" of their participants. Religion, education, linguistic practices, cultural and artistic life, trade unions, and political organizations are thus included within it. Gramsci is well aware, though, that in the modern epoch there is no clear boundary between "private life" and the "life of the state." In a famous formulation, in fact, he includes civil society with "political society" as part of the state. (See Antonio Gramsci, *Selections From the Prison Notebooks*, Quentin Hoare and Geoffrey Nowell Smith, eds. (New York: International, 1971) p. 263.) In our view, the concept of hegemony, through which the dominant social forces acquire the consent of the subordinate ones, in itself presumes an autonomous civil society and a limited capacity for state "intervention" into the realm of "micro-politics," since this "consent" is not given stupidly or blindly but because the needs, interests, and ideas of the subordinate groups are actively incorporated and taken into account in the organization of society.

23. See Theodore J. Lowi, "The New Public Philosophy: Interest-Group Liberalism," in T. Ferguson and J. Rogers, *The Political Economy* (Armonk, NY: Sharpe, 1984).

24. This takes us into the realm of organizational theory, which is beyond the

present scope. An interesting discussion of interagency relationships and their ability to frustrate innovative racial policy is Roland Warren et al, *The Structure of Urban Reform* (Lexington, MA: D.C. Heath, 1973); on the autonomy of state officials see Fred Block, "Beyond Relative Autonomy: State Managers as Historical Subjects," *New Political Science* No. 7 (Winter 1981).

25. Claus Offe has developed some interesting approaches to these issues in his concepts of "selection mechanisms" by which political demands are rendered salient to state institutions, and of "allocative" vs. "productive" types of state policies, which are brought into play to deal with different rules of state decision-making. See, respectively, Offe, "Structural Problems of the Capitalist State," in K. von Beyme, ed., *German Political Studies* Vol. 1 (Beverly Hills: Sage, 1974), and idem, "The Theory of the Capitalist State and the Problem of Policy Formation," in L. Lindberg et al, eds., *Stress and Contradiction in Modern Capitalism* (Lexington, MA: Heath, 1975).

26. See for example Gramsci's remarks on parliamentary democracy, in *Selections from the Prison Notebooks*, p. 80n.

27. These are aspects of hegemony which are beyond our present scope, but consider for example Roosevelt's failure to "pack" the Supreme Court (which constitutionally may have as many as fifteen justices); or the outcry at Nixon's so-called "Saturday Night Massacre" (his firings of Cox, Richardson, and Ruckelshaus were perfectly legal). On the oppositional side, there are enormous difficulties involved in breaking with the supposedly "consensual" aspects of U.S. politics: the logic and justice of the "free enterprise system," anticommunism, the morality and truthfulness of government ("We stand for freedom," etc.). These are examples of a hegemonic domain from which challenges are effectively excluded—and within which basic political unity is therefore preserved.

28. The following discussion assumes the kinds of general racial conditions that have existed in the postwar U.S.: what we have termed racial war of position (e.g., the availability of "normal" political channels for racial politics), and the open existence of racial civil society (e.g., the possibility of minority cultural autonomy, political institutions, observance of traditional customs, linguistic practices, etc.). Obviously these conditions have not existed at all times and all places; indeed the civil rights phase of the black movement was concerned precisely with extending and institutionalizing them in the South. The very success of the southern struggle shows, though, that at least on a national level, these conditions did already obtain. See Chapter 6, below.

29. Gramsci, *Selections from the Prison Notebooks*, p. 182.

30. The main means available to the state for the equilibration of conflicting interests is precisely their incorporation into the state in the form of policies,

programs, patronage, etc. Gramsci argues that various forms of hegemony flow from this process of incorporation: "expansive" hegemony if state-society relations display sufficient dynamism and are not inordinately plagued by crisis conditions; "reformist" hegemony (what he calls "transformism") if political stability requires continuing concessions to competing forces. See also our discussion of "absorption" and "insulation" below.

31. Racially subordinated groups may not be permitted access to the political system; if they are represented, this will take the form of racially defined political organizations, or by organizations which have racially explicit projects and programs.

32. We use this term in the Gramscian sense of social actors whose position and training permits them to express the worldviews, ideas, and sense of social identity of various social actors. Priests, teachers, artists, and entertainers fit in this definition, which is not the same as the standard usage of "intelligentsia."

33. Lack of success terminates the crisis. The result may be a restoration of the previous pattern of unstable equilibrium, or the consolidation of a counter-reformist agenda. On cyclical patterns in contemporary movement politics, see Frances Fox Piven and Richard A. Cloward. See their *Poor People's Movements: How They Succeed, Why They Fail* (New York: Vintage, 1979).

34. As seen from a movement standpoint. From the standpoint of the state, these are reform policies.

35. "The Mexican Americans now view the political system as an Anglo system. They feel that only a Mexican American political system can serve their needs. . . . " Jose Angel Gutierrez, "La Raza and Revolution" [1968], in M. S. Meier and F. Rivera, eds., *Readings on La Raza* (New York: Hill and Wang, 1974) p. 231.

36. Charles V. Hamilton, "Black Social Scientists: Contributions and Problems," in Joyce Ladner, ed., *The Death of White Sociology* (New York: Vintage, 1973) pp. 472–473.

37. Michael Novak, *The Rise of the Unmeltable Ethnics* (New York: Macmillan, 1973); Nathan Glazer, *Affirmative Discrimination* (New York: Basic, 1975).

38. For example, see Gutierrez, "La Raza and Revolution," p. 232. These organizations had often played a challenging role in a previous phase of the reform trajectory; their leaders had been, in many cases, the militants of their generation. We discuss the concept of "trajectories" of reform movements below.

39. Malcolm X (with Alex Haley), *The Autobiography of Malcolm X* (New York: Grove Press, 1965) pp. 53–56.

40. A good example is the incorporation of the Gandhian concept of nonviolence into the civil rights movement. See Chapter 6, below.

41. The dislocation of white identity, of the meaning of "whiteness" in con-

temporary racial conflicts has received relatively little attention. Some social psychological studies have been directed at the identity crisis experienced by whites in the face of minority demands for equality, political rights, cultural/organizational autonomy, etc. The idea that the great Western societies are somehow fundamentally white—which today is espoused by explicitly racist groups like the Ku Klux Klan and the National Front in Britain—seems to us to be an attempt to keep the formerly unquestioned (or barely questioned) subjective coherence of "whiteness" alive. See for example Michael Billig, "Patterns of Racism: Interviews With National Front Members," *Race and Class*, Vol. 20, no. 2 (Autumn 1978) pp. 161–179.

6. The Great Transformation

1. By *racism* we mean those social projects which create or reproduce structures of domination based on essentialist categories of race. The concept of racism is discussed extensively in Chapter 4.
2. This phrase, of course, is Karl Polanyi's term for the introduction of market society in pre-capitalist England. We have appropriated it, with apologies to Polanyi, to indicate the epochal character of the shift to a *socially* based politics in the contemporary U.S.
3. David Edgar, "Reagan's Hidden Agenda: Racism and the New Right," *Race and Class*, Vol. 22, no. 3 (Winter 1981) p. 222.
4. See Chapter 1 for more detailed discussion of this point.
5. Nathan Glazer, *Affirmative Discrimination: Ethnic Inequality and Public Policy* (New York: Basic, 1975) p. 3.
6. Use of the term "elite" is not meant pejoratively. Although the prewar civil rights movement included some episodes of "direct action" and mass mobilization (notably during Reconstruction and in the aftermath of World War I—e.g., the Garvey movement) these were infrequent and antagonistic to moderate programs. Reform strategies concentrated, for reasons of necessity, on lobbying, use of the courts, and appeals to enlightened whites, tactics which depend on knowledgeable elites for leadership and render mass participation counterproductive. In addition, the straitened conditions facing blacks in the prewar period generated a survival-oriented ideology which did not adapt itself well to mass mobilization. For a good history of the black struggle in the 1930s, see Nancy J. Weiss, *Farewell to the Party of Lincoln: Black Politics in the Age of FDR* (Princeton: Princeton University Press, 1983).
7. Douglas McAdam, *Political Process and the Development of Black Insurgency* (Chicago: University of Chicago Press, 1984).
8. Aldon D. Morris, *The Origins of the Civil Rights Movement: Black Communities Organizing for Change* (New York: Free Press, 1984).
9. For representative statements, see Robert A. Dahl, *Pluralist Democracy in the*

United States (Chicago: Rand McNally, 1967); Arnold Rose, *The Power Structure* (New York: Oxford University Press, 1967). Good critiques are Theodore J. Lowi, *The End of Liberalism* (New York: Norton, 1969); Peter Bachrach and Morton Baratz, *Power and Poverty* (New York: Oxford University Press, 1970); Steven Lukes, *Power: A Radical View* (London: Macmillan, 1974).

10. Southern loyalty to the Democrats was assured by the national Party's acquiescence in segregation, and specifically in the disenfranchisement of southern blacks.

11. *Rearticulation* is a practice of discursive reorganization or reinterpretation of ideological themes and interests already present in the subjects' consciousness, such that these elements obtain new meanings or coherence. This practice is ordinarily the work of "intellectuals." Those whose role is to interpret the social world for given subjects—religious leaders, entertainers, schoolteachers, etc.—may on this account be "intellectuals."

12. For a startling and vivid evocation of that rhetorical toolkit, see Zora Neale Hurston, "The Sermon," in idem, *The Sanctified Church* (Berkeley: Turtle Island, 1984).

13. Cornel West, *Prophesy Deliverance! Toward A Revolutionary Afro-American Christianity* (Philadelphia: Westminster, 1982).

14. Robert Moses drew important inspiration from Camus, for example, as noted by Clayborne Carson, *In Struggle: SNCC and the Black Awakening of the 1960s* (Cambridge, MA: Harvard University Press, 1981) p. 46.

15. Eugene Genovese, among others, has argued that religious and cultural forms operating during slavery constituted "pre-political" forms of black resistance. See Genovese, *Roll, Jordan, Roll: the World the Slaves Made* (New York: Pantheon, 1974).

16. Martin Luther King, Jr., quoted in Harvard Sitkoff, *The Struggle for Black Equality* (New York: Hill and Wang, 1981) p. 61.

17. See for example Julius Lester, *Look Out Whitey! Black Power's Gon Get Your Mama!* (New York: Dial, 1968).

18. Quoted in William Julius Wilson, "The Black Community in the 1980s: Questions of Race, Class, and Public Policy," *The Annals of the American Academy of Social and Political Science*, Vol. 454 (March 1981) p. 28.

19. The march had been planned as a unified effort to demonstrate black and liberal support for national civil rights legislation. The SNCC speaker, John Lewis, was forced to censor his remarks by white and black moderates, but even the rewritten speech contrasted sharply with the self-congratulatory tone of the rest of the event:

> The party of Kennedy is also the party of Eastland . . . the party of Javits is also the party of Goldwater. Where is our party?

(Quoted in Carson, *In Struggle*, p. 94.)

20. The white violence culminated a month after the campaign's end in the bombing of the 16th Street Baptist Church (September 15, 1963), which killed four black children in the institution which had been the center of the Birmingham movement. Sources on Birmingham are numerous. A few good ones are David Lewis, *King: A Critical Biography* (New York: Praeger, 1970) pp. 171–209; Martin Luther King, Jr., *Why We Can't Wait* (New York: Signet, 1964); Stanley B. Greenberg, *Race and State in Capitalist Development* (New Haven: Yale University Press, 1980) pp. 235–242; Aldon D. Morris, *The Origins of the Civil Rights Movement*, pp. 229–274.

21. At first promised and then denied white liberal support, the MFDP challengers left the convention profoundly disillusioned. On the MFDP, see Clayborne Carson, *In Struggle*, pp. 108–109, 123–129, 185–186.

22. The "long hot summers" of the middle 1960s were viewed by many blacks (and by the U.S. police at all levels) as a proto-revolutionary situation. Many activists saw the black underclass as "voting with shopping carts," taking what was deservedly theirs, and accelerating the unacceptably slow pace of reform. Moderates, by contrast, questioned the effectiveness of disruption and argued that riots discredited efforts to achieve political reforms. In retrospect we may discount the more extreme claims made by all sides during these years, but during the 1967–1968 period alone, some 384 "racial disorders" were recorded in 298 cities, and these can hardly be considered as unrelated to the atmosphere of black protest which after 1964 engulfed the nation, not just the South. (Data are from McAdam, *Political Process*, p. 227.) Other good sources are Joe R. Feagin and Harlan Hahn, *Ghetto Revolts: The Politics of Violence in America's Cities* (New York: Macmillan, 1973); James W. Button, *Black Violence* (Princeton: Princeton University Press, 1978); Frances Fox Piven and Richard A. Cloward, *Poor People's Movements: Why They Succeed, How They Fail* (New York: Vintage, 1979) pp. 248, 272–273. It should be remembered that measurements and statistics are notoriously unreliable on the subject of riots. For the moderate response, see Bayard Rustin, "The Lessons of the Long Hot Summer," *Commentary* (October 1967); Lewis M. Killian, *The Impossible Revolution, Phase II: Black Power and the American Dream* (New York: Random House, 1975).

23. This trend was most spectacularly demonstrated by the appearance in the national spotlight of George Wallace, the arch-segregationist Governor of Alabama. "Backlash" also took the form of white counterdemonstrations and violence against civil rights marches. Many movement radicals viewed white resistance (especially white resistance in the North) as decisive proof that nonviolent strategy was ineffective in its efforts to lead not only blacks but whites toward greater racial equality and harmony. The "backlash" phenomenon, and Wallace in particular, are considered in greater depth in Chapter 7, below.

24. On March 7th, some 2000 marchers had been ferociously attacked on the Pettus Bridge at Selma. For good analyses of the complexities of the Selma situation, which many see as the point at which southern intransigence was finally ruptured, see Carson, *In Struggle*, pp. 157–162; Lewis, *King*, especially pp. 375–381; David Garrow, *Protest at Selma: Martin Luther King, Jr. and the Voting Rights Act of 1965* (New Haven: Yale University Press, 1978).

25. Many commentators date the black power phase of the movement from the "Meredith march" of June 1966, though this is clearly a somewhat arbitrary periodization.

26. Roy Wilkins, quoted in Robert Allen, *Black Awakening in Capitalist America: An Analytic History* (New York: 1970) p. 78.

27. See Nathan Glazer and Daniel P. Moynihan, *Beyond the Melting Pot* (Cambridge, MA: MIT Press, 1970) p. x.

28. Allen, *Black Awakening*, p. 50; see also Stokely Carmichael and Charles V. Hamilton, *Black Power: The Politics of Liberation in America* (New York: Vintage, 1967) p. 44.

29. See Chapter 7, below.

30. Carmichael and Hamilton certainly did not burn their moderate bridges. Robert Allen wrote that *Black Power* " . . . was largely an essay in liberal reformism . . . ," (Allen, *Black Awakening*, p. 247) a judgment based on the authors' lack of a "revolutionary" political program. The book is better interpreted as one of the first postwar efforts—after those of Cruse and Malcolm X—to understand black oppression in a global context. The authors wish to break with the ethnicity paradigm, but not with the mainstream aspirations of U.S. blacks.

31. James Boggs, *Racism and Class Struggle* (New York: Monthly Review Press, 1970).

32. See his speech, "The Ballot or the Bullet," in *Malcolm X Speaks* (New York: Grove, 1966).

33. See George Breitman, ed., *The Last Year of Malcolm X* (New York: Pathfinder, 1967).

34. Malcolm's chief bodyguard was later revealed to be a police agent.

35. See John Brown Childs, "Afro-American Intellectuals and the People's Culture," *Theory and Society* 13 (1984).

36. Some good sources here are Mark Naison, *Communists in Harlem During the Depression* (Urbana: University of Illinois Press, 1983); Cedric J. Robinson, *Black Marxism: The Making of the Black Radical Tradition* (London: Zed, 1983).

37. See Allen, *Black Awakening*, pp. 153–164, 210–238.

38. Elsewhere in this work we have referred to the "trajectory" of movement/state relationships (see Chapter 5, for example). In respect to the racial history of the postwar period, we understand this trajectory to include both the

encounter discussed here—a "rising phase," so to speak, of the racial minority movements—and that considered in the following chapter as a period of "reaction." See Chapter 7, below.

39. This formulation derives from Marxist state theory. The state provides a political framework for interest concertation—understood in the traditional economically determined meaning of classes, of course, but this is not important for our argument here—which is unavailable to particularistic interests interacting directly. For present purposes the state may be seen as the institutions, policies, conditions, and through which the racial order is organized, enforced, and transformed. For an erudite reading of the Marxist literature on the "factor of cohesion" formulation, see Bob Jessop, *The Capitalist State* (New York: New York University Press, 1982, pp. 16–20. These points are considered in more detail in Chapter 5, above.

40. Two good sources here are Allen, *Black Awakening*; Manning Marable, "Black Nationalism in the 1970s: Through the Prism of Race and Class," *Socialist Review* 50/51 (March–June 1980). See also the concluding section of this chapter.

41. Radical black organizations like SNCC opposed the war, while moderate groups like the Urban League supported it.

42. Huntington has analyzed the black movement as an "ideals vs. institutions" conflict. He dates the onset of this new upsurge from the Greensboro student sit-ins of February, 1960, which seems to us too late. See Samuel P. Huntington, *American Politics: The Promise of Disharmony* (Cambridge, MA: Harvard University Press, 1978).

43. See Chapter 5, above.

44. Consider the transformation of the United Farmworkers into an organized lobbying group for Agricultural Labor Relations Act passage and enforcement, which tended to weaken the Union's ability to mobilize a national support network, and diverted it from servicing and organizing farmworker members.

45. For example a SNCC worker's 1962 letter to President Kennedy: "The people of Ruleville . . . wonder why protection can be given to people 6000 miles away and not be given to American citizens in the South." (Charles McLaurin, cited in Carson, p. 85).

46. The CRS was later to be transformed once again into an *agent-provocateur* center. See Pat Bryant, "Justice vs. the Movement," *Southern Exposure,* Vol. 8, No. 2 (Summer 1980) pp. 79–80.

47. James O'Connor, "The Democratic Movement in the United States," *Kapitalistate* No. 7 (1978); Robert R. Alford and Roger Friedland, "Political Participation and Social Policy," *Annual Review of Sociology* 1975.

48. None of these currents is by any means exclusive. Specific perspectives often contain elements of more than one current. Internal colonialism, for exam-

ple, can be expressed in nationalist or socialist terms. The categories we employ are "ideal types"—they permit the classification of diverse tendencies for analytical purposes.

49. See Rodolfo Acuña's account of the LRUP's trajectory in *Occupied America: A History of Chicanos*, 2nd. ed. (New York: Harper and Row, 1981) pp. 387–391; see also Mario Barrera, "The Historical Evolution of Chicano Ethnic Goals" (MS, 1984), pp. 31–32; David Montejano, "The Demise of 'Jim Crow' for Texas Mexicans, 1940–1970" (ms, 1984), pp. 30–34; John Shockley, *Chicano Revolt in a Texas Town* (Notre Dame: Notre Dame University Press, 1974).

50. See Carson, *In Struggle*, pp. 167–168.

51. The history of minority Marxism-Leninism was interesting as an organizational process. Several of the currently active M-L organizations with substantial minority membership—for example, the League for Revolutionary Struggle, the Communist Workers Party—were formed when racially exclusive groups merged and composed "multiracial" organizations, parties or "pre-parties." The LRS, for example, was formed by a merger of the I Wor Kuen, an Asian American (largely Chinese American) group, with the August Twentyninth Movement, a largely Chicano group. Other M-L organizations began as white "new left" groups and later incorporated substantial numbers of minority members: the Revolutionary Communist Party, Communist Labor Party, and the Democratic Workers Party. By the late 1980s, many of these groups were quite defunct. (This brief survey does not take into account the "old left" groups which can also stake a claim on Marxism-Leninism, such as the Communist Party or Socialist Workers Party; the CP, which traditionally had significant minority membership, has lost much of it in party schisms of the late 1980s and early 1990s. Nor do we discuss here the various social democratic currents).

52. The first "stage" is the creation of a multiclass united front to liberate the colony; the second "stage" is the subsequent pursuit of socialist reconstruction and, presumably, class struggle. The internal colonialist orientation of the 1960s was often explicitly Maoist, as were many other Marxisms of the period.

53. Land struggles were most strenuously pursued by the *Alianza Federal de Mercedes*, founded in 1963 by Reies Lopez Tijerina. The *Alianza* (later renamed *La Confederación de Pueblos Libres*) sought to restore lands originally held by Mexican Americans in northern New Mexico under grants dating from the conquest, and built upon regional traditions of struggle dating from the 19th century. See Reies Lopez Tijerina, *Mi Lucha Por La Tierra* (Mexico, DF: Fondo de Cultura Economica, 1978); Peter Nabokov, *Tijerina and the Courthouse Raid* (Albuquerque: University of New Mexico Press, 1969). Tijerina's politics have been the subject of some debate. His

personalistic and confrontational style and his focus on the tactics of land occupation place him in a venerable Mexican revolutionary tradition. But Tijerina built upon and altered this legacy in the attempt to address modern U.S. conditions. He ran for Governor of New Mexico in 1968, joined Martin Luther King, Jr.'s Poor People's Crusade, and espoused a Pan American and Third Worldist revolutionary philosophy. After extensive harassment, Tijerina was jailed in 1969, and his movement dispersed.

54. Important regional distinctions also affect Mexican American politics in the Southwest. Andrés Jimenez identifies four regions—the lower Rio Grande valley (incorporating the frontier zone with the Mexican states of Nuevo Leon, Tamaulipas, and Coahuila), the upper Rio Grande corridor (extending from the state of Chihuahua north into New Mexico), the Arizona area (incorporating the frontier with the state of Sonora), and California (including the Baja California border area)—each with its particular history of political development, incorporation in the U.S. (and global) economy, and cultural traditions. This obviously leaves aside important concentrations such as Colorado, the Pacific Northwest, and the Midwest. Chicago today is one of the largest "Mexican" cities in the world. (Andrés Jimenez, personal communication, July 10, 1985).

55. For the 19th century heritage, see Acuña, *Occupied America*; Matt S. Meier and Feliciano Rivera, *The Chicanos: A History of Mexican Americans* (New York: Hill and Wang, 1972) pp. 54–95; Mario Barrera, *Race and Class in the Southwest* (Notre Dame: University of Notre Dame Press, 1979). Interestingly, Barrera suggests that "The system of colonial labor appears to have been based on racial rather than ethnic distinctions," (ibid., p. 49) which is consistent with our argument (in Chapter 3, above) that a racial logic structured North American colonialism and was not merely an outcome of that system.

56. Groups such as the Brown Berets, The Crusade for Justice, *El Movimiento Estudiantil Chicanos de Aztlán* (MECHA), and the Mexican American Youth Organization (MAYO) originated at this time. Though asserting their *Chicanismo*, most groups adopted a Mexicanized political style, setting forth their demands in *Planes*, for example. MECHA enunciated its program in *El Plan de Santa Barbara*; Rodolfo "Corky" Gonzales launched *El Plan Espiritual de Aztlán* at a Chicano Youth Conference held in Denver in 1969. Many other groups developed their demands in this manner. See Barrera, "The Historical Evolution . . . ," pp. 27–31; Acuña, *Occupied America*, pp. 357–360.

57. "Commitment to the struggle for Chicano Liberation is the operative definition of the ideology used here. Chicanismo involves a crucial distinction in political consciousness between a Mexican American and a Chicano mentality. The Mexican American is a person who lacks respect for his (sic) cultural and ethnic heritage. Unsure of himself, he seeks assimilation

as a way out of his "degraded" social status. . . . In contrast, Chicanismo reflects self-respect and pride in one's ethnic and cultural background. . . . Mexican Americans must be viewed as potential Chicanos. . . . Chicano Liberation is a means of total Chicano liberation." ("El Plan de Santa Barbara," quoted ibid, p. 34.)

58. These conflicts often revealed important class dimensions within Asian American communities—dimensions which were played up by Marxist-Leninist groups and played down by "entrists" and more moderate nationalists. For example, Asian entrepreneurs were sometimes branded an indigenous "national" bourgeoisie, whose "class interests" conflicted with those of other class forces.

59. *El Grito, Aztlán, El Tecolote*, and *La Raza* were some of these.

60. Paul Wong notes: "The most widely accepted slogans in the white antiwar movement have been 'Give peace a chance' and 'Bring the G.I.'s home.' The Asian-American movement, in contrast, emphasized the *racist* nature of the war, using such slogans as 'Stop killing *our* Asian brothers and sisters,' and 'We don't want *your* racist war.' Paul Wong, "The Emergence of the Asian-American Movement," *Bridge*, Vol. 2, no. 1 (September/October 1972) pp. 35–36.

61. Republican "entrism" has also come into being among minorities long considered to be in the Democratic column, especially since the election of Reagan.

62. Some campaigns led by community organizations continued into the 1970s with varying degrees of success. In San Antonio, where the Communities Organized for Public Service (COPS) was active, a moderate Chicano mayor was eventually elected with a strong community base. Local organizing by Chicano moderates has also continued to flourish or at least survive in Los Angeles and Denver.

63. Of a voluminous literature, see for example Guillermo Flores, "Internal Colonialism and Racial Minorities in the U.S.: An Overview," in Frank Bonilla and Robert Girling, eds., *Structures of Dependency* (Stanford, CA: Stanford University Press, 1973); Robert Blauner, *Racial Oppression in America* (New York: Harper and Row, 1972) pp. 82–110; see also Chapter 3, above.

64. See Chapter 3, above.

65. Consider the history of Indian education, for example, or the perverse hyper-patriotism of the "relocation camps"—Manzanar, Tule Lake, Gila River— in which Japanese Americans were imprisoned during World War II.

66. The internal colonialism framework made more sense in dealing with relatively homogeneous concentrations of minorities, for example New York's Ocean Hill-Brownsville and Bedford-Stuyvesant ghettos (both heavily black), or South Bronx (Puerto Rican). It was less useful where given minority

groups were insufficiently concentrated geographically, or where minority communities were more heterogeneous. Homogeneity, of course, is never more than relative. See Chapter 1, above.

67. See for example Carlos Moore, "Marxism: A Prolet-Aryan Outlook," *Berkeley Journal of Sociology*, Vol. XIX (1974-1975).

7. Race and Reaction

1. *San Francisco Chronicle*, 8 March 1985.
2. In April 1985, the black unemployment rate was 16.3 percent compared to the overall unemployment rate of 7.3 percent. (Department of Labor, Bureau of Labor Statistics). The Center on Budget and Policy Priorities reported that the poverty rate among blacks is almost 36 percent, the highest proportion sice 1968. The Center also noted that while long-term unemployment among whites has increased by 1.5 percent since 1980, among blacks it has increased by 72 percent (cited in Roger Wilkins, "Smiling Racism," *The Nation*, 3 November 1984). For a more recent analysis of an essentially unchanged pattern of racialized poverty, see Gerald D. Jaynes and Robin M. Williams, Jr., eds., *A Common Destiny: Blacks and American Society* (Washington, DC: National Academy Press, 1989) pp. 277–291.
3. Barry Bluestone and Bennett Harrison, *The Deindustrialization of America: Plant Closings, Community Abandonment, and the Dismantling of Basic Industry* (New York: Basic Books, 1982).
4. Howard J. Sherman, *Stagflation* (New York: Harper and Row, 1976).
5. James O'Connor, *The Fiscal Crisis of the State* (New York: St. Martin's Press, 1973).
6. "The advantages for the U.S. of this dollar-based system were formidable. Essentially, it created a unique, built-in demand for dollars, independent of the demand for U.S. products. This need for dollars meant the U.S. could buy more than it sold abroad without fearing that the oversupply of dollars would cause the value of the dollar to drop. U.S. multinationals and banks were in a strong position to invest abroad, since the dollars they were spending were in such demand. This in turn encouraged U.S. military expansion worldwide by allowing the U.S. to keep spending the money needed to support its troops overseas. In short, it was precisely through the enthronement of the dollar at Bretton Woods that the U.S. was able to finance the postwar Pax Americana." ("Bretton Woods: The Rise and Fall of an International Monetary Sytem," *Dollars & Sense* 102 [December 1984].) See also Fred Block, *The Origins of International Economic Disorder* (Berkeley: University of California Press, 1977).
7. In 1984 the U.S. trade deficit with Canada was $20 billion, second only to the nation's $37 billion deficit with Japan. In spite of this, Americans did not harbor negative attitudes towards Canada.

8. Republican Senator John Heinz during a Congressional debate over U.S.-Japan trade relations stated that "In category after category they [the Japanese] are slicing us neatly and thinly off like a piece of sushimi [sic], which they so elegantly do." At a March 8, 1985 hearing, Sen. Heinz noted that when the "Japanese get their little fork into us—or chopsticks . . . they really do stick it to us."

   During a March 20, 1985 hearing, Democratic Senator Ernest Hollings said the Japanese "love all those bowings—they have been doing that for twenty-five years and getting away with it." Cited in *Hokubei Mainichi*, April 16, 1985.

9. Laura Chin and Ada Kan, *Where We Stand in America: A Report on Anti-Asian Violence and Anti-Foreign Sentiments* (Washington, D.C.: The Organization of Chinese Americans, Inc., August 1984). In 1982 Vincent Chin, a Chinese American man was beaten to death in Detroit by a laid-off plant foreman and his stepson who mistook their victim for Japanese and blamed him for the loss of their jobs. The incident further outraged Asian American communities when Wayne County Circuit Court Judge Charles Kaufman allowed the two men to plead guilty to manslaughter (the original charge had been second-degree murder), placed them on three years' probation, and fined them $3,780 each.

10. "Illegal aliens" are equated with "Mexicans" or the "brown flood" in general, even though undocumented workers from Mexico constitute at most 60 percent of the "illegal population." It is estimated that of the 1,086,000 undocumented workers in California between 1970 and 1980, 589,000 were from Mexico. See Thomas Muller, *The Fourth Wave: California's Newest Immigrants* (Washington, DC: The Urban Institute Press, 1984). Despite the numbers, the U.S. Immigration and Naturalization Service directs its enforcement activities at Mexicans. More than 90 percent of arrests of "illegal aliens" are made at the border with Mexico. See Ann Cooper, "Hazy Numbers Complicate the Debate Over How to Slow Illegal Immigration," *National Journal*, 8 June 1985.

11. A Gallup poll conducted in May 1980 revealed that 91 percent of the people interviewed felt that *all* immigration to the U.S. should be halted until the national unemployment rate dropped to 5 percent.

12. See, among a host of similar works, Charles Murray, *Losing Ground: American Social Policy 1950–1980* (New York: Basic Books, Inc., 1984). For a good critical review of Murray's work, see Sar A. Levitan's review in *Society*, Vol. 22, no. 4 (May–June 1985); see also the debate between Murray and Levitan in *Political Science Quarterly*, Vol. 100, no. 3 (Fall 1985).

13. David Edgar has suggested that, "California's tax-cutting referendum Prop. 13 was as much a vote against black welfare as it was a vote for lower taxes." David Edgar, "Reagan's Hidden Agenda: Racism and the New Amer-

ican Right," *Race & Class*, Vol. XXII, no. 3 (Winter 1981) p. 231.

14. In 1982, Metzger ran for the U.S. Senate in the Democratic primary and placed fourth in a field of eleven candidates, garnering 73,987 votes. Bill Wallace, "Racist Group Using Computers and TV to Recruit in Bay Area," *San Francisco Chronicle*, 5 March 1985.

15. "Violence on the Right," *Newsweek*, 4 March 1985, p. 25.

16. Note the ecological language. Some far right groups, perhaps via survivalism, are rearticulating environmentalist themes. The original notion of race-mixing, which occasionally used similar terms, was not nearly as holistic or totalizing. Its frame of reference was eugenicist (i.e., Darwinian) or even Linnaean/Aristotelian.

17. "Jesus Christ Christian" means rejection of the Jewishness of Jesus, an important interpretation for far right antisemites.

18. *Newsweek*, 4 March 1985, p. 25.

19. Tom Metzger himself has suggested this: " . . . the only time you can get a white person's attention, a working person, is when things get tight. Then you can get him to sit down and listen. While he's got his beer, and got his dune buggy, and everything's going good, and he's got a job, he won't listen to you. Once things start to get tight, he starts looking around, what's the problem, and then you can get a foot in the door." ABC News Closeup, "Wounds from Within" with Marshall Frady, broadcast 18 Oct. 1981.

20. Bruce Maxwell, "Radical Rightist Groups Feed on Rural Despair," *San Francisco Examiner*, 5 March 1985.

21. Ethnic, class, national, and religious dimensions of "whiteness" have all been explored by the far right.

22. ABC News Closeup, "Wounds from Within."

23. Vincent Ryan, managing editor of the far-right publication *The Spotlight* said his paper's circulation has been cut almost in half, to 166,000, without "a Carter to push around." *Newsweek*, op. cit.

24. Sara Diamond, "Neo-Nazis in America," *The Daily Californian*, 30 April 1985. More recent confirmation of both this trend and the countertrend of "mainstreaming" neo-Nazis on the new right can be found in James Ridgeway, *Blood in the Face: The Ku Klux Klan, Aryan Nations, Nazi Skinheads, and the Rise of a New Right Culture* (New York: Thunder's Mouth Press, 1990); Elinor Langer, "The American Neo-Nazi Movement Today," *The Nation*, 16/23 July 1990; Julia Reed, "His Brilliant Career," *The New York Review of Books*, 19 April 1992.

25. Jeff Bale says that "highly visible hate groups like the Klan and Aryan nations serve to *distract* attention away from the far more dangerous activities of the 'respectable' authoritarians in positions of real power." Quoted in Diamond, "Neo-Nazis in America."

26. Ironically the only other analogy in recent U.S. history comes from the far

left. The Weather Underground, the SLA, and the Black Liberation Army have played a similar role as "fringe groups" in American politics.

27. Walter Dean Burnham, "Post-Conservative America," *Socialist Review* 72 (November-December 1983) p. 125.

28. Of particular importance was the feminist movement which critiqued the patriachial family, inequities in sex/gender relations, and women's lack of control over their own bodies.

29. Gillian Peele, *Revival & Reaction: The Right in Contemporary America* (Oxford: Oxford University Press, 1984) p. 52.

30. Alan Crawford, *Thunder on the Right: The "New Right" and the Politics of Resentment* (New York: Pantheon Books, 1980) p. 5.

31. The collapse of the family and the decline of traditional values and forms of authority are often cited by the new right as the causes of domestic ills and the decline of the American hegemony in the world. The new right's agenda is therefore filled with anti-abortion platforms, school prayer amendments, and other "pro-family" issues.

32. See Lillian Rubin, *Busing and Backlash* (Berkeley: University of California Press, 1972).

33. More complex scientistic ideologies of racial inferiority are a different matter, and here the new right is actively engaged. See Leon Kamin, Richard Lewontin, and Stephen Rose, *Not In Our Genes* (New York: Pantheon, 1984)) for an excellent account of the modern application of biologism to social and political categories such as race.

34. As a young Alabama politician, Wallace was seen as something of a moderate. But after losing a close election early in his career he made a public vow to "never be outniggered again." He then rose to his second last stand, when as Governor of Alabama in 1962 he "stood in the schoolhouse door" to prevent integration. His third incarnation, as Presidential candidate, required him to moderate his white supremacy and to experiment with "code words." His fourth and current identity, which appeared in the aftermath of the Voting Rights Act and of a 1972 assassination attempt, is once again "moderate."

35. Kevin Phillips, *The Emerging Republican Majority* (New York: Anchor, 1970).

36. Conservative egalitarianism was the principle advocated by ethnicity theorists (of whom Moynihan was a leading personage) in policy matters. Ethnicity theory, as we have argued above (Chapter 1) was and remains the dominant racial theory in the U.S.

37. The "Republicanized" version of minority politics strictly distinguished between moderate and radical features of the 1960s racial movements. Those that had challenged such anachronistic and inessential forms of racial inequality as legalized segregation and discriminatory employment practices (i.e.,

explicit discrimination against individuals) were easily jettisoned. Those features of the minority movements that had questioned the role of race in shaping the U.S. social structure, however, were rejected and marginalized. Collective demands, "institutionalized racism": these issues the Republicans opposed or ignored.

38. See Burnham, "Post-Conservative America."

39. The charge of "secular humanism" is directed at liberals in general, and the welfare state in particular, mainly by new right activists oriented to Protestant fundamentalism. The chief complaint seems to be that liberal (and radical) ideologies have desacralized morality, placing "values" on the same rationalistic terrain as politics, and subjecting them to the "culture of critical discourse." There are also important ties between the critique of "secular humanism" and new right/neoconservative hostility to the "new class" of knowledge workers. For an academically based statement of this critique, see Peter L. Berger, "The Worldview of the New Class: Secularity and Its Discontents," in B. Bruce Briggs, ed., *The New Class?* (New Brunswick, New Jersey: Transaction, 1979), p. 50; the concept of a "culture of critical discourse" fundamental to the ideology of the "new class" originates in Alvin Gouldner's *The Future of Intellectuals and the Rise of the New Class* (New York: Seabury, 1979). Gouldner's perspective, of course, is quite different from that of the right-wing "new class" theorists.

40. Crawford, *Thunder on the Right*, pp. 311–312.

41. Ibid., p. 5.

42. The concept of "status revolution" has its origins in the liberal historian Richard Hofstadter's rejection of the class-based categories of Charles Beard and others whose work on U.S. social movements had reached its high point in the 1930s. See Hofstadter, *The Age of Reform: From Bryan to FDR*, 2nd. ed. (New York: Alfred A. Knopf, 1965).

43. Crawford, *Thunder on the Right*, p. 148.

44. Linda Gordon and Allen Hunter, "Sex, Family and the New Right: Anti-Feminism as a Political Force," *Radical America*, Vol 11, no. 6 & Vol. 12, no. 1 (November 1977-February 1978) p. 12. See also Jonathan Rieder, *Canarsie: The Jews and Italians of Brooklyn Against Liberalism* (Cambridge, MA: Harvard University Press, 1985).

45. Rowland Evans and Robert Novak, "Ed Davis, Toned-Down Favorite," *Washington Post*, 3 February 1978 cited in Crawford, *Thunder on the Right*, p. 104.

46. The term "third world state" is from Phillips who uses it to describe states which have an increasing racial minority population. Phillips writes, "Retention of the Electoral College would probably guarantee a minority-oriented presidential selection process for the 1980s." Kevin Phillips, "Abolish the

Electoral College!," cited in ibid, p. 324.

47. These charges had their origins in the FBI's campaigns to discredit King, in which Robert Kennedy was also involved.

48. Patrick J. Buchanan, "GOP Vote Search Should Bypass Ghetto," cited in ibid, p. 258.

49. Ibid, p. 145.

50. William Rusher, *The Making of a New Majority Party* (Ottawa, Ill.: Greenhill Publications, 1975) p. 31.

51. We also wonder if the "liberal verbalist elite" is not implicitly Jewish.

52. Gordon and Hunter, "Sex, Family, and the New Right," p. 11.

53. Certain left groups allied themselves with the antibusing forces, arguing that the issue was one of class, rather than race. See the articles in *Radical America*, Vol. 8, no. 6 (1974), and Vol. 9, no. 3 (1975).

54. In attempting to portray diversity, the nearly absolute attention which textbooks had formerly paid whites had perhaps been "diluted," though hardly to the extent some groups claimed. Interestingly, a study by the National Council of Teachers in 1978 found that parent protesters were most concerned with books that presented attitudes and lifestyles of those of "different" cultural backgrounds. See Crawford, *Thunder on the Right*, pp. 155–58.

55. Lyndon B. Johnson, "To Fulfill These Rights," delivered at Howard University on June 4, 1965; in Lee Rainwater and William L. Yancey, *The Moynihan Report and the Politics of Controversy* (Cambridge, MA: MIT Press, 1967) p. 125.

56. Nathan Glazer, "The Peoples of America," *Ethnic Dilemmas, 1964–1982* (Cambridge, MA: Harvard University Press, 1983) p. 27. This, of course, was the underside of the ideal of tolerance: implicit threats toward groups that failed to conform. It was precisely these kinds of formulations which led blacks to mistrust white liberals and to preserve "group interests."

57. Glazer, *Affirmative Discrimination*, p. 220.

58. Glazer even went so far as to suggest that if affirmative action programs were effective he might support them out of pragmatic commitment to equality.

> For me, no consideration of principle—such as that merit should be rewarded, or that governmental programs should not discriminate on the grounds of race or ethnic group—would stand in the way of a program of preferential hiring if it made some substantial progress in reducing the severe problems of the low-income black population and of the inner cities" (ibid., p. 73).

59. A typical polemic is Morris Abram, "What Constitutes a Civil Right?" *New*

York Times Magazine, 10 June 1984. In a thoughtful reconceptualization, Lewis M. Killian argues that "From its inception, the Civil Rights movement was fundamentally and unrelentingly 'assimilationist.'" On the other hand, "Black power treated Blacks in the United States as a community, not as a category of individual Americans handicapped and stigmatized on the basis of their color." This distinction corresponds to our argument that the civil rights movement operated largely within the dominant *ethnicity* paradigm of race, while black power broke with the dominant view, invoking the *nation-based* paradigm (and to a lesser extent, the class-based) paradigms of race. If this distinction is recognized, neoconservatism emerges clearly as a reaction to the radical currents of the "great transformation," an attempt to confine racially based demands to an ethnicity-oriented model of politics. See Killian, "Black Power and White Reactions: The Revitalization of Race-Thinking in the United States," *The Annals of The American Academy of Political and Social Sciences* 454 (March, 1981) pp. 43, 47.

60. Abram, "What Constitutes a Civil Right?" p. 60. Of course, many opponents of affirmative action are also "right-to-work" advocates who find the same kinds of faults with the labor laws that those who charge "reverse discrimination" do with affirmative action. At the heart of the right-wing agenda, as James O'Connor has recently argued, is always an ideology of individualism. See O'Connor, *Accumulation Crisis* (New York: Blackwell, 1984).

61. Philip Green, *The Pursuit of Inequality* (New York: Pantheon, 1981).

62. The key work here is Glazer's, particularly *Affirmative Discrimination*, and the later essays in *Ethnic Dilemmas*. Many of the interpretive essays in the massive *Harvard Encyclopedia of American Ethnic Groups* (Cambridge, MA: Harvard University Press, 1982) also share the neoconservative perspective.

63. In our view this threat reflected not so much the radical nature of the 1960s minority upsurge or the reforms it won, but indeed their fundamentally moderate and half-hearted character. A more comprehensive series of reforms, for example, might have extended to redistribution initiatives and full employment commitments, which could have cushioned the blow that whites located in marginal neighborhoods, school districts, jobs, etc. received when affirmative action and similar programs increased competition for semi-skilled work, public education, and affordable housing. But as it was, the threat was real enough.

64. As Rieder demonstrates, however, white ethnic appeals to "fairness" often segue into overt racism, especially as the perceived threats to community, family, and "way of life" increase. For one example among many provided in this work, see Rieder, *Canarsie*, p. 245.

65. Cited in Robby Cohen, "Reagan: A 'Neo-Segregationist,'" *The Daily Californian*, 18 October 1984.

66. Ibid.

67. *San Francisco Chronicle*, 18 February 1980. Her remark was made during a telephone conversation with Mr. Reagan broadcast over loudspeakers for the benefit of the diners. Flustered, Ms. Reagan tried to correct herself by saying " . . . all the beautiful black and white people." Unfortunately, there were no blacks in the room. Reported in Michael Kilian, "GOP Genie Rescues Republicans," *Chicago Tribune*, 25 February 1980.

68. "White Men Were Key to Reagan Landslide," *San Francisco Chronicle*, 27 December 1984.

69. Ibid.

70. Kirk made his remarks on February 3 on NBC's "Meet the Press." This may be in direct response to Kevin Phillips' hostile advice to the Democrats:

   If you Democrats do anything, try to get rid of the party's pervasive image of being the vehicle of every kind of cultural, sexual and ethnic fringe group with a letterhead and stationery. Jettisoning special-interest group caucuses would be a start (Cited in J. K. Yamamoto, "Democratic National Committee Chair Questions Need for Asian/Pacific Caucus," *Pacific Citizen*, March 8, 1985).

71. He argued that their persistence was merely a function of a self-serving bureaucracy:

   I think there are, there is a tendency of some individuals who have positions in organizations that have been created for whatever purpose but for some purpose to rectify some ill, that then once that gets going they're reluctant to admit how much they've achieved, because it might reveal then that there's no longer a need for that particular organization, which would mean no longer a need for their job. ("Rights Groups Unneeded, Reagan Says," *Pacific Citizen*, February 1, 1985.)

72. "Justice Dept. Taking A City to Court Over Hiring Quotas," *San Francisco Chronicle*, April 30, 1985.

73. "Race Questions Cut From Federal Forms," *San Francisco Chronicle*, 25 March 1985. "Jerry McMurry, staff director for the housing subcommittee of the House Banking Committee, said the Reagan administration 'would rather not know' the racial composition of its programs so it cannot be challenged on its civil rights record." An early policy recommendation along these lines was the Heritage Foundation report "Agenda '83," a new right blueprint for the President. One of its major points was an attack on affirmative action—"Agenda '83" argued for a challenge to court-ordered quotas in hiring and promotion and for a new definition of discrimination.

74. The bible in this regard is Charles Murray, *Losing Ground*. See also George Gilder, *Wealth and Poverty* (New York: Basic Books, 1981).

75. See Gary Delgado, "Reverse Distribution: Fiscal Crisis and Black Resis-

tance," *Critical Perspectives of Third World America*, Vol. 1, no. 1 (Fall 1983).

76. In contrast to the new racists, Pendletons stated that Reagan supporters were " . . . performing corrective surgery on the disfigured civil rights laws" (*The New York Times*, March 6, 1985).

77. Black's remarks were made in an interview with Haynes Johnson of *The Washington Post*. Cited in Wilkins, "Smiling Racism."

Conclusion

1. At stake was who represented the legitimate voice of "the People." Community activists who were absorbed into the various state-sponsored bureaucracies were derided as "poverty pimps" who had been "coopted" by "the system" and now sought to preserve their jobs and expand their influence by making the community increasingly dependent upon them. College students were faulted for their often sporadic commitment (revolution according to the academic calendar) and their potentially upwardly mobile status. The "lumpenproletariat" was either glorified as the "vanguard" of third world struggles in the U.S. or denounced as criminal elements and/or "street people" with little collective political consciousness.

2. Samuel P. Huntington,"Chapter III—The United States," in Michel Crozier, Samuel P. Huntington, and Joji Watanuki, *The Crisis of Democracy: Report on the Governability of Democracies to the Trilateral Commission* (New York: NYU Press, 1975).

3. Jonathan Rieder, *Canarsie: The Jews and Italians of Brooklyn Against Liberalism* (Cambridge, MA: Harvard University Press, 1985) p. 6; see also Kevin Phillips' newsletter, *The American Political Report* (Bethesda, MD: The American Political Research Group), 17 May 1985, pp. 4–5.

4. Stuart Hall has used this term to characterize the Thatcher regime in Britain; it has obvious resonance on American shores as well. See Hall, "The Great Moving Right Show," *Socialist Review* 55 (January–February 1981).

5. Such a program would probably rearticulate racial theory in terms of a biologistic conception of race which would locate inequality in racial differences themselves. Some preliminary steps have been taken in this direction, for example in the uses of "sociobiology," but intellectual acceptance of a new biologistic racism has thus far not materialized.

6. According to the present version, state antidiscrimination activity is only justified when the practice of intentional discrimination on racial grounds can be demonstrated. This theory, however, still bears the marks of its liberal origins. For example, Nathan Glazer claims that he would favor more extensive state antidiscrimination activity, even in the face of principle, if on pragmatic grounds it could be shown to be effective. See Glazer, *Affirmative Discrimination* (New York: Basic, 1975) p. 73.

7. Orlando Patterson has described this solution with respect to the black com-

munity: "Ideally the proto-fascist scenario calls for the containment of the black poor in concentrated areas and the use of their labor for the menial but essential tasks that will remain even in the most highly advanced, post-industrial utopia: street cleaning and general sanitation, sewage disposal, hospital attendants, the less technical aspects of the transportation industry, and the filthier and more hazardous types of blue collar jobs." He doubts such a scenario could be implemented due to the "counter-leviathan power of the urban poor." Orlando Patterson, "The Black Community: Is There a Future?" in Seymour Martin Lipset, ed., *The Third Century* (Stanford, CA: The Hoover Institution Press, 1979), p. 280–281.

8. This section draws on Howard Winant, "Postmodern Racial Politics in the United States: Difference and Inequality," *Socialist Review* 90/1 (February 1990).

9. The heart of his organizational base, PUSH, in fact employed an updated version of Urban League tactics, pressuring large firms to grant economic concessions (chain restaurant franchises, hiring quotas and set-asides, programs for local community hiring and on the job training, etc.) to blacks under the threat of boycotts and other sanctions. We do not wish to disparage this strategy unduly, for we believe it did accomplish certain incremental changes, but it still must be seen as very moderate—black capitalism, movement-style.

10. Recall that the Jackson campaign had a major beef with the Democratic Party in 1984: the runoff primary system in the South, which in his view limited black electoral chances there.

11. Much of this account draws on the work of Manning Marable, who was one of the few analysts who recognized early on the significance of Jackson's challenge to the Democratic Party. While Marable is not uncritical, he understands the change Jackson represented from Democratic "business as usual." See his *Black American Politics: From the Washington Marches to Jesse Jackson* (London: Verso, 1985). In contrast, Adolph Reed's analysis failed to capture the Jackson campaign's potential for polarizing the party and posing sharply the question of its future direction and constituency. Reed's preoccupation with the lack of in-depth democracy in black politics led him to neglect the insurgent aspects of the 1984 Jackson candidacy, which was in fact an anti-establishment effort not only in the Party overall, but in its black apparatus as well. Reed's focus on elite competition is too narrow. See his *The Jesse Jackson Phenomenon* (New Haven: Yale University Press, 1986).

12. Two books by William J. Wilson, *The Declining Significance of Race: Blacks and Changing American Institutions,* 2nd ed. (Chicago: University of Chicago Press, 1978), and *The Truly Disadvantaged: The Inner City, The Underclass, and Public Policy* (Chicago: University of Chicago Press, 1987), played an important role in catalyzing these debates.

Notes

Epilogue: Closing Pandora's Box—Race and the "New Democrats"

1. Quoted in R. W. Apple Jr., "Riots and Ballots," *The New York Times*, 2 May 1992.
2. For a fuller discussion of the political implications, see Michael Omi and Howard Winant, "The Los Angeles 'Race Riot' and Contemporary U.S. Politics," in Robert Gooding-Williams, ed., *Reading Rodney King, Reading Urban Uprising* (New York and London: Routledge, 1993).
3. Michael Kramer, "Two Ways to Play the Politics of Race," *Time* (18 May 1992); *Business Week*, "Situation Critical But Not Hopeless" (18 May 1992).
4. The exceptions here were of course those few leaders and legislators who represented, or at least identified with, the urban poor, such as Maxine Waters, Congresswoman from South Central L.A.
5. *The New York Times*, "Excerpts From Speech by Bush in Los Angeles," 9 May 1992.
6. Ibid.
7. The term *neoliberalism* has a general meaning which parallels its usage here to apply to Clinton's racial politics. It refers to a newer, refigured conception of the classical political liberalism associated with the mainstream Democratic Party's politics from Roosevelt to Johnson. The refiguring is important as a series of lessons supposedly to be learned from the party's post-1960s losses: not only regarding race, but also involving the Democrats' symbiosis with social movement politics, their affiliation with "big government," etc. Thus a neoliberal politics generally seeks to balance between the conservative orientation adopted by the Republican Party in the Reagan-Bush years, and the legacies of the New Deal and Great Society. See Charles Peters and Philip Keirling, eds., *A New Road for America: The Neoliberal Movement* (New York: Charles Scribner's Sons, 1985).
8. Allan Bloom, *The Closing of the American Mind: How Higher Education Has Failed Democracy and Impoverished the Souls of Today's Students* (New York: Simon and Schuster, 1987); Dinesh D'Souza *Illiberal Education: The Politics of Race and Sex on Campus* (New York: The Free Press, 1991); Roger Kimball, *Tenured Radicals: How Politics Has Corrupted Our Higher Education* (New York: Harper and Row, 1990); Arthur M. Schlesinger, Jr., *The Disuniting of America: Reflections on a Multicultural Society* (New York: W. W. Norton & Co., 1992); Robert Hughes, *Culture of Complaint: The Fraying of America* (New York: Oxford University Press, 1993).
9. On May 4, 1991, President George Bush told students at the University of Michigan that "The notion of political correctness has ignited controversy across the land. And although the movement arises from the laudable desire to sweep away the debris of racism and sexism and hatred, it replaces old

prejudices with new ones." (Quoted in Patricia Aufderheide, ed., *Beyond P.C.: Toward a Politics of Understanding* (Saint Paul, MN: Graywolf Press, 1992) p. 227.)

10. Eugene D. Genovese, "Heresy, Yes—Sensitivity, No," *The New Republic* Vol. 204, no. 15 (15 April 1991); C. Vann Woodward, "Freedom and the Universities," *The New York Review of Books*, 18 July 1991. Todd Gitlin, "From Universality to Difference: Notes on the Fragmentation of the Idea of a Left," *Contention*, Vol 2, no. 2 (Winter 1993).

11. William Julius Wilson, "The Right Message," *The New York Times*, 17 March 1992.

12. William Julius Wilson, *The Truly Disadvantaged: The Inner City, the Underclass, and Public Policy* (Chicago: University of Chicago Press, 1987).

13. Ibid., p. 120.

14. Kathryn M. Neckerman and Joleen Kirschenman, "Hiring Strategies, Racial Bias, and Inner-City Workers," *Social Problems* Vol. 38, no. 4 (Nov. 1991); see also Joe R. Feagin, "The Continuing Significance of Race: Antiblack Discrimination in Public Places," *American Sociological Review* Vol. 56, no. 1 (February 1991).

15. Thomas Byrne Edsall and Mary D. Edsall, *Chain Reaction: The Impact of Race, Rights, and Taxes on American Politics* (New York: W. W. Norton & Co., 1991).

16. In 1988, the percentage of presidential votes cast in the suburbs was 48.3 percent. By contrast, rural areas constituted 22.2 percent of the presidential votes cast, while the central city areas accounted for 29.5 percent (Edsalls, *Chain Reaction*, p. 229).

17. Ibid., p. 231.

18. Governor Bill Clinton and Senator Al Gore, *Putting People First: How We Can All Change America* (New York: Times Books, 1992).

19. A pledge Clinton broke soon after his inauguration. In *Putting People First*, he had promised to "stop the forced repatriation of Haitian refugees," which had been the Bush administration's policy. Clinton continued the policy.

20. Clinton and Gore, *Putting People First*, pp. 64–65.

21. Andrew Hacker, "The Blacks & Clinton," *The New York Review of Books*, Vol. XL, no. 3 (28 January 1993) p. 14. See *The New York Times*, "Excerpts From the Platform: A 'New Covenant' With Americans," 15 July 1992.

22. Tim Rutten, "A New Kind of Riot." *The New York Review of Books*, Vol. XXXIX, no. 11 (11 June 1992) p. 52.

23. This account neglects third candidate H. Ross Perot, who withdrew from the race shortly after the riot, and then reentered several months later. Perot's racial significance was marginal in our view.

24. Andrew Hacker, *Two Nations: Black and White, Separate, Hostile, Unequal*

(New York: Charles Scribner's Sons, 1992); Thomas Byrne Edsall and Mary D. Edsall, *Chain Reaction* (New York: W. W. Norton, 1991); Derrick Bell, *Faces at the Bottom of the Well: The Permanence of Racism* (New York: Basic Books, 1992); Studs Terkel, *Race: How Blacks and Whites Think and Feel About the American Obsession* (New York: The New Press, 1992).

25. Andrew Hacker, *Two Nations*, pp. 134–46.

26. One way Hacker maintains and rationalizes his bi-polar framework is to suggest that some groups, such as Asian Americans, may over time be absorbed into a new expansive definition of what "white" is. See Hacker, *Two Nations*, pp. 9–11.

27. We are indebted to Elaine Kim for this point. For a discussion of the media silencing of Korean Americans in the wake of the L.A. riot, see Elaine Kim, "Home Is Where the Han Is," in Robert Gooding-Williams, ed., *Reading Rodney King, Reading Urban Uprising.*

28. Clint Bolick, "Clinton's Quota Queens," *The Wall Street Journal*, 30 April 1993.

29. R. W. Apple, Jr., "President Blames Himself for Furor Over Nominee," *The New York Times*, 5 June 1993.

30. Quoted in Peter Applebome, "Where Ideas that Hurt Nominee Thrive," *The New York Times*, 5 June 1991.

31. "[President Clinton] . . . said the treatment of blacks and whites as two separate communities in the United States—as 'we and they'—'runs completely counter to all my ideas about a single society.'" (R. W. Apple, "President Blames Himself," p. A8.)

32. David Wellman, *Portraits of White Racism* (New York: Cambridge University Press, 1977) p. 35.

33. We are grateful to Jerry Watts for suggesting some of these points.

34. Debates in the black community over such matters as black conservatism, sexism and homophobia, and the crisis of the family demonstrate this problem. See Cornel West, "The Pitfalls of Racial Reasoning," in Toni Morrison, ed., *Race-ing Justice, En-gendering Power: Essays on Anita Hill, Clarence Thomas, and the Construction of Social Reality* (New York: Pantheon, 1992). A Chicano version of these debates was occasioned by the publication of Richard Rodriguez's autobiography, *Hunger of Memory: The Education of Richard Rodriguez* (Boston: D. R. Godine, 1981).

Index

Abram, Morris, 130, 207n.59, 208n.60
Absorption, racial state and, 86, 106, 138
Acuña, Rodolfo, 80
Affirmative action: social projects and concept of racism, 72–73; and racial reaction of 1970s, 116; neoconservatism and, 128–131; attack on by Reagan revolution, 134, 135, 209n.73; and "right-to-work" advocates, 208n.60
African American studies, 187n.60
Afrocentrism, 59
Agnew, Spiro, 126
Agricultural Labor Relations Act, 198n.44
Agricultural policy, 191n.21
Alianza Federal de Mercedes, 199n.53
All African Peoples Revolutionary Party, 177n.16
Allen, Robert, 103, 177n.27, 197n.25
American Conservative Union, 122
An American Dilemma (Myrdal), 16–18
Antibusing movement, 127
Antistatism, cultural politics of new right, 125–128
Apartheid, 177n.17
Appiah, Kwame Anthony, 181n.5
Aryan Nations, 119
Asian Americans: ethnicity theory and ethnicity among, 23; informal quotas for university admissions, 77–78; racial

categories in 19th-century California, 82; social movements and collective identity, 89; nationalism and community control issues, 109; cultural nationalism and civil rights movement of 1960s, 109–110; recent immigration and divisions within communities, 144; and bipolar model of race, 154, 214n.26; and variations within racial identities, 162n.3; class dimensions among, 201n.58; racist nature of Vietnam War, 201n.60; violence against, 203n.9; Los Angeles riot and, 214n.27. *See also* Japanese Americans
Assimilation and assimilationism: and ethnicity-based paradigm of race, 15, 48; debate with cultural pluralists within ethnic group paradigm, 16–18; and controversy concerning black cultural heritage, 167n.17
Authoritarian populism, 123, 140
Aztlán, 41, 109

Backlash. *See* Racial reaction
Bale, Jeff, 204n.25
Baraka, Imamu Amiri, 41
Bargaining power theory, 30–31
Baron, Harold, 50
Barrera, Mario, 200n.55

Index

Beard, Charles, 206n.42
Becker, Gary, 24, 25, 170n.4
Begue, Brian, 53
Bell, Derrick, 153
Berg, Alan, 118
Berreman, Gerald, 166n.8
Beyond The Melting Pot (Glazer &
  Moynihan), 18
Biologism: as paradigm of race, 14–15;
  racial categories and, 55; Enlightenment
  justifications for racial difference,
  63–64; slavery and, 165n.2; new right
  and scientist ideologies of racial
  inferiority, 205n.33; and rearticulation
  of racial theory in terms of, 210n.5
Birmingham campaign of April–May
  1963, 101, 196n.20
Birth of a Nation (1915 film), 118
Black, Merle, 135
Black capitalism, 124
Black Liberation Army, 205n.26
Black Nation Thesis, 43–44
Black Panther Party, 139
Black power: radicalization of civil rights
  movement, 101–104; and nation-based
  paradigm of race, 208n.59
*Black Power: The Politics of Liberation in
  America* (Hamilton), 103
Blacks: ethnicity theory and ethnicity
  among, 22; as exception to immigrant
  pattern in ethnicity theory, 167n.21. *See
  also* Civil rights movement; Culture;
  Nationalism; Politics; Race; Racism
Blauner, Robert, 45–46, 70–71,
  163–164n.1–2, 179–180n.46–49
Boas, Franz, 65
Boggs, James, 103
Bolick, Clint, 155
Bonacich, Edna, 32–33
Bond, Julian, 107
Bootstraps model, of ethnicity paradigm,
  21–22
Boston busing controversy of 1970s, 127
Bowles, Samuel, 172n.23
Bretton Woods system, 115, 202n.6
Briggs, Cyril, 103
Brown Berets, 200n.56
Buchanan, Patrick J., 126
Burawoy, Michael, 174n.38, 179n.46
Burnham, Walter Dean, 121
Bush, George: and Reagan administration

record on civil rights, 133; on Los
  Angeles riot of 1992, 146, 153; use of
  racial code words, 182n.12; on political
  correctness, 212n.9
Busing, school: new right and racial
  reaction, 127; racial policy of Reagan
  administration, 134
Butler, Richard G., 119

Cabral, Amilcar, 39
California, racial categories, 82
Carmichael, Stokely, 39, 103, 177n.16,
  186n.50, 197n.30
Censorship, new right and textbooks,
  127–128, 207n.54
Census, racial categories in, 3, 162n.5,
  163n.6
Chain Reaction (Edsall), 149–150
Chicago school (sociology), 10
Chicanismo, 109, 200–201n.56–57
Chicano movement: cultural nationalism
  and concept of *Aztlán*, 41; nationalism
  and civil rights movement, 108–109;
  local organizing by moderates, 201n.62.
  See also Hispanic Americans; Latinos;
  Mexican Americans
Chinatowns, 109
Christian fundamentalism, new right and
  backlash politics, 122
Christian-Patriots Defense League, 119
Churches, black, 98, 99
Church of Jesus Christ Christian, 119,
  204n.17
Civil Rights Act (1964), 101, 106, 133
Civil Rights Commission, 140
Civil rights movement: and ethnicity
  paradigm of race, 19, 167–168n.23,
  207–208n.59; Cruse's criticism of, 40;
  evolution of concept of racism, 69;
  racial formation theory and interpretation of, 95–97; emergence of, 97–98;
  and politics of identity, rearticulation,
  and opposition, 99–101; radicalization
  of the black movement, 101–104;
  encountering and reforming the racial
  state, 104–106; challenging paradigms
  and strategic divisions of, 107–112;
  1985 commemoration of in Alabama,
  113; decentering of political unity in
  1980s, 138–139; prewar and postwar
  compared, 194n.6; summers of middle

Index

146–147; progress toward racial since 1965, 157; and neoliberalism, 212n.7

Democratic party: 1948 confrontation between integrationists and segregationists within, 16; origins of new social movement politics, 99; challenge to segregationist delegation at 1964 convention, 101; electoral/institutional entrists and, 110; response to Reagan's success among white male voters, 134; Jackson presidential campaign and, 142–143, 211n.10; racism and Southern loyalty to, 195n.10

Democratic Workers Party, 199n.51

Department of Housing and Urban Development (HUD), 83, 134

Direct-mail solicitation, new right and backlash politics, 122

Discovery, age of and discourse on race, 61–62

Disruptive state interventionism model, class paradigm of race, 26

Doeringer, Peter, 30, 172–173n.26

Dolan, John T., 122

Donovan, Raymond, 134

Du Bois, W. E. B., 36, 38, 39, 65, 108, 184n.32

Economics: class paradigm of race and, 24–35; dislocations of 1970s as context for racial reaction, 114–115; far right and dislocations of 1980s, 119–120; theoretical debate over nature of contemporary, 169n.3

Edgar, David, 97, 203n.13

Edsall, Thomas and Mary, 149–150, 153

Edwards, Richard, 30–32

Electoral college, 126

Electoral districts, social projects and racism, 74

Electoral/institutional entrism, 107, 110, 111

Elite, use of term, 194n.6

Ellison, Ralph, 67

The Emerging Republican Majority (Phillips), 124

Engels, Friedrich, 9, 42

Enlightenment, discourse on race, 63–64

Entrism, electoral/institutional, 107, 110, 111

Essence, race as, 54–55

Essentialism: scientific justifications for racial difference, 64; differentiation of race from racism, 71–72; denial of differences within racial groups, 72; definition of, 181n.6, 187n.57; concept of strategic, 188n.61

Ethnic group, definition of, 14

Ethnicity theory: definition and implications of, 4–5, 12; as paradigm of race, 14–23; nation-based paradigms and critical rejection of, 37; theoretical inadequacies of, 48–50; organization of modern civil rights movement within, 96, 167–168n.23; and neoconservative debate on affirmative action, 128, 129; alliance with neoconservatism and new right, 131–132; challenges to by radical theories of race, 139; resurrection of in 1980s, 141; blacks as exception to immigrant pattern, 167n.21; conservative egalitarianism and, 205n.36

Eugenics movement, 64

Europe, age of discovery and discourse on race, 61–62

Exchange, class paradigm of race, 24, 26

Fairness for the 90s (Republican National Committee), 77

Falwell, Jerry, 122

Family values, agenda of new right, 205n.31

Fanon, Frantz, 39

Far left, 204–205n.26

Farmers Liberation Army, 119

Farrakhan, Louis, 73

Far right: racial reaction of 1980s, 118–121; and racist ideology of pre–civil rights movement days, 140; compared to new right and neoconservatives, 141; rearticulation of environmentalist themes, 204n.16

Federal government. *See* State

Federal Reserve Board, 106

Feminism: and reinterpretation of gender, 68: importance of movement, 205n.28. *See also* Gender; Sex discrimination

Frazier, E. Franklin, 17, 167n.17

Friedman, Milton, 25

Galton, Francis, 64

Garvey, Marcus, 38–39, 103, 108, 176n.12

Gender: and race and class as regions of hegemony, 68; Reagan's 1984 success among white men, 133–134; as social construct, 181n.4. *See also* Feminism; Sex discrimination

Genovese, Eugene, 195n.15

Geronimo, 80

Gerrymandering, 74

Ghost Dance, 80

Gintis, Herbert, 172n.23

Glazer, Nathan: assimilationism and ethnicity paradigm, 18; civil rights movement and ethnicity paradigm, 19, 98; on justification for state antidiscrimination activity, 20, 210n.6; ethnicity paradigm and dynamics of group incorporation, 21; and Blauner on internal colonialism, 45, 46; opposition to affirmative action, 128, 129–130, 207n.58; on ethnic groups and national interests, 168n.29

Glenn, Evelyn Nakano, 68

Gonzales, Rodolfo, 41, 200n.56

Gordon, David M., 30–32

Gordon, Milton, 19, 20, 21, 21, 167n.22

Gore, Al, 150–151

Gossett, Thomas F., 183n.26

Gould, Steven Jay, 183n.26

Government. *See* State

Gramsci, Antonio, 66–67, 80, 191n.22, 193n.30

Green, Philip, 130

Griffith, D. W., 118

Group rights, neoconservative debate on affirmative action, 128–131

Guinier, Lani, 155, 188n.68

Hacker, Andrew, 153, 154, 180n.2, 214n.26

Hall, Stuart, 24, 210n.4

Hamilton, Charles V., 103, 186n.50, 197n.30

Hamilton, William, 134

Harlem Renaissance, 36, 39

Hate crimes: opposition to legislation by Reagan administration, 134–135; debate over banning of hate speech, 188n.69

Hegel, Georg, 191n.22

Hegemony: concept of and racial dictatorship, 66–69, 191n.22; model of racial state, 84; decline in U.S.

international in 1970s, 115; neoliberal project and racial in 1990s, 148; forms of and state process of incorporation, 193n.30

Heinz, John, 203n.8

Helms, Jesse, 126, 182n.12

Heritage Foundation, 122, 127–128, 209n.73

Hill, Anita, 68

Hispanic Americans: cultures of resistance, 80; racial categories in California, 82. *See also* Chicanos; Latinos; Mexican Americans

History: racism as theme in American, 1, 79; centrality of race in American, 4; U.S. as racial dictatorship, 65–69; origins of racial politics in the U.S., 79–84; context for racially based reaction, 114–116; contemporary crisis in U.S., 138

Hofstadter, Richard, 206n.42

Holliday, George, 145

Hollings, Ernest, 203n.8

Humphrey, Hubert, 132

Huntington, Samuel P., 198n.42

Identity: social movements and collective, 88–89; dominant racial ideology and reconceptualization of racial, 91; new collective racial during 1950s and 1960s, 97; origins of new social movement politics, 99–101, 163n.7; crisis of and far-right white supremacist organizations, 120; variations possible within, 162n.3; dislocation of white, 193–194n.41

Ideology: social structure and racism, 74–75; trajectory of racial politics, 86–87; racial movements and rearticulation of dominant racial, 89–91; attempts to rearticulate racial in conservative direction, 114; popular and use of racial themes as framework for major problems, 115–116; racial reaction and rearticulation of racial, 117–118, 127; continuities between present-day and past versions of racial, 189n.5

Illusion, race as, 54–55

Immigrant analogy, ethnicity paradigm and, 16, 19–20, 21

Index

Index

racial neoliberalism of 1990s compared to, 148, 156; new class and, 171n.17
Neoliberalism: racial politics of 1990s, 147–157; use of term, 212n.7
Neomarxism, 172n.21
Neo-Nazis. *See* White supremacy movement
New class, cultural politics of new right, 125–128, 171n.17
New Deal, 99
New right: political projects and racist views of difference, 58, 75; rearticulation of racial ideology and restructuring of racial politics, 91; use of code words to disguise racial issues, 118; and racial reaction of 1980s, 121–124; cultural politics, antistatism, and the new class, 125–128, 171n.17; compared to neoconservatives on politics of ressentiment, 130; convergence of with neoconservatism on politics of racial reaction, 131–32; racial policy of Reagan administration, 134, 135; compared to far right and neoconservatives, 141; mainstreaming of neo-Nazis, 204n.24; family values and agenda of, 205n.31; scientist ideologies of racial inferiority, 205n.33
Newton, Huey P., 104
New World, European exploration and discourse of race, 61–62
Nixon, Richard, 124
Nkrumah, Kwame, 39
Novak, Michael, 128

Offe, Claus, 192n.25
OPEC nations, 115
Organization of Afro-American Unity, 39

Padmore, George, 39
Pan-Africanism, 37, 38–39, 103, 108
Park, Robert E., 10, 15, 16, 65, 165n.4, 165–166n.7
Patriarchy, new right and reassertion of, 123
Patterson, Orlando, 210–211n.7
Peele, Gillian, 122
Pendleton, Clarence, Jr., 1, 5, 135
People v. Hall (1854), 82
Periodicals, new right, 122
Perot, H. Ross, 213n.23

Peterson, William, 14
Phillips, Howard, 122
Phillips, Kevin, 124, 126, 145, 206n.46, 209n.70
Phipps, Susie Guillory, 53–54, 180n.1
Piore, Michael, 30, 172–173n.26
El Plan Espiritual de Aztlán, 200n.56
Polanyi, Karl, 194n.2
Political correctness, identity politics and debate over, 148, 212n.9
Politics: centrality of race in American, 2, 138–144; determination of racial categories, 3; stratification theory of race, 27–29; cultural nationalism and, 42; spectrum of racial formation, 58–59; rejection of biologistic notions of race and, 64–65; trajectory of racial, 77–79, 84–88; origins of racial in U.S., 79–84; contemporary change in racial order, 88–91; new social movements and issues of identity, rearticulation, and opposition, 99–101; civil rights movement and reformation of racial state, 104–106; challenging paradigms and strategic divisions of civil rights movement, 107–112; historical context for racially based reaction, 114–116; far right and racial reaction in 1980s, 118–121; new right and racial reaction of 1980s, 121–124; neoconservatism and racial reaction in 1980s, 128–132; Reagan revolution and racial reaction, 133–136; influences on future of racial, 144; racial in 1990s, 147–159; access to by racially subordinated groups, 193n.31; importance of suburbs in 1980s, 213n.16
Populism: new right and authoritarianism, 123, 140; antistatism and cultural politics of new right, 125
Populist Party (far right), 119
Postcolonialism, nation-based paradigm of race, 47
Poverty: and Vietnam war in 1960s, 105; economic reversals of 1970s, 116; rate of among blacks, 202n.2
Prager, Jeffrey, 172n.25
Problem, posing of race as, 55
Progressivism, and ethnicity-based paradigm of race, 15
Projects, racial: racial formation as

222

Sowell, Thomas, 187n.55

Split labor market theory, as approach to class conflict theory of race, 30, 32–34, 35, 173n.36, 174n.43

Srole, Leo, 166n.9

Stagflation, 115

Stalin, Joseph, 43

Staple, Gregory C., 175n.5

State: racial formation theory and expanded model of, 4; and racial dimensions of social structure, 57; trajectory of racial politics, 77–79, 84–88; origins of racial politics, 79–84; historical development of racial, 81–82; model of racial, 83–84; contemporary change in racial order, 88–91; civil rights movement and reformation of racial, 104–106; as target of white supremacists, 119; sophistication of contemporary racial, 143; conflicting 1960s activities of federal courts and federal urban policies, 190n.16; equilibration of conflicting interests and policies of, 192–193n.30; justification of antidiscrimination activity, 210n.6

Status revolution, concept of, 206n.42

Stereotypes, racial, 59–60

Stratification theory, as approach to class paradigm of race, 27–29

Structural assimilation, 21–22

Student Nonviolent Coordinating Committee (SNCC), 101–102, 198n.41; 198n.45

Subjectivity, black collective and civil rights movement, 98, 99–101

Suburbanism: new patterns of segregation in 1990s, 150; influence on politics in 1980s, 213n.16

Superexploitation, and internal colonialism, 46

Supreme Court: new right and racial reaction, 126; racial policy of Reagan administration, 134; restrictions of antidiscrimination laws, 186n.51, 188n.62

Symbionese Liberation Army, 205n.26

Tax policy: and racial state in 1960s, 106; and racial reaction of 1970s, 116

Terkel, Studs, 153

Terrorism, far right and, 121

Textbook, new right and censorship of, 127–128, 207n.54

Thomas, Clarence, 68

Thurmond, Strom, 123

Thurow, Lester, 170n.4

Tijerina, Reies Lopez, 199–200n.53

Trajectory, defined, 78, 85, 197–198n.38

Treaty of Guadalupe Hidalgo (1848), 82

The Truly Disadvantaged (Wilson), 149

United Farm Workers, 118, 198n.44

Universalism, neoliberal racial project and, 155–157

Universal Negro Improvement Association (UNIA), 38

Universities: informal quotas for Asian American admissions, 77–78; increase in black attendance, 171n.16

Unstable equilibrium, trajectory of racial politics, 84–88

Urban League, 198n.41

Van den Berghe, Pierre L., 164n.6

Vasquez, Tibúrcio, 80

Veterans Administration, 134

Victimology, traditional racism and, 158

Vietnam War: war on poverty and, 105; Asian American view of as racist, 110, 201n.60; black organizations and, 198n.41

Viguerie, Richard A., 122

Voltaire, 63

Voting rights: drives in South, 105; Guinier's views on, 155. *See also* Electoral districts

Voting Rights Act (1965), 74, 133

Wallace, George, 123–124, 196n.23

Walter-McCarran Act of 1952, 81, 184n.35

War of maneuver, racial, 81

Warner, W. Lloyd, 166n.9

War of position, racial, 81, 192n.28

Washington, Booker T., 38, 102–103, 108

Waters, Maxine, 212n.4

Wattenberg, Ben, 125

Weather Underground, 205n.26

Weber, Max, 65

Welfare state: and racial reaction of 1970s, 116; racial policy of Reagan administration, 135